Decency and Difference

Decency remains one of the most prevalent yet least understood terms in today's political discourse. In evoking respect, kindness, courage, integrity, reason, and tolerance, it has long expressed an unquestioned duty and belief in promoting and protecting the dignity of all persons. Today this unquestioned belief is in crisis. Tribalism and identity politics have both hindered and threatened its moral stability and efficacy. Still, many scholars and policymakers continue to undertheorize its political character by isolating it from the effects of identity politics. *Decency and Difference* argues that decency is a primary source of political tension that has long shaped the struggles for power, identity, and justice in the global arena. It distinguishes among basic, conservative, and liberal strands of decency to critically examine the many conflicting and competing applications of decency in global politics. Together these three strands reflect the long and uneven evolution of decency from the British and American empires to a global network of justice. This powerful book exposes the gaps of decency and the disparate ways it is practiced, thus addressing the global challenge of configuring a diverse political ethic of decency.

Steven C. Roach is Professor of International Relations and Graduate Director at the School of Interdisciplinary Global Studies at the University of South Florida.

CONFIGURATIONS: CRITICAL STUDIES OF WORLD POLITICS

Patrick Thaddeus Jackson, series editor

Recent Titles:

Decency and Difference: Humanity and the Global Challenge of Identity Politics
Steven C. Roach

State of Translation: Turkey in Interlingual Relations
Einar Wigen

The Politics of Intimacy: Rethinking the End-of-Life Controversy
Anna Durnová

Angry Public Rhetorics: Global Relations and Emotion in the Wake of 9/11
Celeste Michelle Condit

The Distinction of Peace: A Social Analysis of Peacebuilding
Catherine Goetze

India China: Rethinking Borders and Security
L. H. M. Ling, Adriana Erthal Abdenur, Payal Banerjee, Nimmi Kurian, Mahendra P. Lama, and Li Bo

The Politics of Expertise: Competing for Authority in Global Governance
Ole Jacob Sending

Making Human: World Order and the Global Governance of Human Dignity
Matthew S. Weinert

The Politics of Subjectivity in American Foreign Policy Discourses
Ty Solomon

For a complete list of titles, please see www.press.umich.edu

Decency and Difference

Humanity and the Global Challenge of Identity Politics

Steven C. Roach

University of Michigan Press
Ann Arbor

Published in the United States of America by the
University of Michigan Press
Printed and bound by CPI Group (UK) Ltd, Croydon, CR0 4YY

First published November 2019

A CIP catalog record for this book is available from the British Library.

Library of Congress Cataloging-in-Publication Data

Names: Roach, Steven C., author.
Title: Decency and difference : humanity and the global challenge of identity politics / Steven C. Roach.
Description: Ann Arbor : University of Michigan Press, 2019. | Series: Configurations : critical studies of world politics | Includes bibliographical references and index.
Identifiers: LCCN 2019025038 (print) | LCCN 2019025039 (ebook) | ISBN 9780472131624 (hardcover) | ISBN 9780472126156 (ebook)
Subjects: LCSH: Political ethics. | Political culture. | Identity politics. | Justice. | Reconciliation—Political aspects. | Power (Social sciences)—Political aspects.
Classification: LCC JA79 .R58 2019 (print) | LCC JA79 (ebook) | DDC 172—dc23
LC record available at https://lccn.loc.gov/2019025038
LC ebook record available at https://lccn.loc.gov/2019025039

Cover illustration: Henry M. Stanley with a boy named Kalulu (1872).

For Emmett and Renée

Contents

Digital materials related to this title can be found on the Fulcrum platform via the following citable URL: https://doi.org/10.3998/mpub.9394344

Foreword

Decency is one of those notions that, at first glance, seems to be an unqualified good. One might raise questions about the limits of being polite or the downside of being civil, but who could possibly oppose being *decent*? It is precisely such taken-for-granted commonplaces that critical social science has a mission to interrogate, since what is unremarked can easily be the precise place where subtle forms of social power persist and exercise their most profound shaping effects. Steven Roach has conducted just such an interrogation in this book, showing how the notion of "decency" functions in ambiguous—both benign and baneful—ways.

Roach adopts a critical-theoretical approach to the problem of humanitarian ethics, disclosing the role played by "decency" at the core of such ethical approaches. Roach's approach is critical not merely because it raises some questions about the double-edged effects of an ethics based on notions of human decency, but more importantly because it embeds this seemingly self-evident notion of decency in a complex history that is anything but inevitable. It did not have to be the case that we inhabit a world in which a putatively secular notion of decency grounds much global ethical discussion, but a variety of contingent historical processes have led us to this point, and have given us a heritage on which contemporary discussions are built. Roach's book de-naturalizes that foundation and frees us to ask critical questions about it—questions that might lead to a reconstitution of what he calls "deep pluralism" as a way forward. His careful tracing of the complex genealogy of decency also allows us to distinguish between humane decency and the liberal notions of toleration and civility that often accompany it; one of his chief conceptual contributions is opening up space to think through decency outside of the liberal world order.

Importantly, Roach's book is not an argument from first principles, but is firmly grounded in empirics. His three case chapters show the ethic of decency at work and, in particular, illustrate how tensions within the notion of decency *itself* produce problematic resolutions of a variety of conflicts. It is not enough to insist on decency, since this presumes a view of human beings that ignores affect and emotion; reincorporating those into our model of human beings suggests that ties to local cultural values cannot simply be set aside in the name of some common notion of restraint in support of universal rights. Instead, we need to think about clashes of value from the starting point of concretely involved individuals with emotional connections to different forms of life, which will both help us explain otherwise-puzzling outcomes and allow us to think seriously about the role that humane sentiment might play in a revisioned global ethics. "Decency" is more a site of contestation than a doctrinal pronouncement, and restoring that contestation to public view may enable responses to the present-day rise of populist exclusivity that any particular and narrow construal of decency forecloses. Indeed, Roach suggests, some of the present rise of populism around the globe may stem from a too-narrow understanding of decency and the emotional backlash that it promotes. Through the case chapters we see how this dynamic happens, and perhaps learn how to avoid it; that understanding may give us hope for the future.

In the end, this integration of the critical-theoretical and the explanatory is part of what the *Configurations* series is all about, and I am pleased to have Steven Roach's book be a part of the series.

Patrick Thaddeus Jackson
Series Editor, Configurations

Preface and Acknowledgments

When I began to research this book in the spring of 2011, decency seemed to be on the rise in global politics. President Barack Obama—who frequently used the term "common decency" to defend the dignity of persecuted civilians—was in the last year of his first term of office. Meanwhile, the Arab Spring protests, which had been sparked by a street vendor's sacrifice, brought democracy and accountability to Tunisia and other autocratic Arab states, such as Egypt. But the optimism and hope generated by these events would of course prove short lived. The Migrant Crisis of 2015, the Syrian War, the emergence of the Islamic State, and the rise of right-wing populism ushered in a new era of reactionary and repressive rule.

This led me to recast decency in a far more critical light. I began to ask the hard question of what a decent international order really meant. Was decency supposed to be the last line of defense against reactionary politics? And yet, if it was intended to serve as the moral, albeit weakening, bulwark of the liberal international order, was this because, not in spite of, itself? Decency, it seemed, had always constituted a moral silo defense that was based on an unquestioned belief in the common good. But what if this silo was itself contributing to the decline of decency by restricting our understanding of the politics of decency? Was it appropriate to rely on this unquestioned belief to morally defend the international order, especially when doing so ignored the possibility that such orthodoxy had become the source of the problem, not the solution to the rising turmoil of identity politics? In the end, I felt that in ignoring this reality, I would be doing an injustice to a concept that has long stood (and rightfully so) for an evolving moral threshold of justice.

Still, I do not pretend to offer any definitive answers to these above questions. My aim rather is to understand decency's complex evolution and contradictions, that is, to address the perils of applying it to world politics. In effect, we need to start seeing decency for what it is: namely, a vital yet affected part of the ongoing struggle for justice and dignity protection. We should therefore stop being lulled into thinking that there is one common way to practice decency, or, even worse, that some people inherently lack the sensibility to practice it. Nor should we think of decency in relativistic terms or without any reference to international customary law. With decency, the challenge is to rethink what it means to practice the good and conduct oneself morally in relation to others. In short, it is to project restraint in ways where one becomes willing and open to being shaped by the customs that inform alternative rules of behavior.

In writing this book, I also realized something else: that decency tends to mirror our biases rather than neutralize them. Understanding the political tensions of decency thus involved confronting some of my own cultural biases. I became both a skeptic of and a critical believer in liberalism, which, in projecting decency's progressive qualities in politics, also becomes complicit in its retrogressive character. Still, this is the encounter we need to have with decency, if we are to engage its realistic, moral potential, while never refraining from calling for a global test of decency, especially when the desire is to make all persons respect the dignity of others. To have a reliable test of decency, then, we also must test decency itself.

The completion of this book would never have been possible if not for the love and support of my wife, Erica, and the many discussions I had with her regarding my idea of decency. I would also like to express my deep gratitude to Patrick Thaddeus Jackson for his helpful and insightful suggestions. Throughout the writing of the book, I also received invaluable inspiration and comments from Francisco Cardoso Gomes de Matos, a poet laureate of dignity, whose optimism and indefatigable writing remains a constant, if not daily, reminder about what the world can still become when it commits itself to the peace and dignity of humankind. I also would like to thank the editors of the University of Michigan Press, Elizabeth Demers, Danielle Coty, Melody Herr, and Kevin Rennells, for their editorial advice and assistance and their unceasing efforts to bring this book to publication.

In addition, I am grateful for the comments and assistance that colleagues and friends offered me in informal and formal venues, including

Yavuz Akdag, Anthony Burke, Martin Coward, Francois Debrix, Milena Diaz, Antonio Franceschet, Peter Funke, Kevin Gray, Kyle Grayson, Patrick Hayden, Derrick Hudson, Murad Idris, Ed Kissi, Alex Koutsoukis, James Libengood, Evelin Lindner, Robert Oprisko, Murid Partaw, Jacqueline Carol Reich, Dawn Rothe, Manu Samnotra, Brent Steele, Steve Tauber, Harry Vanden, and Jongseok Woo. I also received invaluable input from the anonymous reviewers of this manuscript and benefited from a generous grant from the Humanities Institute at the University of South Florida that helped finance my research for chapter 6. In addition, I would also like to thank Routledge for permission to reprint "Decency and the Liberal International (Dis-)Order," *Globalizations* 13, no. 6 (2017) and to Springer Publications, for permission to reprint "Multilayered Justice in Northern Uganda: ICC Intervention and Local Procedures of Accountability," *International Criminal Law Review* 13, no. 1 (2013).

During the writing of this book, our family lost an ever-trusted companion, our beloved beagle. But we also brought into this world two human beacons of light: my son, Emmett, and daughter, Renée. It is to them that I dedicate this book.

CHAPTER ONE

The Idea of Decency

A good part of the struggles of mankind centre round the single task of finding an expedient accommodation—one, that is, that will bring happiness—between this claim of the individual and the cultural claims of the group, and one of the problems that touches the fate of humanity is whether such an accommodation can bet reached by means of some particular forms of civilization or whether this conflict is irreconcilable.

—Sigmund Freud, *Civilization and Its Discontents*

For it seems that the name of virtue presupposes difficulty and contrast, and that it cannot be exercised without opposition. Perhaps this is why we call God good, strong, liberal, and just, but we do not call him virtuous: his operations are wholly natural and effortless.

—Montaigne, *On Cruelty*

In 1954, at the height of Army-McCarthy hearings in the U.S. Congress, Senator Joseph McCarthy accused a U.S. Army sergeant of having ties with a communist organization. His attorney, Joseph Welch, defended his client by stating, "Until this moment, Senator, I think I never really gauged your cruelty or your recklessness. . . . Have you no sense of decency, sir?"[1] Welch's statement marked a pivotal moment in American politics. In helping to shift public opinion against McCarthy's red-baiting and fearmongering, it showed how the hearings threatened a core value of America's civic identity. In today's increasingly polarized environment, it is fair to say that decency has lost much of this desired political effect. One could even argue that its appeal has become increasingly based on political expediency (and mere political politicking) rather than actually improving and upholding respect for the rule of law and the basic rights of people.[2] This is not to say that it has become a political liability or some moral sleight of hand, but rather, as some have suggested, that we need to do more to defend its role in stabilizing and regulating moral conduct in the political arena.[3]

But it is also this normative view that raises the question of what makes decency so stable, or so deeply tied to our sensibility of nondomination and the preservation of the rule of law.[4] Why is decency something we always instinctually defend and rarely, if ever, critically examine in the political arena? Is it simply that decency is so deeply rooted in the secular and liberal imagination, or what it means to be human in the modern age, that it must always be treated as a given, incontestable virtue of preserving humanity? And yet, does treating decency in this way cause us to overlook something more important: namely, its intricate and open-ended part in the struggle to realize and preserve justice, peace, and order in world politics? If these questions tell us anything, it is that scholars and theorists continue to undertheorize its political function in the global arena. This might explain the growing uncertainty surrounding its secular liberal and religious applications in this arena and what these conflicting applications mean for consistently enforcing the many broad standards of decency, such as fair treatment and the protection of basic needs. Decency, it seems, plays a very conflictual role in society. And yet, few are willing to accept this possibility. Indeed, the tendency is to largely overlook this, which only reinforces the problematic need to dogmatize decency, or to assert an unquestioned secular and religious belief in its stable foundations. In effect, we tend to isolate decency from the contentious identity politics that shape it. My goal in this book is to engage this politics and its relationship to decency. I argue that decency constitutes a primary source of political tension that has shaped the struggle for power, identity, and justice in the global arena.

By confronting decency's perilous part in promoting dignity, peace, and security, then, I shall challenge the idea that decency can and should always function independently of the political forces (tribalism and nativism) threatening it. My idea is that decency plays a problematic yet constructive, interlinking role in identity politics. To morally isolate it from the political threats of tribalism and nativism, in other words, is to reinforce a hollow faith in its ability to neutralize and overcome the destructive effects of reactionary politics. For example, the political scholar Francis

Fukuyama, argues that decency should be treated as a creedal value of national civic identity, which exists independently of the political tensions between the nationalist politics of right-wing populists and the liberal identity politics of recognition.[5] His point is that while liberal identity politics (such as liberal pluralism and multiculturalism) caused the emergence of nationalist identity politics, it is decency that, if properly applied, can umpire and resolve the conflict.[6] Like Fukuyama, Paul Krugman, the well-known *New York Times* columnist and Nobel Laureate in Economics, claims that right-wing populism suppresses the moral "forces of decency" or the desire to practice tolerance and the rule of law.[7] While this may be true, Krugman's claim seems to offer a somewhat rarefied view of decency in the political arena, since it suggests that "the forces of decency" are primarily, if not exclusively, concerned with promoting the liberal principles of fair and respectful treatment and protecting the rights of all persons.

In reality, the "forces of decency" are both more complex and volatile than this. Not only do they involve promoting liberal principles but they also embody competing tensions among basic, liberal, and conservative claims to justice and order. The basic and conservative claims focus on protecting essential needs and preserving and respecting traditional customs, respectively. When these two strands conflict with the liberal features of decency (or liberal decency), such as equal treatment under the law and impartiality, or when these claims are used to advance competing political agendas, they can produce hostility and even political polarization. Nigel Farage, for example, the populist leader of the British Independence Party, declared Brexit to be a victory for "decent people," or the white working class negatively affected by the effects of globalization, that is, inequality and unemployment.[8] Moreover, at the recent U.S. Senate Judiciary Committee confirmation hearings of Judge Brett Kavanaugh, Republicans and Democrats used decency to support their contrasting political views on sexual abuse. The Republicans, for instance, stressed the moral unacceptability of injuring the judge's reputation, while the Democrats insisted on the need to hold the judge to account for his sexual misconduct.[9] These conflicting applications of decency seem to suggest that decency intensifies more than it reduces political pressures, as both sides seek in their own way, to justify and reclaim decency as a force for the good.

Still, this does not mean that decency is in permanent crisis or on a rapid decline in the political arena. Instead, it shows how much we have neglected to understand decency as a force of political change. The question therefore is how should we confront the dangers of advancing decency in the political arena, especially when defending it as source of the good contradicts the need for upholding its standards of treating all persons and cultural customs with respect.[10] In the absence of any critical notion of decency, decency can mean whatever one feels is necessary to advance a political agenda. As Pankaj Mishra writes of the current political climate, "People everywhere find themselves in thrall to the sentiment, generated by the new media and amplified by the social media—that anything can happen anywhere, to anybody any time."[11] For Mishra, the divisiveness of identity politics is not novel but part of a larger cyclical process in which today's politics of anger (concentrated in the white working class) mirrors eighteenth- and nineteenth-century nativists' attempts to gain political advantage by condemning liberal virtues and values.[12] Today's right-wing global populism, in his view, is simply a different version of the hostile sentiment that has been driving and countering the liberal politics of decency.

For many normative theorists, confronting decency has either meant uncovering its minimalist function of promoting respect, tolerance, and consensus, or revealing the moral basis of transcending harmful cultural customs.[13] John Rawls's idea of decency, for instance, is about preserving a shared respect of the common good or what he calls an overlapping consensus on the requirements for justice, peace, and the toleration of other peoples' customs and values.[14] David Miller advocates a similarly, if not more minimalist, notion of decency to justify what is most basic to justice and the responsibility of fulfilling basic needs and rights.[15] Critics of minimal decency, however, argue that it remains too restrictive to capture its potential of promoting basic human rights and global justice.[16] The goal, in their view, is to treat decency as a source of compassion for ending human suffering.[17] But like the minimalists, they, too, accept the idea of decency as an unquestioned expression of the common good, that is, as a value that lies prior to the political and moral conflicts it is supposed to neutralize and resolve. The problem with treating decency in this manner is that it divorces it from the politics that shape and drive its role in the global arena. It suggests that the only way to appreciate decency is by detaching it from the political tensions that structure its application and standardization in international relations.

My primary aim in this book is to engage these political tensions and contradictions of decency in the global realm. By focusing on its evolution from the national to global level and the conflicts between its universal and particular applications, I shall probe the competing and contradictory elements of basic, conservative, and liberal decency. As we shall see, these distinctive strands help to expose propriety gaps in decency or the conflicting ways that decency is practiced in global politics. At the same time, they also reflect a deep-seated human sentiment for respect that is as protean and diverse as it is difficult to modulate. Thus, compared to the concept of civility,[18] which, as the Oxford English Dictionary states, concerns "politeness, courtesy and consideration . . . and the minimum degree of courtesy required in a social situation," decency stresses a sense of properness or an inner sensibility about what is appropriate and fitting for the circumstances.[19] Civility and decency in this sense involve two different denominations: the civil manners that allow us to communicate with others and the set of principles and social obligations that enable us to cooperate and reach mutual consent.[20] But unlike civility's outward display of these manners and principles, decency demonstrates how the inner traits of sensibility, such as integrity, tolerance, and courage, can be cultivated to deepen awareness of the value of practicing these manners and rules for protecting the dignity of all persons. Decency, in other words, is not just about conforming to an acceptable and uniform set of conventions and principles. It also concerns the diverse nature of sensibility or the multiple ways to justify, in practical terms, the rules that protect people from undue, serious harm. This diverse dynamic thus expresses the moral dissonance of decency and its varied applications in the political arena. More importantly, it raises four sets of issues for critically examining its complex role in global politics.[21]

First, how has decency, which once reflected the proper manners of respect and modesty, become so intermeshed with liberal norms, individual rights, and equal dignity? The intricate and seemingly binding ties between liberalism and decency, as we shall see, grew out of the Enlightenment's struggle against injustice and oppression. They were part of the emergence of secular reason, or the invention of a new science of democratic freedom and morality that marked the progressive role of moral sentiments in politics and the ideas of Adam Smith, Jean-Jacques Rousseau, Voltaire, Immanuel Kant, and John Locke, among others. Together, these thinkers recognized, to varying degrees, that improper moral conduct and a lack of respect were the product of unreasonable laws and rules. Proper moral conduct and dignity in this sense were no longer confined to ecclesiastical and aristocratic circles but became part of a new politics of decency in which reason as a natural sentiment would be applied to combat harm and suffering and to promote the rule of law and tolerance.

The liberal politics of decency championed the natural capacity for reason and for judging others impartially. Yet for all that it represented in terms of moral progress and a new social democratic order, it could not do away with the habits, tastes, and manners that constituted the political and social ties to tradition and privilege. These conservative elements still, to this day, shape our understanding of decency and the limits of liberal decency in society. Thus, liberal decency did not eclipse conservative decency; it became intertwined with it in both positive and negative ways, as we shall see.

The second set of issues concerns whether decency can support a pluralist liberal system capable of balancing the universal constraints on killing or harming a person's dignity against the recognition of different identity claims. How durable or flexible, in other words, are these normative constraints in the global realm? And can they hold up to the increasing pressures of liberal identity politics or the measures designed to accommodate the rights and needs of traditionally marginalized groups, particularly when doing so seems to provoke many to see these measures as reasons for preserving past cultural norms and social traditions? But more importantly, does upholding such normative constraints redound to the advantage of the most powerful liberal-democratic states in a way that turns decency into a political tool for advancing the interests of hegemonic states?

The British Empire adopted a range of liberal constraints, such as due process and neutrality, to expand their liberal empire. For Daron Acemoglu and James Robinson, erecting these constraints was part of "the virtuous circles" in world politics, in which, as they put it, "inclusive institutions were based on constraints on the exercise of power and on a pluralist distribution of power in a society enshrined in the rule of law."[22] In the nineteenth and early twentieth centuries, British decency was spread overseas through civic imperialism and the duty to civilize and educate others overseas. Not only did it serve as a central trait of national identity but it also drove Britain's global vision of moral progress. Yet it was this vision that also remained blind to and, in most cases, justified the mistreatment and oppression of colonial peoples. Such mistreatment also contradicted what was practiced in Britain (in terms of kindness and restraint), which suggested that decency was never truly extended to the global realm; rather, it was applied in a way that reinforced not only the narrow interests of

British citizens and officials overseas but the self-serving civilizational standards of equal and fair treatment. In short, the gap between the national and global practice of decency explained the need for forcibly spreading British morals to other peoples, who had to be educated in proper British manners to appreciate and abide by the liberal constraints of decency.

However, the end of World War II would mark the rise of an international set of decency standards based on the expanded rule of consensus, greater inclusion, human rights protections, and nondiscrimination. Decency in this international context seemed to work beyond the nationalist limits of moral propriety by providing institutional mechanisms that advanced cooperation and promoted the equal dignity of all peoples. This made it possible to internalize the normative constraints of decency on a broad scale and to end the very discriminatory effects of colonial oppression (via decolonization) that had defined the mistreatment of non-European peoples. Still, it was an international order that required U.S. willpower and assistance to defend the common decency standards of the international community. When, for instance, President Barack Obama responded to Muammar Qaddafi's indiscriminate killing of innocent civilians in 2011 by stating that "these actions violate . . . every standard of common decency," he sought to condemn Qaddafi's blatant disrespect for the decency standards against killing.[23] Obama's words reflected a heightened need to protect Libyan civilians from serious harm. So great was the need that it has been applied to living and dead civilians, alike. After the downing of the Malaysia Airlines Flight 17 over eastern Ukraine in July 2014, for example, Australian and Dutch leaders accused the separatist forces in eastern Ukraine of preventing the recovery of the bodies of the victims and lacking "human decency."[24] For them, blocking access to the dead bodies amounted to an inexcusable offense against human dignity, one that underscored the need for erecting a global test of decency to uphold the dignity of all persons.

Still, the eastern Ukrainian secessionists that these leaders condemned were part of a nationalist movement (or nationalist identity politics) that had already begun to destabilize international norms. Their movement was part of a much larger trend of delegitimizing the international institutions—such as NATO, the United Nations, and the European Union—that were expected to enforce the rules of international order. But rather than confronting this threat to international order, many continue to treat decency as a universally shared pragmatic ideal of protecting all persons, even though, as I have argued, the source of these threats stem from prejudice, hate, and resentment that have long shaped decency in national and global politics.

A third set of issues concerns the role of emotions in countering or furthering human decency, that is, whether decency represents a felt, moral connection with others. Does the moral threshold we settle on in terms of a shared common good constitute the basis for preserving what is most basic to humanity, namely, a deeply felt, abiding respect for others' dignity? Martha Nussbaum argues that love and compassion constitute the moral judgments that enable us to measure the values defining our duties and commitments to justice.[25] Her transcultural perspective holds that love and compassion can overcome the negative effects of shame and distrust by forging deeper emotional attachments to justice and the common good. Political emotions reflect how these attachments direct our actions toward universal norms of human rights protection. Conceptualizing emotions in this way means that we learn to free ourselves from the negative constraints of state power, which, in turn, suggests that we can and should treat political emotions as part of an expanding threshold of decency in world politics or the emergence of a decent world society in which all persons learn to respect and abide by the liberal norms of dignity protection.

But populist attacks on liberalism continue to dampen enthusiasm for this idea. More than anything, they have demonstrated how the fear of normative constraints can also subvert the emotional content of such constraints (e.g., political correctness), and end up, as Rogers Brubaker puts it, creating a condition of "an affective disinvestment from the politics as usual."[26] "The idea of popular sovereignty," Brubaker writes, "may be drained of its emotional potency, leaving only cynicism and distrust in its place. . . . The affective constellation that sustains populist politics can thus shade over into a constellation that undermines populist politics as much as it does other forms of representative politics." Here, the attacks on the ends of liberal morality (equal representation and respect) become a means of reacting against the normative constraints of decency. This is one way that politics can be seen not simply as an end but as a relation that comes into existence through the conflict of sensibilities.[27]

To speak of an affective politics, then, is to distinguish between emotion and affect. While emotion expresses a set of feelings that register a partial expression of affect (or conscious threshold of acting on a particular set of memories and habits), affect represents the emergence of feeling or an event of passing beyond this threshold of emotion. Affect, in other words, is about understanding the primal forces of emergence and the unconscious experience of intensity that enables us to conceptualize the political reality of decency and the intensity of emotion.[28] To get from affect to intensity, as Brian Massumi reasons, we also need to accept the necessary existence of constraints and to understand how they can be flipped into greater degrees of freedom.[29] Political affect, in this sense, is about confronting the ontological realm or political reality of decency, that is, decency's normative structure and the hidden sources of its political and cultural tensions.

Finally, this brings us to a fourth set of issues regarding the relation between decency and difference. What role has decency played in either mitigating or reinforcing the tension between reason and cultural pluralism? Why, in other words, is being tolerant and respectful of different cultural practices necessary for upholding and promoting these different practices? Or does decency necessarily involve one universal set of standards for evaluating the worth and potential of these cultural practices to contribute to peace and justice? At the global level, we might say that the standards against harming persons justify top-down liberal internationalist interventions to protect these persons; that such standards require the acceptance of freedom and equality to further accommodate different cultural practices and values. This is what liberal pluralism assumes: that individual freedom and equality justify and therefore guarantee the needed respect and accommodation of different values and practices.

The trouble with this idea, however, is that it often requires a notion of moral fitness and common sensibility to measure the unreasonable, moral deviations from decency standards. In other words, when certain procedures, norms, practices, and values fail to meet (or fit in with) these international standards, these "other" practices tend to be considered as morally unfit. Such moral unfitness, in turn, helps to justify the reasons for exclusion and top-down accommodation. Yet, in doing so, it also raises the question of what determines a lack of moral propriety. Can we say that the institutionalization of decency standards has given way to an overarching notion of moral fitness and uniformity globally, but that such a process has suppressed the local interventions capable of complementing these standards? And does this mean that capacity building is about bridging this moral fitness gap by devolving power to local communities, or by combining local and international rules, as we have seen with hybrid criminal courts that are based on a combination of local and international legal norms and customs? The answer will invariably depend on our efforts to contest the moral orthodoxy of decency, or the fixed belief in a moral threshold of fitness, and to advance the coexistence of different proprieties and cultural habits in international relations.[30]

Formulating a heterodox idea of decency, therefore, is about articulating the plurality of ways of practicing decency to promote dignity protection. It is an idea that requires us to chart the possibilities of working beyond the statist and secular limits of liberal pluralism and to show how these limits reinforce the hegemonic liberal discourse of the modern states system. In *Pluralism*, William Connolly challenges the secular idea of separating religion and politics in liberal democratic states. In his view, contesting this idea or treating it as agonistic in global politics may actually be a desirable thing in terms of promoting dialogue, civic participation, and representation. This at least is what his notion of "deep pluralism" (or "new pluralism")[31] sets out to do. By showing how the global sphere opens up the possibilities of promoting identity and difference, one learns to engage one another for who they are and what they represent. This, in turn, means a more direct confrontation with the effects of exclusion and marginalization that lie in between sovereign boundaries and a borderless world, allowing us to reveal the widening social gaps produced by global political pressures, including open borders, the rapid transmission of knowledge, and social media.[32] In effect, the problematic tension between decency and cultural difference is symptomatic of the longstanding and unquestioned belief in separating religion and politics in democratic states. By thus contesting the need for this in global politics, we may begin to shed more light on the political difficulties and moral possibilities of advancing decency in the global arena.

Meaning, Divergent Sentiments, and Global Moral Propriety

When the renowned political theorist Isaiah Berlin was asked to define decency, he remarked that it was "the only kind of life which we think that human beings should follow, if they are not to destroy each other. I can say that is the only kind of life which we think that human beings should follow. These are general truths but this does not assume something unalterable."[33] Decency, in this sense, expresses an exclusive moral threshold of basic mutual respect, that is, a deep-seated moral duty to treat others fairly in the absence of which there could be no moral life or dignity protection. Moreover, it requires us to keep an open mind about how to apply that duty since, as Berlin suggests, new social circumstances might change the accepted norms and moral reality for carrying out such a duty properly. For Berlin, there were essential virtuous qualities that linked this duty with proper moral conduct; they included bravery, generosity, kindness, fairness, integrity, tolerance, and restraint. Together, these dispositions enabled a person to conduct his or her life in accordance with the accepted rules of moral behavior; more importantly, they determined the moral fitness (or test of character) to apply these rules. The Oxford English Dictionary defines this condition as "the fitness to the circumstances or requirements of the case . . . fitness, seemliness, propriety." The dictionary traces decency's modern origins to a 1567 commentary on Horace's poetry, in which morals and manners conveyed "the Decencies for stirring youth." In Thomas Hobbes's *Leviathan*, decency was equated with a "condition of orderly and social life"—or what Hobbes called "small morals"—that represented "conformity in behavior, speech, or action to the standard of propriety or good taste" as well as to "compliance with recognized notions of modesty or delicacy; freedom from impropriety."[34] Possessing moral propriety, in other words, was about exhibiting a refined sensibility, befitting of someone with a stately, dignified character. It meant that any freedom from impropriety could only be suitably tested in the company of one's respected peers.

Class privilege in early modern Europe (1500–1800) determined who possessed the manners, tastes, and decorum, such as ladies' wear and how to grieve and express oneself with delicacy. Social etiquette was thus reserved for only the ecclesiastical, aristocratic, and middle classes, which used it to justify and uphold an exclusive social order. In this way, decency's small morals (or moral tastes and manners) helped maintain the aristocracy's virtual monopoly on honor, courage, and propriety in public.[35] Breaking this monopoly meant combating the effects of moral privilege and superstition. For many eighteenth-century Enlightenment thinkers, the struggle required reasoned moral judgment, not moral taste, to legitimize public authority and inclusion. Only through reasoned judgment could one begin to end the unfair, brutal, and arbitrary treatment of persons—such as slavery and torture.[36]

By the end of the early modern period, then, decency entered the public consciousness as a sensible entitlement to fair and equal protection against harm. It constituted a new moral threshold of justice and democratic rule in which reasoned judgment legitimized individual liberty, equal dignity, autonomy, tolerance, and the rule of law. These liberal features of secular decency came to comprise what I shall call liberal decency. At its core, liberal decency reflected a new, tempered faith in reason and the human capacity to resolve societal problems; it instilled its believers with the determination to counter the effects of class prejudice and to institute new laws protecting one's freedom and dignity.[37] Its emergence thus heralded a political sensibility or belief in moderating and guiding the revolutionary zeal for democratic order and its constitutional rules protecting the rights, dignity, and needs of all individual citizens. As the central pillars of this new democratic order, the newly adopted French and U.S. constitutions codified the civil rights and key constraints on governmental authority, such as the infringement on the rights of citizens. But while liberal decency may have marked a radical, political shift from the exclusionary morality of decency—in terms of maintaining class-based manners, tradition, and moral etiquette—it also continued to maintain an uncomfortable relationship with these small morals throughout the nineteenth century. Great Britain's imperial projection of its manners and moral conduct, as we shall see, would show just how contradictory this relationship would become.

Virtue and Universal Value

To understand this complex relationship, we need to appreciate both the breadth and depth of decency's role in politics. This means taking stock of its virtuous moral qualities and the value it places on acting reasonably and sensibly toward others. Again, these qualities consist principally of restraint, courage, kindness, respect, and toleration, which together inform one's sense of duty for treating individuals fairly and recognizing the need for protecting them against the harm or injury that degrades their dignity. This sense of duty also requires trust in the laws, policies, and institutions that secure and protect the rights and social needs of all persons, in particular the most disadvantaged or innocent. To possess human decency is to demonstrate a shared belief in maintaining these protections of the life and dignity of all persons. It is to realize that there is something more basic to humanity than simply the protection provided by the faith in God; that "humane decency," as Christopher Hitchens famously put it, "does not necessarily derive from religion but precedes it."[38] In essence, decency means believing in and practicing the shared virtue of nonkilling, which can be found in many religions, including the Judeo-Christian commandment of thou shall not kill, and the virtue of ahimsa in Hinduism, Jainism, and Buddhism.[39] Ahimsa, for instance, refers to "non-injury to living beings in thought, word, and deed," and sees harm as caused by one's thoughts and intent to injure living beings and the environment. More importantly, it holds that God's all-pervasive presence in nature "creates," as one source puts it, "an attitude of sublime tolerance and acceptance towards others"; hence, a respect for all other living beings' capacity to feel and be injured.[40] Moreover, in Islam, *sabr* denotes the restraint from injuring others through persistent devotion, even though this does not mean that one cannot injure others in order to defend against a much larger, external source of harm.

Decency therefore speaks to the intrinsic value we place on preserving and dignifying all human life.[41] It finds its deepest expression in the humane sentiment that we evoke to respect and protect all living beings, including nonhuman animals (and their feelings and cognitive abilities), and in cultivating the virtue of nonkilling. "Nonkilling," as Francisco Cardoso Gomes de Matos states, is "a deeply humanizing responsibility,"[42] which Article 3 of the Nobel Laureates Charter defines as the "right not to be killed and the responsibility not to kill others."[43] Critics, though, argue that the realities of killing place undue restrictions on this virtue of nonkilling and that there will always be a moral cause of preventing unjust and indiscriminate killing (of combatants in war).[44] While it may be difficult to draw any clear-cut distinction between nonkilling and the morally just cause of killing—or the just war principle of protecting noncombatants in war—this should not detract from the aim of cultivating the virtue of nonkilling, or, for that matter, instilling the fundamental responsibility to not kill innocent civilians.[45] For decency's broad appeal lies precisely in the idea of not perpetrating violence against those who are likely to suffer the most from the effects of violence, such as women and children.

The virtue of nonkilling thus reflects a deep-seated moral commitment to and conviction to treat all persons with respect and protect the needs and rights of the most vulnerable or excluded. Decency in this context serves as an end in itself, or as a goal that is valued for its own sake. As one of the more controversial standards of decency, the abolition of the death penalty constitutes the legal obligation to respect the dignity of those convicted of serious and heinous crimes. The standard stresses rehabilitation, lighter sentences, and, in general, the rules applying to fair and proper treatment in prison (i.e., no extended solitary confinement).[46] One could even argue that it has affected how authorities administer the death penalty in countries that practice capital punishment, insofar as it pressures these officials to seek out more humane ways of killing the convicted. Still, the difficult challenge of turning the abolition of the death penalty into a uniform standard in world politics is that the global arena is composed of sovereign countries with different customs and habits. Countries with laws allowing capital punishment not only see such punishment—and the brutal ways of administering it—as a means of deterring criminal behavior but also as a commitment to upholding the integrity of its cultural customs and conventions. Yet for all that it is worth, the respect paid to these countries' sovereignty can also quickly devolve into political conflict or diplomatic crisis, when, for instance, a citizen from a country that has banned capital punishment is accused and convicted of a nonviolent crime (e.g., drug smuggling) and sentenced to death.

Accordingly, competition and class conflict help to define the instrumental value of protecting the needs of individuals in international relations. When decency is treated as simply a means to an end, it can convey the conflicting political aims of or controversial reasons for doing away with the practices and symbols of abusive and unfair treatment. For example, the defense of the historical customs of the old (Dixie) South in the United States, such as the flying of the Confederate flag, deeply offends many persons' sense of racial justice. Yet, when the decision is made to remove the flag out of respect for those offended, it can engender a hostile defense of these customs. Justifying this decision in terms of common decency, or a shared sentiment toward treating all persons regardless of race with dignity and respect, may not be adequate to offset these tensions.

The trouble with using common decency in world politics is that it often presumes that a fixed, overarching standard of conduct exists to evaluate proper moral conduct and even moral fitness. Enforcing this standard means that the most powerful countries can use their influence to impose their own moral customs and values on other countries. In international relations, we often see how one powerful group or state can use its influence to punish actions that violate the rules and norms regarding the disrespect of life and mistreatment of innocent civilians (e.g., torture). Propriety is how we express the practice of these decency norms, or how entities should conduct themselves in accordance with these norms and standards. It represents in this sense a structural tendency (or parameter) of decency, a process of learning to reproduce these rules and norms of decency. But propriety also varies from culture to culture to reflect the many ways in which local cultural customs enable persons to fulfill these norms and standards of decency. Political propriety, then, refers to the actions and decisions taken by persons to fulfill these norms, while moral propriety expresses the moral conduct needed to internalize and structure decency in society.

The global dimension of moral propriety, as I shall explain in greater detail below, constitutes the open-ended global network of institutions, norms, and standards that help to determine what is and is not appropriate behavior for preserving and promoting global justice (e.g., human rights, health, and environmental protection). For many, the idea of global or universal decency expresses a basic human value found in all cultures, that is, a human value that partakes of higher orders of values (e.g., hedonism, self-enhancement, stimulation, achievement, security, conformity, tradition, benevolence, and universalism) and an "openness to change, conservation, self-enhancement, and self-transcendence," as Shalom Schwartz writes.[47] The practical, social, and material importance of this basic meaning of decency is what I call "basic decency," namely, the value of protecting the essential needs and conditions of upholding the dignity of all persons, regardless of nationality, race, sex, or religion. These needs involve the survival and security of persons, including adequate shelter, access to food and water, decent wages, a safe work environment, and free movement.

But basic decency, I contend, did not take root in global politics—at least not in practice—until the mid-twentieth century. From the late eighteenth to the mid-twentieth century, decency in global politics tended to mask the effects of projecting the civic, imperial power of nations. The idea of Great Britain, as discussed earlier, was rooted in a grand vision of moral progress predicated on the mission of civilizing others.[48] Great Britain's ambition of spreading its civic virtues of generosity, bravery, and kindness seemed to stem from a belief in the superiority of its military power and special responsibility to enforce the civilizational standards at the time. Yet its own prudish behavior at home—replete with its own moral constraints—revealed a dark side: the tendency to mistreat others who failed to meet their standards of civil conduct.

Tradition and the Dark Side

Although Victorian decency constituted a key feature of Britain's global vision of moral progress, it also raised the question of how British manners and proper civil conduct could justify racial prejudice and the unfair application of civilizational standards. These two negative factors suggest that British decency was never truly intended to accommodate others, but rather served as a tool for extending its influence overseas. If this is true, then the primary goal of its global vision was to preserve national customs, beliefs, manners, and political norms.

Preserving tradition and manners is what underscores the conservative strand of decency. It can be traced back to Edmund Burke's idea of a natural order that was based on the maintenance of traditional morals, laws, virtues, reasonability, restraint, and proper manners. The idea of an evolving natural order was that tradition and customs formed the basis of human development. The people comprising this order were those ruled by self-restraint and reason, while those judged to be outside of this order were driven by instinct and blind passion. Burke identified the latter in terms of the radical proponents of the French Revolution, who in acting out of a blind passion for justice, rejected the virtuous elements of this order.[49] This was not to say that the radicals lacked reason; only that they showed an unreasonableness when it came to recognizing the virtues of political reform.[50]

Burke in this sense embraced an incrementalist view of natural order. For him, order evolved gradually through tolerance or the recognition of other people's varying degrees of development and reason. This seemed to make him both a moral conservative and progressive, meaning that his idea was neither reactionary nor exclusive. Rather, it reflected the universal needs of exercising moral restraint overseas. That said, Burke's idea seems to point to a (unintended) reactionary dimension of conservative decency, or the collective desire of preserving a fixed social order. In its most benign form, this dimension characterizes a narrow sentiment of justice, in which championing the exclusive rights and needs of people conflicts with moral progress or the inclusion of underrepresented, marginalized peoples. And yet, in its most virulent form, it characterizes an irrational desire to destroy a prevailing social order that is considered to pose an existential threat to a traditional system of values. Decency is this most extreme scenario is turned into a source of anger by zealots who advocate the killing of innocent civilians as a means of resurrecting a past social order.

This inversion of decency, or the politics of indecency, finds its clearest expression in the messianic movements that embrace a purist model of the past, as highlighted by the Islamic State or ISIS, the Lord's Resistance Army, and Nazi Germany. These movements of anti-decency attack the very core of decency and its applied standards at the national and international levels, by seeking to eliminate both conservative and liberal sentiments of decency altogether. The Nazis, as is well known, adopted the symbols of blood and soil to justify a new master race and the killing of millions of innocent civilians. In *Homage to Catalonia*, George Orwell, in recounting his wartime experience in the Spanish Civil War, wrote that "the whole experience has left me with not less but more belief in the decency of human beings."[51] Orwell, it could be argued, had already begun to anticipate the need for resurrecting decency at the international level, where this time, it could be shored up through consensus and participation to combat indecency at the national level and to restore the elements of Victorian morality within a new liberal international order.

From Basic Decency to Global Moral Propriety

The emergence of basic and liberal decency at the international level represented the new rules, policies, and norms of protecting the essential needs, entitlements, and dignity of all persons. In providing a key component of the post–World War II liberal international order, it helped reinforce many of the liberal features of this new order, including impartiality, nondiscrimination, consensus-making, and the rule of law. Yet, in as much as it seemed to represent a new beginning in international politics, it did not, I argue, transcend the reactionary tendencies of conservative decency. Instead, it contained and suppressed them within what would become a divided United Nations. Still, it did mark the emergence of a broad consensus surrounding the laws, codes, and standards (e.g., adequate shelter, access to food and clothing, work protections, and access to legal counsel) of conventions and protocols, such as the 1949 Geneva

Conventions, as well as the creation of effective international forums for deliberating on issues related to international peace and security.[52] Indeed, the new rule-based liberal international order managed to embed the humanitarian norms, practices, and values that formed the basis of several key human rights documents and institutions, including the Universal Declaration of Human Rights,[53] the Genocide Convention,[54] the Refugee Convention,[55] and a retooled International Labor Organization (on workers' rights). The new international human rights regime thus helped standardize decency by putting into practice the rules and norms designed to overcome many of the exclusionary effects of national ideology and civilization standards (and their projection of racial, nationalist sentiment). The Universal Declaration of Human Rights, for instance, championed neither the natural rights of individuals nor the materialism of group rights; rather, it adopted the word "persons" to appeal to both sides and to promote equal dignity.

But the subsequent Cold War rivalry between the United States and the Soviet Union stymied this standardization process inside the UN. Not only did it help sideline human rights in the public diplomacy of the United States and other states' foreign policies but it also offset many of the gains made in the UN General Assembly, such as decolonization and international protections against racism. This had the unfortunate effect of encouraging political divisions along ideological lines and increasing the tension between social and economic needs and cultural rights. In an effort to resolve this tension, international policymakers and leaders adopted various mechanisms on minority rights protections, including the 1975 Final Act of Helsinki[56] and the African Union's African Charter on Human and Peoples' Rights.[57] Such mechanisms became emblematic of a growing commitment to combat severe harm and to promote further diversity and inclusion. The two most prominent examples of this trend were the Torture Convention (1984) and the Single European Act (1986);[58] both testified to the increasing solidarity around human rights that culminated in the 1989 uprisings in Eastern Europe and the eventual fall of the Soviet Union.

The Soviet Union's collapse of course allowed the United States to emerge as the sole superpower. Under its leadership—and the influence of many other liberal democracies—a sweeping realignment of state interests occurred, creating new incentives for promoting human rights protection and for voluntarily complying with new norms. Such incentives marked the emergence of a uniform set of rules and norms in global policymaking and new normative constraints on a range of issues, including child conscription, discrimination against women, abolishing the death penalty (for the sake of protecting human life against cruelty, especially in the case of juveniles and the mentally impaired), criminal accountably for gross human rights violations (e.g., the International Criminal Tribunals and the International Criminal Court), and special protections of minority rights (e.g., multiculturalism). In effect, the new laws represented the projection of liberal decency and the need to interfuse its features with those of basic decency. Basic human rights, or the rights considered essential to enjoy all other rights, became an important conceptual link between these two strands.[59] By this I mean that in signifying the essential "claims" to security and subsistence, basic rights could also be conceived as fundamental claims to fair and respectful treatment and dignity protection.

Nonetheless, by the early 1990s, the idea was that voluntary cooperation and compliance and governing by consensus could nurture the mutual trust required to sustain and enforce the normative constraints of the new international order. For some, the new global network of institutions, rules, laws, and norms (or a global civil society) provided the global resources to solve many of the problems that the state could no longer effectively manage, such as environmental pollution.[60] The new faith in the problem-solving capacity of global institutions testified to a growing sense of human interconnectedness that demanded the appropriate moral conduct to promote and uphold global justice.[61] Indeed, it represented something very new: a more open-ended notion of moral propriety in global politics, one that was very different from the moral propriety practiced at the national and international levels. The global dimension of moral propriety signified the practical possibilities of committing to and abiding by a uniform set of norms and rules of moral conduct in various issue areas of global politics. But as promising as it sounded, it also represented the challenge of maintaining an open field of inclusion, that is, the open-ended possibilities of spreading decency to resolve the cultural, social, and political sources of group and individual humiliation and exclusion. The main effect, or what I call the "propriety effect," was that this global dimension increased the range and intensity of tension between the uniform application of decency standards and the political and moral proprieties of underrepresented groups. Cultural pluralism and identity politics, in other words, were no longer outside forces whose effects could be transcended, but rather became integral drivers of this tension associated with the openness of global moral propriety. In this sense, global moral propriety created the political tensions it sought to modulate through a complex set of interactive domains or modes of institution building, including moral cooperation, capacity building, participation (in shaping the norms and process of governance), and dialogue (intercultural).

Moral cooperation stressed not simply strategic but deeper, substantive moral commitments among a diversity of actors to further global justice, most notably, environmental protection, criminal accountability, health, and security. By comparison, capacity building referred to two aspects: (1) the efficient utilization of political and social resources to build and diffuse responsibility (at regional and local levels) as well as to adapt to new risks and challenges; (2) and the actual recognition of autonomous capacity building, or the basic rights of individuals to develop and be protected from humiliation. Meanwhile, participation reflected the new opportunities for those affected by violence and injustice to shape the affairs of global and transnational institutions. Whether this meant participating in the European Parliament or upholding the International Criminal Court's (ICC) legal focus on a victim's right to participate in prosecutorial proceedings, participation complemented the second aspect of capacity building by providing novel opportunities to shape the outcomes of institutional policymaking. Intercultural dialogue, by comparison, which began to emerge in the late 1990s, has aimed to facilitate integration and communication among different cultural groups.[62] It stresses the need for negotiations and communication that advance open and respectful exchanges of ideas among different groups, individuals, and organizations. Both UNESCO and the European Council, for instance, have adopted broad agendas of intercultural dialogue to end the exclusionary treatment of, or discrimination against minorities, and to prevent conflict though communication.

In short, global moral propriety came to represent an uneasy and rapid extension of basic and liberal decency, one that targeted the effects of underrepresentation through the internalization of norms—understood as the acceptance of norms as appropriate standards of behavior in the identity of actors—and created the opportunities for persons to become directly involved in shaping the issues and matters related to justice and peace (e.g., the ICC). It was thus predicated on a human sentiment that was as vital as it was difficult to govern. Yet it did not transcend nor assure the permanent and stable progression of values beyond statist or nationalist identity politics (and its reactionary and normative pressures). To embrace this transcendent idea was to overlook the fact that states have long proved unwilling to fulfil their commitments, especially when preserving national customs takes precedence over emergent, yet contested, global norms (e.g., LGBTQ rights). Rather, it reflected how the effects of these universal commitments can shape the political reality of decency in global politics.

Whether one is referring to the Kyoto Protocol (1997), or the separate but more widely adopted instrument of the Paris Climate Agreement in 2015,[63] the Responsibility to Protect established in 2005,[64] or the Global Compact, moral cooperation and capacity building reveal the challenge of advancing decency by facilitating intercultural dialogue and participation. In this way, moral commitments and capacity building continue to form a double-edged sword in global politics, for in creating the possibilities of integration and further consensus, they also expose the perils of upholding the normative constraints against harming innocent civilians. The built-in tension between the special recognition paid to underrepresented persons via cultural pluralism, immigration reform, and multicultural politics and the general idea of not harming and disrespecting innocent civilians shows how decency can become complicit in its own unrealistic capacity to stabilize and resolve the conflict of global identity politics. In short, the resurgence of reactionary, conservative decency manifests the far more intense political effect of extending basic and liberal decency globally through identity politics; it confirms, in other words, how championing the instrumental value of decency remains integral to identity politics and to the reversal of liberal democratic norms.

The important point to stress, then, is that in the post–Cold War era, global populist pressures manifest the friction that is built into the reality of promoting global moral propriety's openness. It thus becomes unrealistic to proclaim, much less defend, the stable existence of a decent international order, or to draw on this notion to justify a global test of decency, as we saw in the political leaders' condemnation of the downing of Malaysian Airlines Flight 17.[65] By reinforcing the need for universal decency, these calls only end up disguising the complex source of friction between these standards and the reactive attempts to defend the identity and difference of current and past proprieties. Again, this is not to say that we should stop believing in universal decency, or that such an ideal is inherently problematic and counterproductive. Rather, it is to suggest that in pursuing this ideal, we also need to confront the political perils of applying an unquestioned belief in the common good in world politics. This critical pursuit involves understanding how the imposition of either liberal or conservative decency, or both, can create effects that contradict what it means to be decent, or to protect the needs and rights of the most innocent.

In distinguishing between global moral propriety and a global decent society, I want to show the importance of contesting what I referred to earlier as the orthodox idea of decency in global politics.[66] For unlike the idea of a decent world society, which seeks to affirm and preserve a shared baseline of values and beliefs or a common good, the idea of global moral propriety concerns the difficulties of working beyond the limits of this belief, limits that arise from the fragile notion of a uniform application of the rules of dignity protection and the normative constraints of the global order. The focus on a decent global society only makes this task harder by assuming that there is an unquestioned belief in, or a priori baseline of values supporting a stable sense of the common good. The idea of global moral propriety, therefore, allows us to register the diminishing and intensifying degrees of interaction of its domains, that is, to explicate the potential interaction of political and moral proprieties.

By the same token, global moral propriety has yet to reach its moral potential. By representing the practical difficulties of promoting a uniform set of standards, it shows how the pressures to conform to these uniform rules can trigger the unwieldy responses and reactions that become unmanageable and that reverse the moral progress made in expanding the laws and policies protecting the most disadvantaged people against harm. This is an idea I shall explore by theorizing whether a deeper sense of liberalism's emphasis on identity politics can also be construed as an attempt to realize its moral potential by embracing a schedule of group-differentiated rights designed to preserve and transform cultural identities. Liberal multiculturalism, for instance, treats these rights as a means of reconciling cultural pluralism and liberalism and overcoming the liberal (procedural) constraints of the global order (e.g., impartiality).[67] But, as Will Kymlicka, the liberal communitarian architect of this approach, admits, there remains the "global challenge" of spreading multicultural values to developing countries and preventing illiberal forces from capturing the liberal architecture. Liberal multiculturalism thus seems to beg a question it cannot fully answer: namely, how targeted group rights can intensify the propriety effect discussed earlier. Does the application of a uniform set of liberal rules and principles that targets and recognizes the needs of groups necessarily transform identities and free us from the effects of culturally insensitive rules and norms? Liberal identity politics leaves much to be desired in terms of diversifying decency in global politics. But its shortcomings also bring us to the nationalist identity politics that now opposes and threatens it.

Global Identity Politics and Its Challenges

The global challenge posed by nationalist identity politics is that it disrupts and weakens the rules-based liberal international order. The liberal international order of course has proved both resilient and flexible in its capacity to govern and manage social relations and cultural diversity.[68] It is an arrangement rooted in the idea of decency, insofar as it seeks to promote fair and equal treatment of individuals and states and to offer the rules and procedures protecting these entities from harm and humiliation As the primary institutions of this order, the United Nations, the World Trade Organization (WTO), the North Atlantic Treaty Organization (NATO), the ICC, the G20, and Brazil, Russia, India, China, and South Africa (BRICS) have all been responsible for promoting cooperation and consensus-making on issues related to the advancement of global justice, such as freedom of movement, free trade, human rights, peace and security, accountability, environmental protection, and the rule of law. In some cases, this has required states to surrender some of their sovereignty to international authorities, such as the ICC. But the trade-off between sovereignty and global authority has also pushed up against the idea of an evolving social contract among states, international authorities, and nongovernmental actors. As Jeff Colgan and Robert Keohane write, the international liberal order was "made up of free-market societies that nevertheless preserved welfare states and labor-market policies that allowed for . . . compensation for those who lost out from trade liberalization, and validation of the self-worth of all citizens" through interventions designed to uphold the dignity of persons.[69] The welfare state, in other words, constituted a bargain between socialist programs and capitalist market forces, one designed to protect the worker and domestic economy (e.g., the workers' right to collectively bargain and to strike) against the negative repercussions of the free market.

But when increasing foreign competition began to challenge these standards and the unions that supported them, officials stressed the need for more personal investment and less state intervention. They resorted to regressive tax policies that could steer more money away from infrastructural development, such as public schools and transportation, and into the hands of private investors. This ended up eroding much of the safety net protecting workers' rights while challenging the very notion of embedded liberalism, which had justified new social programs and prioritized the state's role in distributing resources fairly. The rise of neoliberal policies and principles, such as lower taxes, privatization, market efficiency, and personal responsibility, reduced the need for many social entitlements that were designed to protect workers' needs against the effects of unbridled capitalism.[70]

Still, the disaffection of the working and middle classes proved deep and profound. And it left many resentful and unwilling to take up the mantle of personal responsibility advocated by global elites (e.g., political and organizational leaders, experts, corporate leaders). In short, the white working class's growing resentment reflected not simply the loss of jobs. It also highlighted the rapid erosion of a social order that had once protected their rights to decent wages while also shielding them against the threats of unskilled workers and automation. By now, the migrants willing to work for less had become the objects of ire for much of the white working class, which increasingly saw itself as the victim of immigration. In appealing to this anti-immigration sentiment, right-wing populist leaders have stressed a return to cultural heritage and law and order in various parts of the world, including Europe, the United States, India, and Latin America.

Global populism has thus become the catch-all term of nationalist identity politics. Today, it poses the most challenging threat to the standards, constraints, and principles comprising the international liberal order.[71] With its tacit ties to white nationalism, it has managed to mobilize political discontent against the liberal international order and the extended qualities of liberal decency, in particular the rights of immigrants. In effect, global populism has come to represent the rise of reactionary, conservative decency, which hast created a gap between liberal and basic decency and exposed the limits of conservative decency itself. The erosion of the trust in the common good, which had once united the working class (albeit somewhat tensely) and managerial elites in the national bargains/contracts and global compacts that interweaved basic and liberal decency, has come to represent the effects of instability that only an authoritarian leader can control. Fear and suspicion in this regard become a means of deepening this distrust of institutions. For instance, claims that the rules-based international system is rigged heighten the political uncertainty that populist leaders manipulate by appealing to the traditional decency of their followers. The effect of such uncertainty is the rapid erosion of the credibility of knowledge and facts or the heralding of a willful ignorance that uses the term "fake news" to condemn any criticism of its leaders.

In addition to this gap between basic and liberal decency, nationalist identity politics exposes mounting political tension between conservative and basic decency. For example, the Indian constitution, which eliminated many religious codes upholding the Hindu caste system and helped pave the way for affirmative action programs benefiting the Dalits, the lowest caste, has not prevented the discrimination and growing violence perpetrated against the Dalits. In recent years, Guijars, a higher caste, have committed several unprovoked, brutal attacks against the Dalits, which included beheadings and scalping.[72] They have been emboldened by the Bharatiya Janata Party's (BJP) nationalist agenda, which draws on its belief in Hindu supremacist roots to champion traditional Indian society that existed long before the Indian constitution was written and India was modernized.[73]

Religion has in some cases become the source of increasing tension between basic and liberal decency, particularly in French society. For example, when the French government decided to ban the burka, which covers the entire body of Muslim women (the French Parliament also in the past banned the veil), it restricted the religious freedom and customs of Islamic women.[74] Fueled in large part by the outrage caused by an Islamic man from Tunisia who mowed down several hundred people, killing 86 and injuring nearly 300, the ban recalled a similar event in the 1950s when France (and Italy) had outlawed the bikini. While France's highest court, the Council of State, overturned the ban on the burka, the reactionary sentiment against Muslims managed to turn women's bodies into a "battleground," while at the same time challenging the normative constraints of basic decency and the propriety of Muslim women by targeting their desire to preserve their cultural heritage.[75] It is tempting to conclude at this point that the reversal of basic decency, or these gaps in decency, stems from the external pressures placed on decency. But this, I argue, would overlook how insincerity and bias can also become interfused with the global dimension of decency. There is, in other words, a political separation we encounter between the idea of decency as impartiality and the full inclusion of cultural differences.

The Cant of Decency

The reactionary politics of decency is the most overt expression of this separation, for it reflects the political tendency to fracture and contradict decency's moral threshold of courage, sincerity, and kindness. Such a tendency also symptomizes what I call the "cant of decency" (as a virtue): that is, the insincere, hypocritical, and even scandalous talk of morality in politics. Cant reflects why some attack others for lacking the very moral qualities that they themselves have expressed little moral commitment to upholding. This has become especially prevalent in the United States where many conservatives are quick to attack the liberal bias of the media, while professing to be fair and honest. In a Fox News segment of the *The O'Reilly Factor* (a news program), for instance, Jesse Watters and Bill O'Reilly discussed their interviews with the Chinese people on the street, referring to them as polite people. In response, Christopher Kang, the national director for the National Council of Asian Pacific Americans, condemned the segment for its "shocking level of callousness and lack of decency."[76] In effect, Kang was attacking the reporters for how they disingenuously sought to promote the word "polite" by being impolite toward these polite people.

The cant of decency stems largely from a growing cynicism toward scientific knowledge and the political elites. Tom Nichols, for example, argues that the loss of respect for expertise allows "the least competent people . . . to be the ones least likely to realize they are wrong and others right, the most likely to respond to their own ignorance by trying to fake it and the least able to learn anything."[77] The idea that knowledge itself is the enemy means that we no longer need to be beholden to accepted facts; that the freedom from the truth can serve as a political means of subverting the responsibility to uphold any general truth(s). Indeed, when Ben Carson, a former Republican presidential candidate and advisor to President Trump, insisted that the Khizr Khan family apologize to Trump for accusing him of not reading the U.S. Constitution, it was evident that he was seeking to justify decency based on a rhetorical question posed by Khan about Trump's not knowing the U.S. Constitution. One can also point to Trump's impulsive accusations of corrupt U.S. election officials in the absence of any evidence to substantiate such claims of corruption. This tactic has the contradictory effect of undermining the decent work performed by the workers of these institutions and the integrity of the elections process. In short, cant divests decency not only of its virtuous elements but also of its desired emotive qualities (e.g., empathy toward victims), as alluded to earlier.

Still, it would be overly simplistic to say that cant is merely a reaction of nationalist identity politics against the decency standards of the global liberal order, and that there is only a cant of virtue and not value per se when describing what we discussed earlier as the presumptive link between liberal decency and world order. After all, Jair Bolsonaro, the newly elected populist president of Brazil, who, despite modeling himself after President Trump, came to power because, not in spite of, his sincerity to root out corruption and restore Brazil's economy and safety. As suggested earlier, the core idea of decency, or its primal sentiment, predates the rise of liberalism or the secularization of this virtue. On the other hand, in the political arena, decency, which did not materialize into its secular, liberal form until the eighteenth century, has become largely synonymous with the liberal values and openness of global moral propriety. To recall, the idea of liberal decency was that all oppression and harmful practices were inherently unjust. But this also suggested that the liberal inventors of this idea were the tacit proprietors of this morality, that is, the ones who would bring justice to European society and beyond. In universalizing moral propriety, it was thought, they had produced the opportunities for a top-down application of decency that could enable others to adjust their cultural rules and customs to their invented standards of decency.

This self-serving notion of liberal moral propriety points to a second, albeit soft and latent form of the cant of decency, one that concerns the exclusive extension of liberalism to accommodate the rights of others, or rather, how liberalism's preexisting subject determines how one should think about and realize proper moral conduct on a wider political scale. The idea is that because decency expresses what is most essential to human coexistence via the basic freedoms and equal dignity, its core sentiment remains strictly coterminous with liberal values. This tacit, coexistent relationship is what naturalizes or universalizes these values, or both, and strips basic decency of its nonideological, diverse, and even protean content. Decency, in this sense, tends to reinforce a universal faith in the common good, because of human rights and other standards. It is when one uses decency interchangeably with the universality of liberal values that one necessarily suppresses others' creative and distinctive relation to this sentiment. This second tacit form of the cant of decency, then, is only loosely related to the more overt first level form of cant. But it is the second form, I claim, that helps explain the driving forces of the former and why, for that matter, liberalism can become delusional of itself or its high-minded aims of transforming world order.

This deeper extension of the cant of decency to global politics thus opens up the social and cultural gaps between international and local standards of decency. And it does so in a negative way: by unveiling the fractured tension between decency and liberalism (between civilized and uncivilized) and the political effects of broadening the scope of the humane sentiment underlying the international liberal order. But again, decency is anything but narrow and simplistic, since its open-endedness is always liable to collude with the moral exceptionalism of national, civic ideology in global politics. By this, I mean that liberalism, as the dominant ideology, can tacitly project such exceptionalism, as illustrated by a former advisor to Václav Havel who was asked to comment on Havel's political legacy:

> Many will ask what made Havel exceptional. The answer is simple: decency. He was a decent, principled man. He did not fight against communism because of some hidden personal agenda, but simply because it was, in his view, an indecent, immoral system. . . . : he was one of the last of a now-extinct breed of politicians who could lead effectively in extraordinary times because their first commitment was to common decency and the common good, not to holding power.[78]

Exceptionalism is what helps to explain the problematic role of U.S. and British decency in erecting and enforcing the rules, principles, and normative constraints of the international order. In both countries, the liberal and conservative strands of decency, which have played such a vital part in projecting moral values and manners overseas, involve many problematic, conflicting sentiments and issues. When projected through empire or these states' hegemonic power, these effects are often disguised in an effort to spread a universal notion of decency that applies to all peoples. But, in reality, empire obscures these effects by exposing the tendency to exclude or suppress other cultural and moral proprieties. In other words, whatever poses a difficult fit with the global liberal standards ultimately requires some form of rigid adjustment to these standards.

In sum, expanding liberal decency in the global realm reveals an imperfect and often strained link between liberalism and basic decency. Even the application of a uniform set of decency standards creates effects that global institutions seem unable to fully manage. Moreover, accommodating differences in a top-down manner only seems to mirror the problems encountered in the early twentieth century when Europe sought to manage the development of "backward peoples" via the League of Nations mandate system. The idea of global moral propriety, then, is that these tensions and contradictory effects should become the starting point of an analysis of decency, especially if we are to better wrestle with the challenge of diversifying decency rather than merely seeking to restore it through the revamping of the existing liberal rules and principles of the global order.

Overview of the Book

In chapter 2, I shall examine how the secular politics of decency emerged in the eighteenth century. In particular, I will address how the liberal foundation of such politics involved new ways of thinking about the relationship between justice and decency and freedom and religion and how it introduced the idea of basic decency at the national level (in the context of the French Revolution). This period in history would also reveal the tension and gaps in religious and natural sentiment and between liberal and conservative decency in national politics. I then move on to analyze how decency came to play a complex and contradictory role in Great Britain's empire or global vision of moral progress. The projection of British decency, as already pointed out, became tacitly aligned with the civilizing mission and the application of civilizational standards that were largely restricted to European states. This exclusionary effect arose from the intellectual conflict between naturalism and positivism and the subsequent prevalence of positivism, which helped justify and disguise the racial prejudice dividing British decency and cultural pluralism. Rather than reconciling reason and traditional manners, British civic imperialism came to symbolize the repression of difference and the consequent need to preserve British cultural heritage overseas. Not only were there few moral constraints on harming others, but the constraints that existed served merely as the tools for inculcating British customs and manners. In this way, British decency, I argue, reflected an unstable tension between imperialism and cultural pluralism. Overcoming this tension and the prejudice/bias that drove it would introduce a basic, practical challenge of promoting peace and security at the international level, or how, in this case, the United States' more open-ended, albeit strained notion of liberal and basic decency could be projected through the post–World War II liberal international order.

The central aim of chapter 3 is to examine the rapidly evolving notion of liberal decency at the international level, first by analyzing its conceptual framework, and then by showing how its extended application helped define the parameters of global moral propriety. Such open-ended parameters reflected, as noted above, a uniform set of rules and principles and an expanding threshold sense of decency that seemed to lie at the heart of the idea of a decent international society. But rather than unifying liberal theorists, the idea exposed divisions regarding its limits and universality. Here, I engage Rawls's use of decency to justify the law of peoples or the limits of liberal morality in global politics. I contend that the conflict between Rawls and cosmopolitan proponents of decency in international relations centers principally around the interpretation of capacity building at the individual and collective levels. The burden of globalizing moral propriety is that it cannot escape the effects of its statism or autonomous capacity building. The result is a fissiparous defense of decency in global politics, in which the ideological strands of decency contradict the basic decency that connects them.

This makes the problem of working toward a diverse sense of decency even more complex, for it suggests that only liberalism can effectively meet the challenges of multicultural representation. The question, therefore, is how liberal multiculturalism can meet the global challenge of moral propriety when its effectiveness remains tied to liberalism and an exclusive focus on the European Union (EU) to demonstrate how best to work beyond the statist constraints placed on cultural identity. In drawing on William Connolly's deep pluralism, I claim that the global challenge of identity politics requires rethinking of the very notion of pluralism in global politics. Here, I critically examine how Connolly's notion of pluralism contests the statist limits of liberalism and how, contra Connolly, identity politics is built into global moral propriety and its many open and closed reflexes, e.g., nationalist identity politics. It is these open-ended reflexes, in other words, that allow us to understand the challenge of advancing participation and intercultural dialogue and diversifying decency globally.

Chapter 4 addresses this interactive potential of decency in terms of the politics of affect. I distinguish between emotions and affect in order to understand the divisive and oppressive outcomes of global political pressures. The global politics of affect directs our attention toward the ontological dimension or political reality of decency. It does so by addressing an important issue raised in chapter 3: namely, how decency offers a root, unconscious source of tension involving cultural identity politics or the emotional intensity characterizing conflictual proprieties. More positively, though, it helps to shed light on the advantage of confronting this source, namely, the reflexive and interactive potential of the modes of global moral propriety. The idea of extending decency via the emotional intensity of love and compassion, then, creates a false notion of moral potential and expansion of its normative constraints. The potential for freedom, in other words, cannot simply be about getting beyond all formal constraints in order to realize the moral potential of connecting and interacting with others' moral and cultural beliefs and norms. It is about realizing the mutual interaction of practicing different proprieties and diversifying the sense of decency in global politics.

This is a theme that I examine in the three following case study chapters (5–7) of the book. In chapter 5, I analyze two contrasting outcomes of the struggle for Islamic identity in Egypt: the feminist struggle within the Cairo Women's Mosque Movement and the rejection of the moderate Islamist politics of the Muslim Brotherhood. Egypt has long remained a complex case of reconciling Western liberalism with national and religious customs. While the government has sought to accommodate Islamist demands and women's rights, it has failed to overcome the tensions between the reactionary and progressive sentiments of decency and to work toward balancing the preservation of Islamist values against liberal democratic principles. Still, such conflict is both complex and nuanced, since it involves interpretations of Islam that have either sought common ground with liberal secular values or have (subsequently) advanced a militant, extremist form of Islamism. These social and cultural gaps between Islam and secularism, I argue, stem from deeply, opposing political proprieties that are raising the political stakes of maintaining basic and liberal standards of decency.

Chapter 6 turns attention to the issue of reconciling global and local justice. Here I critically examine the possibilities of achieving a mutual complementarity of justice procedures and practices. The challenge with integrating international and local justice norms lies in showing that state politics is not the decisive (or default) reality in determining the potential for complementarity. The question this raises in terms of the ICC's operations in northern Uganda is how the application of its rules of procedure is creating the opportunity to diversify the interests in global justice. I argue that the ICC offers a framework for integrating the different legal and political proprieties, but that working toward this goal requires analysis of a bottom-up complementarity discussed in chapter 4. In this way, my aim is to explore the affective limitations of the ICC and relational sensibilities or proprieties of justice regarding the legal and political differences between international and local justice. The latter, as we shall see, signifies a procedural difference in justice between the formal and informal modes of justice and addresses the need of overcoming the top-down effects of the complementarity principle through mutual interaction.

The central idea I explore in chapter 7 is how the EU's transnational moral propriety has succeeded in resolving the long-standing oppression of the Roma. I shall examine the sticking points and disparities between the Roma's political mobilization and their traditional customs. In particular, I analyze how Roma political activism has come to signify the intensifying political stakes and challenges of bridging the moral propriety gap between the Roma community and the EU, as well as the rising conflict between state-run populist politics and EU legislation. As such, I will probe the historical and political sources of this discrimination against the Roma in Eastern and Western Europe, before moving on to assess how the EU's transnational moral propriety has failed to overcome the persistent, discriminatory stereotypes in various countries (such as Poland and Hungary), despite the Roma's efforts at building a political coalition consisting of different NGOs and based on EU laws on minority rights.

And finally, in the concluding chapter, I take up the question of why confronting the difficult political reality of decency can and should be a good thing. I argue that in seeing decency's political reality, we can also become better at recognizing and advancing its core qualities or redressing the harmful effects against the most vulnerable parts of the population. In the context of Trumpism, this also means understanding its role in deepening the crisis of decency and exploring new opportunities and possibilities of engaging decency's political reality.

CHAPTER TWO

The Making of a Basic Human Value

All the pleasing illusions which made power gentle and obedience liberal, which harmonized the different shades of life, and which, by a bland assimilation, incorporated into politics the sentiments which beautify and often soften private society are to be dissolved by this new conquering empire of light and reason. All the decent drapery of life is to be rudely torn off. All the superadded ideas, furnished from the wardrobe of a moral imagination, which the heart owns and the understanding ratifies as necessary to cover the defects of naked, shivering nature, and to raise it to dignity in our own estimation, are to be exploded as a ridiculous, absurd, and antiquated fashion.

—Edmund Burke, *Reflections on the Revolution in France*, 1790

The supremacy of it is stated with such violence, the victorious confrontation of these values with the lifestyle and beliefs of the colonized is so impregnated with aggressiveness, that as a counter measure the colonized rightly make a mockery of them whenever they are mentioned. . . . In the period of decolonization the colonized masses thumb their nose at these very values, shower them with insults and vomit them up.

—Frantz Fanon, *The Wretched of the Earth*

By the mid-eighteenth century, decency had come to mean something more than simply the public display of proper tastes and manners. It was now an emerging feature of a political consciousness that championed reason, virtuous sentiments (in justice), and the protection of individual dignity. But in expressing the larger societal need for ending corruption, torture, slavery, and even war, it also reflected a source of great political tension between reformists and revolutionaries during the Enlightenment. Many of those who advocated revolution and rapid political reform situated its virtuous elements of tolerance, courage, and kindness within a new liberal order based on freedom, equality, and the rule of law. By comparison, the most conservative reformists valued its elements for the sake of preserving the manners, traditions, and customs of the nation. Edmund Burke, as mentioned earlier, claimed that the revolutionary and, to a lesser extent, reformist politics of decency amounted to a betrayal of moral progress and civic order. For him, revolutionary politics elevated moral impulse above the forces of reasoned restraint and threatened to undermine a natural order predicated on the respect for tradition.

But Burke's idea of a natural order was neither exclusionary nor averse to rights protection, but rather sought to promote the reconciliation of tradition and dignity protection. It found its greatest expression in the civic character of Britain's national identity and its nineteenth century civic imperialism that revealed the many incongruities between preserving British customs (and rights) and tolerating cultural differences overseas. Yet, in this latter context, one also encountered a fundamental flaw of Great Britain's global vision of moral progress: namely, its seeming appropriation of exclusionary civilizational standards to justify the spread of British civility to other parts of the world. Rather than resolving conflicts overseas, British decency, I argue, increased political tensions and weakened this vision. In effect, the global politics of British decency produced an exclusionary dynamic of civic order that contradicted the notion of moral progress.

One of my aims in this chapter is to analyze this exclusionary dynamic by examining the various social tensions and contradictory effects of Great Britain's civic imperialism. In particular, I will address the difference between British decency and cultural pluralism as well as scientific reason and natural law, showing how Great Britain's idea of civilizing colonial peoples destabilized its liberal empire and engendered and legitimized identity politics overseas. Applying British decency globally thus reflected the profound difficulties of extending liberal decency to the global realm. My other aim is to examine the various ideas and debates that gave rise to liberal and conservative decency, including those which pitted the reformists (or the moderates who focused on moral sentiments) and the revolutionaries (or materialists) within Enlightenment circles. I then move on to show how Victorian morality and liberal empire became rife with the social tensions that reinforced the shortcomings of British exceptionalism. Finally, I examine how these unresolved tensions of British decency would give way to war and crisis, before addressing the role played by American decency in constructing the human rights and decency standards of the post–World War II liberal international order.

Moral Propriety and the Natural Order

In seventeenth-century Europe, the ecclesiastical and aristocratic orders used their influence to define and restrict the parameters of decency. For ecclesiastical authorities and their followers, decency characterized the pietistic qualities of humility and charity that affirmed devotion and submission to God's will. It was about demonstrating an unquestioned respect for and abidance by God's good graces and dignity.[1] Yet, in aristocratic circles, decency had less to do with this inner devotional quality than with cultivating the personal moral habits and manners that could distinguish a member of the upper classes from the lower classes. Showing decency in public was in other words a class privilege that entitled the aristocrats to follow an accepted social etiquette that enabled them to exhibit their worth or dignity in these circles.[2] Thomas Hobbes, however, saw these rules of etiquette as a superficial means of advancing moral judgment, calling them "small morals," which, as he put it, played "an insignificant role in how one judged civil matters."[3] For him, decency had less to do with promoting justice and civil laws than with how the upper classes flaunted their moral tastes and showed an insouciance to the need for just laws and peace. If anything, it expressed the sort of low-mindedness that reinforced an ecclesiastical and aristocratic order ruled by ignorance, corruption, and the vagaries of superstition.

In the mid to late eighteenth century, however, this social order began to crumble. A new high-mindedness of French and Scottish Enlightenment thinkers (in response to rapid industrialization and a rising middle class) began to replace the superficiality of decency and to call attention to its secular character, or the need for harnessing its individual moral traits of kindness, fairness, and courage to the liberal ideals that would reform and even revolutionize society.[4] Decency, in other words, expressed a new secular and ethical undertaking of justice, in which the primary goal was to advocate the ideals of freedom, equality, and the rule of law (especially impartiality) to combat the unjust laws of the ecclesiastical order. For Peter Gay, "the politics of decency" amounted to a novel and protean awareness of injustice, one that informed the high-minded yet practical campaign to end torture, slavery, war, and unjust penal laws.[5]

Liberal decency was thus about engaging a new politics of reasoned or commonsense morality. Moreover, it was an engagement that sought above all to strike a balance between revolution and rapid reform, rather than breaking entirely from the past. Reason was to be treated as a natural sentiment, which, unlike materialist or scientific reason (as I shall discuss below), was thought to function independently of past moral beliefs and values and was borne from a deistic, providential order where God allowed human reason to govern societal affairs.[6] Deistic reason emerged from the ideas of Baruch Spinoza, the Dutch philosopher of the seventeenth century, who theorized that human reason abided by its own natural laws.[7] He claimed that reason was a natural substance, whose properties existed independently of God's will.[8] In this way, he sought to dispel the necessity of God's active intervention in human affairs (or miracles), by theorizing that reason required the verification of the natural causes of events to overcome the political tendency to rationalize ecclesiastical dogma.

His idea of material and natural reason would have a profound influence on Enlightenment thinking. As Jonathan Israel argues, Spinoza played a formative, if not vital, role in shaping the materialist ideas of the philosophes of the French Enlightenment, including Denis Diderot, Claude Helvétius, Baron D'Holbach, and Bernard Le Bovier de Fontenelle.[9] For these thinkers it was the material elements of reason (its mechanical and causal properties), not its deistic qualities, that mattered. Their aim was to formulate a "reason-based" morality that was understood to function independently from the biases and prejudice of the clergy and aristocrats and their oppressive laws; hence, to validate the objectivity of law and to promote a humane and egalitarian society on this scientific basis.[10]

As the radical proponents of change, then, the philosophes treated reason as a progressive mechanism for resolving many contentious social issues, which still remain relevant today, including equal rights for women, gay men, and lesbians. But the trouble with this idea was that it considered religious sources of morality as obstacles to material and moral progress. This seemed to beg the question of how reason was itself formed, and whether scientific reason could provide a reliable basis for governmental action. As Israel put it, "The philosophes' radical focus on reason created a harmful chasm between government and the source of moral authority, making it much harder to 'direct the citizens' passions toward the common good."[11] In dismissing the role of religious mores in the development of a secular democratic society, the philosophes seemed obligated to start anew. But, in reality, it meant that the government lost an important and unique ally in the present and future struggle against injustice, as we shall see with America's Founding Fathers' invention of a public religion.

Many thus sharply criticized the philosophes for their dismissal of religion, arguing that it showed precisely the intolerance that had plagued the ancien régime.[12] But the criticism only seemed to harden the philosophes' conviction in reason's design: that it had to validate a permanent, fixed interest in justice.[13] Anything otherwise would mean becoming subservient to nature and allowing the irrational impulses and prejudice that resided in nature to thwart moral progress. Still, there were questions that remained unanswered. Was, for instance, their intolerance of natural law theory and metaphysics rooted in a rejectionist attitude that threatened to undermine their radical vision of progress? And what did their dismissal of natural law mean for decency's place in the liberal imagination, that is, with permanently securing the rights and duties of citizens, or imagining their eternal existence, which Spinoza and Locke had conceived in terms of reason as a natural sentiment of freedom? Finally, were the philosophes divorcing themselves from the idea of human fallibility and disembodying reason of this evolutionary quality?

For reformist-minded Enlightenment thinkers, such as David Hume, Adam Smith, Montesquieu, and Voltaire, the answers to these questions lay in the feelings that informed reason and its utility for reforming society in accordance with liberal ideals and moral virtue. Indeed, discarding this affective quality of reason constituted something inherently contradictory: namely, the emergence of negative feelings and intolerance that bred corruption. Jean-Jacques Rousseau, for instance, went so far as to argue that the philosophes' idea of a new secular morality was nothing more than an ill-conceived attempt to wipe the philosophic slate clean.[14] Divorcing reason from the passions, in his view, was tantamount to surrendering reason to the orthodox belief that only physical evidence could substantiate reason itself. This, in turn, led him to ask if reason could be cultivated in ways that did not require such evidence, but that proceeded on a basis in which the sense of human imperfection could provoke the passions capable of moving and directing reason. After all, not all past customs, habits, and values were inherently undesirable or oppressive. Locating their place in a new society became a challenge of linking decency's qualities of kindness and tolerance to the moral and secular duty of treating all people with respect.

But laying the moral groundwork for this connection required revolutionary and often counterintuitive thinking. Prior to the seventeenth century, tolerance, for instance, was considered by Catholics as a source of conflict, even a moral vice to be avoided, less one allowed enemy forces to gain advantage. However, John Locke, writing in the early eighteenth century, theorized that if intolerance drove sectarian violence, then toleration might well summon the reasoned judgment capable of containing sectarian violence.[15] As he put it, it was necessary to conceive that "toleration or the imposition be the readyest way to secure the safety & peace & promote the welfare of this Kingdom," "that part where in lyes the dignity of man, which could it be imposed on would make him little different from beast."[16] Tolerance was desirable under these circumstances, since it allowed both sides to recognize the dignity of each other. By suspending negative judgment of others, one learned to exercise not only proper restraint but the courage to see others as reasoning human beings, persons who were neither irrational nor prone to violence. Tolerance, in other words, allowed one to confront his irrational biases and impulsiveness, while intolerance projected these irrational biases.

In his long essay, *A Treatise on Tolerance* (1763), Voltaire claimed that the penal system had become steeped in such irrational bias.[17] Here, he recounts the wrongful, brutal execution of Jean Calas, a merchant living in Toulouse, who was accused of killing his son on hearsay testimony and then sentenced to a painful death by the wheel (where they broke and severed the limbs). The spectacle symbolized the dramatic effect of intolerance at the time. As Voltaire sardonically writes: "You know that intolerance begets either hypocrites or rebels; what an appalling choice! Finally, would you wish to uphold by the power of the executioner the religion of a God who died at the hands of executioners and who preached only gentleness and patience?"[18] No one in other words could exercise direct, unmediated judgment of God; only God himself could do this. The burden thus fell on men to administer the law humanely and sensibly, so that reasonability, and not foolishness, would determine how justice was properly carried out. Voltaire had, in this sense, become the wry champion of the rule of law, "the man," as Gay writes, "who shrugs his shoulders at the foolishness of the world and rails at the persecuting spirit of priests who will never become a fanatical assassin of dissenters."[19]

For Voltaire, then, tolerance was not just a political principle; it was also a political virtue that stood for the reasonable application of the law (without prejudice and malice). Indeed, it required the presumption of one's innocence, followed by the elimination of any unreasonable doubt to prove one's guilt. Only in this way could the rule of reason or burden of proof protect one from the harmful effects of prejudice and superstition. But upholding such a burden reflected the struggle against an ignorance that informed a spirit of inequality, which, as Montesquieu wrote,

> is when some singularly cowardly souls grow vain from the greatness of their servitude and when they believe that what makes them own everything to the prince makes them owe nothing to their homeland . . . everyone will come to love this license, the restraint of commanding will be as tiresome as that of obeying had been . . . that there is no natural right of holding another person in slavery, any limited justification for it must come from practical necessity and reason, in particular, a knowledge and understanding of the abuses and dangers of slavery. . . . Nothing brings the condition of the beasts closer than always to see freeman and not be one. Such peoples are the natural enemies of society, and it would be dangerous for them to be numerous.[20]

For Montesquieu, slavery degraded the self-worth of all men. Its justification assumed that some men were by nature unequal; that nature enabled men to discriminate on this basis. But this was hardly the spirited design of nature. Nature, in other words, was never meant to reinforce the dominance of one people over another. To say that it did meant divesting faith in humankind's capacity to know, communicate, and respect the difference in applying the laws of other cultures. No culture, then, had carte blanche power to hold others in servitude, to treat them as if they were beasts. Even if there was limited justification for treating persons as subordinates, it did not, as Montesquieu suggests, derive from any fixed or rigid law of natural inequality. In Montesquieu's view, all people were born with the natural right to be free from slavery. No lack of manners or refined customs could ever justify one's natural right over others, much less any unequal and cruel treatment. For Hobbes, such an idea was why we needed to distinguish between small and large morals in order to work beyond the unruliness and anarchy of the state of nature. The small morals in this case referred to the decorum that he associated with the "decency of behavior," which was about how "one should salute another, or how a man should wash his mouth, or pick his teeth before company and such other points of small morals."[21] Decency, in this sense, was a superficial moral insofar it assumed an insignificant role in promoting the duties of the social contract. That is to say, it made very little political difference in determining how one feared war or was motivated to voluntarily choose to transfer his right to a political authority. As skeptical as Hobbes was of decency's role in politics, he seemed to understand how its insignificance was related to the weak and exclusionary political system at the time. Without the ambitious political goals of liberal decency to oppose the manners and morals of the corrupt upper classes, conservative decency remained largely isolated from the political pressures and forces that would later shape it. It was not until the mid-1700s, as I have suggested, that we began to see these tensions and pressures emerge. But even then, many were seemingly reluctant to link the liberal ideals of freedom and equality with any humane standard of decency, or to see decency's liberal make-over as a pragmatic force for political change.

For some, the decorum of decency was simply too weak a moral virtue to cultivate man's liberal and humane sentiment toward peace and equality. Rousseau, for instance, suggested that decency was tied to the emergence of self-interest or *amour propre* (self-love), which meant that it was removed from the first sentiment of man's existence, his self-preservation. Rousseau treated this first sentiment of existence as the purest expression of human nature. It was, in other words, something that required a robust notion of morality to guide the ethical conduct of man. The concept of decency, he believed, was incapable of generating the unity and peace that could defend against or even overcome tyranny and inequality. "From that moment on," as he states of the emergence of tyranny, "there would no longer be any question of mores and virtue, for wherever despotism, in which decency affords no hope, reigns, it tolerates no other master . . . there is neither probity or duty to consult, and the blind obedience is the only virtue."[22] Although Rousseau appeared to link decency with despotism, he also advocated the sympathy and passion that embodied the humane sentiment for justice. Rather than replacing decency, the need for sympathetic action helped lay the grounds for liberal decency. For it suggested that the despotic function of decorum was inherently tied to its isolation from nature and any common humane sentiment. Rousseau in effect was exposing the political effects of this isolation, e.g., unaffected competition, narrow self-interest (to place oneself above others), and growing political inequality.[23] In so doing, he seemed to suggest that decency was part of a growing political awareness of justice, in which the conscious separation of decency from despotism could produce human flourishing or cultivate a common political sentiment of justice about ending human suffering.

Kant also appeared to distinguish between conservative and liberal decency by treating propriety/manners as an insufficient, albeit necessary, part of the idea of practical morality. "We are civilized," he wrote, "to the point of excess in all kinds of courtesies and proprieties."[24] Moral propriety was inadequate since "states' vain and violent schemes" could still hinder the development of men's moral natures, thereby preventing us from becoming what he calls morally mature.[25] The condition of moral underdevelopment involved man's moral predicament of unsocial sociability, through which man sought to be a part of society while remaining isolated as a self-interested person seeking honor and prestige. The question was how a person could cultivate a moral propriety capable of transcending this condition, which had hindered the realization of perpetual peace among nations. Was there a way of cultivating reason as a precondition for becoming aware of this antagonism and the prejudice and fears that drove one to treat others as common unequals? Kant's moral immaturity was predicated on the idea that the concepts we use to understand political reality were themselves unstable (when determined strictly on the basis of reality) and therefore incapable of cultivating any humane sentiment or sense of moral duty. If we were to conceptualize and practice liberal decency, then, it was necessary to recognize the tension between our belief in these liberal ideals of freedom and equality and the self-interest underlying their application to society. Overcoming this tension meant becoming morally mature, or morally autonomous.

To summarize: decency assumed a new role in advancing the ambitious political goals of the Enlightenment, which included liberating society from the effects of corruption and instituting reason and the rule of law. The difficult task facing most thinkers was making sense of the uncertainty surrounding decency's own fitness as a moral concept of justice and equality. Indeed, for many the central issue was how to cultivate decency in the emergent political consciousness of justice while overcoming whatever residual, reactionary elements remained of its former isolation from politics.

Common Sentiment and Impartiality

To address this challenge, Scottish Enlightenment thinkers embraced the cognitive features of common sentiments. By treating common sense as a natural sentiment, they believed in the possibilities of moral development and sensibility. Thomas Reid, for example, argued that our stored beliefs and thoughts amounted to a shared human knowledge about truth, meaning that the knowledge human beings held of the truth could be distinguished from that of animals. One's repository of knowledge was the result of years of stored beliefs and thoughts, which existed independently of the rational inquiry derived from sense perception. There was, in short, virtue in sentimentalizing the past and in expressing one's feelings about the beauty of justice and truth. As the philosopher Lord Shaftesbury put it, "If in reality, there be any sense of this kind . . . it must consist in real Antipathy or Aversion to Injustice or wrong, and in real Love towards Equity and Right, for its own sake and on the account of its own natural Beauty and Worth."[26] In Shaftesbury's view, we first needed to sense what existed prior to empirical knowledge and moral judgment. Like Kant, who reasoned that aesthetic judgment required disinterestedness in the beauty one perceived, Shaftsbury believed that when we sensed the beauty in justice and truth, we also became better judges about injustice and corruption.

A true judge of injustice, therefore, learned to refine his sentiments and passions, that is, love, sympathy, trust, and hate, and to orient them to the beauty of justice. Appreciating the truth of justice as beauty, in other words, meant rising above our conflicting interests and biases to properly judge objects and others in a disinterested and impartial manner. For many, impartiality came to be viewed as a core sentiment of valuing human life and the rules and principles that formed our moral judgment. In his *The Theory of Moral Sentiments* (1759), Adam Smith theorized that feelings and sentiments constituted the general rules and principles of morality. For him, these general rules of morality reflected an innate capacity to reason and to evaluate how passion affected our behavior. More importantly, they allowed us to imagine ourselves as an impartial spectator—the condition in which we insert ourselves into another's situation to judge the effects of one's biases on the person being judged.[27] A person, as he put it,

> must first of all, endeavor, as much as he can, to put himself in the situation of the others, and to bring home to himself every little

> circumstance of distress which can possibly occur to the sufferer. He must adopt the whole case of his companion with all its minutest incidents; and to strive to render as perfect as possible, that imaginary change of situation upon which his sympathy is founded.[28]

The impartial spectator constitutes the imaginary observer within us, the one who judges our actions and behavior and allows us to feel the pain or joy of others. As David Raphael points out, this means that "the agent can identify himself with the imagined spectator to the extent of obliterating the natural feelings of self-regard."[29] Smith's idea was that the actual experience of another person's suffering could never produce its mirror twin in us. Individuals experience things and suffer in different ways, which prevents any one moral viewpoint from dominating others. As he wrote: "Nature, it seems, when she loaded us with our own sorrows, thought that they were enough, and therefore did not command us to take any further share in those of others, than what was necessary to prompt us to relieve them."[30] Imagining was never a limited exercise, but an example of what Smith called a dulling effect of our volatile impulses and feelings.[31] Such an effect expressed how moral standards could, in one sense, be internalized to constrain and channel the blind energies of passion, and in another sense, show how in wanting to end the suffering and humiliation of others, we also needed to moderate our passions.

The challenge for Smith, then, was to demonstrate how this stored knowledge that lies prior to truth allowed us to dull the effects of passion and to remain steady in the face of pain and suffering. Concerning this, he states:

> The little sympathy which we feel with bodily pain is the foundation of the propriety of constancy and patience in enduring it. The man, who under the severest tortures allows no weakness to escape him, vents no groan, gives way to no passion which we do not entirely enter into, commands our highest admiration. His firmness enables him to keep time with our indifference and insensibility.[32]

By a propriety of constancy, Smith meant that any firmness of judgment had to keep track of the effects of one's indifference. To avoid becoming indifferent, or isolated in this sense from the influence of the passions and sentiments of others, one had to learn how to engage and control the reflexes of emotions and passions and to modulate the acute sensitivities to the suffering of others.[33] This humane difference made Smith a skeptic of any notion of universal reason that was assumed to function mechanically or independently of prejudice. As I have suggested, Smith believed that in order to become an impartial observer of one's judgment of others, one also needed to remain self-vigilant of the tendency to prejudge different customs and beliefs based on an assumed set of universal standards. This was another way of saying that when power collaborates with reason in rationalizing the use of force, it could also uncritically confirm one's beliefs. For this reason, universal morality had to be deeply negotiated by the agent, such that "by pursuing his own interest," as Smith claimed, "he frequently promotes that of the society more effectually than when he really intends to promote it."[34] In other words, to judge others fairly was to recognize the diverse ways of cultivating a common, humane sentiment.

Smith nonetheless remained cautious when it came to endorsing the universal values of reason, freedom, and fairness. His idea was that these ideals reflected a diverse range of feelings and customs, which needed to be examined cross-culturally. Smith's cross-cultural analysis, as Jennifer Pitts remarks, remained an attempt to engage the "generosity towards the evaluation of others' viewpoints against an awareness that the convention of Europe may also be causing undue harm. European customs and manners were embodied in reason, albeit not in a way that was exclusive to the European standards of society and technological progress."[35] Still, the question was how Smith's relational notion of European propriety was tied to the advancement of a secular, European education that could rid the world of superstition. In *The Wealth of Nations*, he argued that

> though the state was to derive no advantage from the instruction of the inferior ranks of people, it would still deserve attention that they should not be altogether uninstructed. . . . The more they are instructed, the less liable they are to delusions of enthusiasm and superstition, which among ignorant nations, frequently occasion the most dreadful disorders.[36]

In Smith's view, education was the best way to develop and internalize moral constraints against mistreating others. An education embodying European moral propriety was for him the best way of advancing humanity, for in contributing to the public good and working toward an inclusive political system, one would always need the resources for learning how to interact with persons with different cultural views. On this idea, Benjamin Constant, the French philosopher and liberal critic of Napoleon Bonaparte, wrote that "a sense of public decency will spread to the most indecisive and will carry along the time. . . . nobody . . . dare to remain neutral, lest he should betray himself."[37] The publicness of decency not only marked the need to prove one's honor and dignity to the citizenry—rather than simply within aristocratic circles or an ecclesiastical order—but also raised the challenge of preserving the traditional sources of honor, respect, bravery, and sincerity against the modern democratic pressures of institutionalizing the liberal features of decency, such as impartiality and tolerance.

The new public challenge, then, involved navigating the normative constraints of liberal decency; that is, showing how the shared belief and conviction in the rule of law, freedom, and reason could support and advance proper moral and civil conduct. It also meant downplaying and even dismissing for that matter, the role of traditional manners and customs in maintaining public honor, respect, and dignity. But the trouble with ignoring this role was that many Enlightenment thinkers seemed to overlook the limitations and difficulties of extending liberal decency to the global arena. In particular, they failed to appreciate the role of the liberal state in elevating self-serving notions of liberal decency, which, in the case of British decency, would reveal its dark side in global politics.

Burke's Conservative Decency and Geographical Morality

It was this looming darkness that Edmund Burke seemed to anticipate in his political writings about decency. As already mentioned, Burke's idea was that British decency overseas reflected the evolving ties between privilege and rights and the universal duty to preserve and respect traditional customs and manners. Burke insisted that Britain had a duty to respect India's governing institutions. In his response to Lord Hastings' public statement that India's system was despotic and its people savage, Burke was critical of Hastings' intolerance of the Indian government. Here, he intended to show that England's duty to respect the customs of other countries arose from the universal law of nations. English propriety, in other words, should not determine how the Indian people were to be judged or whether they were capable of being civil and just, for this only meant upholding the superiority of English standards of civility and justifying the disrespect and mistreatment of Indian citizens. In Burke's view, it was unreasonable and arrogant to presume the inherent immorality of the Indians. As he put it, "with everything respectable destroyed without us and an attempt to destroy within us every principle of respect, one is almost forced to apologize for harboring the common feelings of men."[38] If British moral standards only applied to the British, then, for Burke, this could amount to a "geographical morality" that undermined the universal law of nations. As Pitts writes, "geographical morality referred to systematic refusal to extend the moral and legal standards that the British recognized in Europe to Indians, as members of distant and alien societies."[39] For Uday Mehta, this criticism seems to make Burke "a champion of British liberalism . . . and its deference to gradualism and to its internal conceptual space, which relies on a teleology of progress and hence the genuine commitment to political paternalism."[40] His point is that Burke was not the conservative thinker who sought to preserve the traditional social order against liberal demands for reform; rather, he believed that respecting and valuing human life was a vital part of sustaining an evolving natural order in global politics.

Much like Smith, Burke treated education as a means of overcoming the effects of geographical morality and challenging British imperialism. In this way, he maintained a soft view on imperialism that was predicated on the belief that Britain had the most at stake in enforcing the incipient international norms at the time, such as antislavery. In 1833, for instance, Britain would become one of the first countries to ban colonial slavery on moral grounds. The new law illustrated how honor and kindness had coalesced to structure the moral constraints of the British Empire. By this time, it had become more honorable to express one's feelings openly about the suffering of slaves and to show one's feelings of shame.[41] As Kwame Anthony Appiah writes: "British honor, colonial shame; the honor of Liverpool and Manchester and the honor of the newly empowered middling classes: these all helped mobilize the people who went beyond the moral commonplace that slavery was an evil and built a movement to compel Parliament to end the slave trade."[42]

Honor was not simply an unchanging virtue or fixed moral code. It was an integral part of reform or gradual social change. Such an idea seemed to reflect the political stakes of defying the laws of gradual change, showing why the French Revolution for that matter, had come to represent a threat to tradition and social restraint. "We look up," Burke writes, "with awe to kings; with affection to parliaments, with duty to magistrates, with reverence to priests. . . . Why? Because when such ideas are brought before our minds, it is natural to be so affected."[43] For him, the French Revolution stood for excessive democratic zeal, which was fueled by an irrational impulse for absolute equality. It showed how revolutionaries had progressed too far.[44] But in threatening to upset the natural order of society, the revolutionaries' zeal also threatened to wipe away years of political and social progress. For civic morality to continue to evolve, it was important to preserve the cultural heritage and customs that could hold these destructive impulses in check. This meant, among other things, treating the constitution as an evolving idea of society and anchoring reformist laws in good deeds, actions, and acquired manners.[45]

But whether or not such liberal reform proved Burke's opposition to imperialism was an open issue. For some, Burke's conservative decency remained integral to his support of British imperialism. Daniel O'Neill, for example, argues that Burke, far from being a thinker cut out of British liberalism or a challenger to British imperialism, was a deeply conservative imperialist, operating, as he puts it, with a "deeply illiberal logic of empire."[46] Burke, he claims, was not only strictly opposed to women's rights but also supported American slavery and the uncivilized status of Africans. Both positions made him the kind of conservative thinker who treated British imperialism as a vital expression of British honor and tradition. Thus, to appreciate the value of Burke's sense of decency, we also need to keep in mind the tension between liberal and conservative decency, and how his conservative sentiment at home informed his more liberal views abroad.[47] His deep respect for Britain's cultural heritage, in other words, seemed to suggest his own support for the right of other cultures to be protected from the effects of imperialism or [Britain's] presumption of their inferiority and savagery. And yet, it was his strong advocacy for British education that also tended to favor colonialism, including the moral imperative of civilizing the savages and backward peoples, as we shall soon see. Either way, it is difficult to determine if he would have actively fought the imposition of British moral standards on colonial peoples in Africa, as this would have meant suppressing the social conventions of Britain's civic imperialism and restricting his idea of natural order. The most one can conjecture is that he likely would have endorsed education as a tool for inculcating order and civility in the natives.

In the end, Burke's political idea of decency was ultimately about maintaining restraint and adhering to gradual reform. To the extent that he sought a more genuine notion of the law of nations, he remained a guardedly cautious imperialist. Yet he seemed to anticipate the growing tension between moral inclusion or equal dignity and the global role of British moral propriety (and its collusion with nineteenth-century civilizational standards). At the core of his idea of British decency was the need for cultivating tradition and preserving one's cultural heritage and customs. More than anyone else of his time, he recognized the perils of combining decency with an imperialism that, rather than extending the natural order, constituted an imminent threat to this order's stability and the shared idea of global moral progress.

Victorian Decency and Civic Imperialism

By the mid-nineteenth century, England had greatly expanded its colonial possessions overseas, increased industrial output, and made considerable scientific progress under the rule of Queen Victoria (1837–1901). Together these factors enabled England to fulfill its global vision of moral progress, of bringing civility to the high seas and to other countries. British decency in this sense came to define Britain's plan to export its customs and liberal values overseas. But the strong sense of civic spirit that drove this extension of British identity to the global arena, and that was so vital to its moral mission overseas, also disguised the growing social anxiety and fear of political disorder at home.[48] In the early nineteenth century, in fact, Britain had begun to face a series of rising social ills that included public absenteeism, shabby work, homelessness, public drunkenness, and debauchery (high rates of prostitution).[49] Many in the upper and middle classes thus sought to distance themselves from these ills and the effects of industrialization. The middle class felt particularly vulnerable because of its newly acquired wealth and status and was quick to label the working class as lazy, licentious, and impulsive, for fear that they could easily fall back into poverty. Indeed, the repression and social anxiety of the middle class helped characterize the prudish behavior of the British during the Victorian era. But more importantly, it compelled many in the middle class to see decency as a way of affirming or safeguarding their social status and escaping the effects of the day-to-day social reality of poverty.[50] This was how British decency, I shall argue, took on a more public, albeit challenging civic role in defining liberal empire, for it meant exhibiting the "reasonableness" required to show civility, bravery, and generosity in public and beyond. Decency had in this way become integral to Great Britain as a civilizing power.[51]

The idea was that Great Britain had reached a point in its history when it could firmly project its exceptional character and civic virtues overseas. But it was an idea based on a profound tension between its global vision as a moral crusader overseas and its economic and political instability at home. Britain's civic imperialism was not the result of a long line of heroism or hero worship, but primarily rooted in the fear of the social, political, and moral dangers heralded by the social degradation and urban squalor of industrialism. Championing courage and fortitude meant elevating a selfish individualism above the corrupting effects of materialism, capitalism, and luxury. It was a "flowering of republicanism," Duncan Bell writes, that "placed duty, individual and communal virtue patriotism, disdain of luxury, and the privileging of the common good, at the center of the political universe."[52] Britain's self-denying altruism projected a civic and virtuous patriotism that seemed to outstrip the need for utilitarianism and its principle of maximizing pleasure to measure the social value of morality, as derived from Jeremy Bentham's pleasure/pain calculus.[53] Civic imperialism, in other words, had come to stress practical, virtuous action and self-discovery.[54] And British citizens were expected to exercise due diligence, a seriousness of character, earnestness (in terms of living by accepted rules), self-help, and respectability.[55] Such elements formed, as Asa Briggs puts it, England's own virtuous mission "to discover and secure moral order which would enable them to improve the standard of living and to connect powerfully in a country that had travelled far and fast in the 1780s."[56] It was a mission as much driven by a need to escape the effects of industrialization as it was to improve one's capacity to work beyond and control these effects. The concern with self-improvement thus reinforced a shared need for a strict(er) moral propriety to deal with the growing social anxiety about poverty.

But instead of leading to honest engagement with these psychological effects, such propriety produced a countervailing hypocrisy toward dissent in England.[57] Lord Byron referred to such hypocrisy as the "cant of virtue," which, as already mentioned, reflects an insincerity of speech. Cant, he wrote, "is a thing of words with the smallest influence upon human actions: the English being now wiser, no better, and much poorer and much divided amongst themselves as well as far less moral, than they were before the prevalence of this verbal decorum."[58] For Byron, the path toward truth began with a return to heroism and the celebration of our fallible nature."[59] It was about recognizing that cant stood in the way of this celebration and heroism. In terms of British decency, it reflected how people had learned to distance themselves from the truth of social decay rather than confronting its effects (e.g., drinking and prostitution) or the immoral reality that so many sought to ignore and stigmatize. In the early period of Victorian England (1830–48), for example, cant showed how the British had managed to wear their morality on their sleeves, marking a departure from the sincere passion of Romanticism (e.g., the Romantic poets) in which, as R. Jay Magill writes, "sincerity was a way to earnestly express feelings, to trumpet the truth of oneself and not simply to please God."[60] As one of the most celebrated British Romanticists, Byron claimed that the constraints placed on any strong display of emotion in public detracted from "maintaining a considerable respect for compassion."[61] On the other hand, it was precisely these constraints that drove the commitment to civic duty and that defined the social reality of one's everyday anxiety.[62]

There was little way of escaping this contradiction between insincerity and civic virtue. Indeed, by the 1830s, it had become possible to lead a scandalous private life while at the same time retaining one's good name—just as long, as Ben Wilson notes, "the private did not intrude upon the public."[63] The only way to deal with the tension, it seemed, was to embrace the proper manners that could give the impression that one had risen above these effects. And yet, as Wilson goes on to point out, this also meant giving decency the "unnatural form of manners that hypocritically subjected the lower orders to standards of behavior and self-denial that were not observed by their betters."[64] In time, such hypocrisy would come to characterize the high-mindedness underlying civilizational competence, that is, a civilizing prowess that emphasized the methods of scientific inquiry. For Norbert Elias, the civilizing process remained a product of a vast array of conglomerated molding pressures. Within this web, he explains, individuals learned to impose their own self-constraints by virtue of the "immanent regularities of society" and self-restraint.[65]

> The denser the web of interdependence becomes in which the individual is enmeshed with the advancing division of functions, the larger the social spaces over which this network extends and which become integrated into functional or institutional units—the more threatened is the social existence of the individual who gives way to spontaneous impulses and emotions, the greater is the social advantage of those able to moderate their affect.[66]

Elias concludes that the civilizing mission was, on the one hand, an irreversible process that exhibited an uneven pattern of evolutionary progress. On the other hand, it was a process that revealed the growing confluence of scientific reason and naturalism, as we saw earlier.

Civilizational progress came to reflect Britain's increasing fascination with scientific theory. Its deepening interest in science stressed, as Benet Davetian puts it, "a reliable and permanent value system and the ambitions of scientists to rationalize an evolutionary view of the world."[67] The world, it could be said, was on a path toward perfection, where, as Davetian argues, "the civilizing process brought on by the Victorian revolution was the high point of evolution. . . . and transferred the moral mission onto international turf."[68] Victorian England's embrace of scientific theory became a driving force of civil imperialism, because it provided a means of unveiling the inner workings of nature and the ability to use this new knowledge to cure Great Britain's social ills at home and overseas.

As one of the most prominent examples of British scientific progress in the nineteenth century, Charles Darwin's *On the Origin of Species* (1859) exposed the internal mechanisms of natural progress. Darwin's theory was based on the idea of natural selection, which held that changes over time were due to the variations of physical properties of species. Natural selection represented a truth based on a testable set of ideas and propositions derived from the laws of nature.[69] This seemed to have the effect of elevating England's moral propriety, since it suggested that its own moral fitness could be derived from the social laws of natural selection. In other words, the development of good manners was not merely a subjective quality, but an objective trait of the British who possessed higher morals and intellectual faculties because of their race. Social Darwinism, as it would eventually become known, was about showing how the racial superiority of the British validated their moral fitness and paternalistic responsibility to civilize others. In 1876, for example, Queen Victoria took on the new title of Empress of India.[70] This meant imposing the (self-) discipline and education needed to more directly manage and cultivate the Indian people's humane sentiments.

The Queen's view was also shared by many prominent liberal philosophers. In *On Liberty* (1859), John Stuart Mill argued that while all peoples could attain knowledge and self-development through proper education and legislation, only the civilized states and their peoples could implement and enforce civilizing standards.[71] Like so many (liberals) during this time, Mill believed that the natives required tutelage/special guidance to internalize the civil rules and norms of Britain. This led him, in turn, to restrict the application of his harm principle to European peoples only, even though the principle held that civilized countries could not impose their laws on others unless the people's actions had harmed others. Still, he insisted on the need to treat native savages fairly and to assume their given capacity to become civilized. In the end, it was this moral conviction in improving the races that became coterminous with preserving British moral propriety and upholding the new international legal standards of the civilizing mission.

Standards of Civilization and a Contradictory Vision

In 1873, the Institute of International Law began to interpret the concept of civilization, which set the stage for erecting the standards of civilization. The standards were largely the product of scientific thinking that focused on the objective qualities of international law. Such qualities "allowed," as Casper Sylvest claims, "for the positivist distinction between is and ought to be blurred, but in an intellectually acceptable fashion which in turn made the 'scientific' study of law compatible with a measure of moralism."[72] The compatibility between natural law (or morality rooted in human nature) and the scientific basis of law depended on the narrow application of both approaches to standardizing civility in international law.

The standards of civilization were nonetheless part of a larger movement to erect a liberal international order in Europe and beyond. European states stood at the forefront of this movement, given that many had either committed to or had already institutionalized liberal values and principles. As such, the leading European states had come to believe that newly codified civilizational standards could verify and measure the civil development of states and civilizations. According to Gerrit Gong, a civilized state had to conform to the following criteria:

> (1) the guarantees of basic rights, i.e., life, dignity and property; freedom of travel, commerce, and religion; (2) the state existing as an organized state with some efficiency, and with some capacity to organize for self-defense; (3) it adheres to the laws of war, while maintaining a system of courts, codes, and published laws which guarantee legal justice for all within its jurisdiction, foreigners and native citizens alike; (4) it fulfills the obligations of the international system by maintaining adequate and permanent avenues for diplomatic interchange and communication; (5) it conforms to accepted norms and practices of civilized international society, in which certain practices such as polygamy and slavery were not considered civilized.[73]

States that met these criteria were part of what came to be known as the "Family of Nations," a network comprised only of European states. Together, though, these states pledged their commitment to uphold the principle of the Comity of Nations adopted in 1862 and to promote the courtesy and friendship of nations as well as the mutual recognition of judicial and executive acts. This exclusive club of civilized states shared the idea that sovereignty was an evolving principle that was based on the capacity to act in accordance with existing rules of war, to uphold the dignity of persons, and to promote the emerging norms of civilized international society. This self-serving idea of sovereignty testified to the growing influence of positivism in the study and application of international law. Compared to the natural sciences, positivism was about merging science with law and moving beyond the natural law tradition that had for centuries served as the paradigmatic standard for evaluating moral progress and the evolution of the law of nations.[74]

Modern natural law theory held that right and authority were justified by reference to an extralegal structure or agency. The idea was that individual reason existed prior to the state,[75] and that from this abstract basis one learned to inquire and become aware of the value of the obligations and responsibilities of individuals. As such, the rights of all were borne from nature, not from the state or by God via a providential natural order. Positivist law, on the other hand, was about the man-made laws that could be deduced from observable facts of social behavior. The state in this respect constituted a concrete entity whose practices, laws, rules and decision-making processes provided the main source of facts. As one of the founders of positivism, Auguste Comte helped lay the basis for its application to law in the nineteenth century.[76] For him, social knowledge was predicated on measurable outcomes in behavior or results that could be verified through statistical analysis. Positivist knowledge would finally produce the certainty and social progress that natural law theory had not. Thus, in making this connection between legal and methodological (philosophical) positivism, it is important to note that legal positivism was not about verifying the effects of social forces or events; rather, it was an approach designed to address the legitimacy of legal norms and rules, such as state sovereignty. Methodological positivism, by comparison, focused on the facts and tools that allowed us to measure the effects of social and natural phenomena and to verify the social perceptions and biases informing legal positivism. This is how the above theories on the social development of the human species (e.g., Darwin's natural selection theory) came to support the moral stature of Western civilization and the idea that new civilizational standards could legitimize the advanced state of Britain's empire in relation to other peoples.

Accordingly, while the new civilizational standards presented an opportunity for Britain to apply its power pursuant to international law, they also became, as Andrew Fitzmaurice states, a "liberal apology for the civilizing mission," which, in uniting evolutionary theories of progress with the evangelical dimension of Victorian society (in terms of moral and human progress or ridding human misery/suffering), made it possible to justify the maltreatment of other peoples.[77] It was an apology, however, that also signified the growing tension between positivism's false evidence of social disparities in intelligence and naturalism's idea that all peoples were born equal and endowed with reason.[78] Racial prejudice, in other words, had wedged itself between decency and cultural difference, to the extent to which it rendered any pragmatic effort to manage the tension fruitless. In short, decency was no longer capable of serving as a moral virtue of impartiality and universal code of respect. Instead, it had become an outlier virtue, meaning that it now played an active role in rationalizing the effects of harm, bias, and disrespect that it sought to modulate. This outlier status reflected a much larger contradiction of decency's role in global affairs: that inasmuch as it had become displaced from its natural sentiments, it was this displacement that showed how nature could be appropriated to evaluate or judge the worthiness of others.[79]

The conflict between natural and positivist law, therefore, demonstrated just how fractious the relationship had become between international law and liberalism. As Fitzmaurice writes:

> While it is true that both international law and liberalism emerged in an imperial context, that context must be understood to include both pro- and anti-imperial voices. Liberalism may have been constituted by consensus about the desirability of liberty, rights, duties, and the sanctity of property, but it was characterized by a dialogue about how to achieve these objectives and by divisions over fundamental issues such as whether the origin of rights was inside or outside of states.[80]

As this passage suggests, it was never clear if either positivism or natural law served the interests of the colonizers, or even why the native savages were assumed to possess no natural right to property. Neither approach alone seemed to determine the course of the adoption and implementation of the standards.[81] If anything, the tension between these approaches reflected the conceptual difficultly of reconciling the pragmatic Western ideals of freedom and equality with the different cultural customs of other nations. Inasmuch as British decency may have helped soften this tension, then, it also signified how a socially elevated moral propriety could come into conflict with liberalism's emphasis on freedom from restraint. For Herbert Spencer, the liberal philosopher of the Victorian Era, it suggested how, in the process of social evolution, "usage can precede law" and receive an authoritative endorsement that reinforced the limitation of liberalism (or enforcement of its principles).[82] The limitation of liberalism seemed to reflect the overreliance on British decency to work beyond this limitation. In effect, decency had reinforced this limitation by becoming a nonnegotiable condition or requirement for inclusion in the civilized world.

In the 1870s, Victorian international lawyers began to confront this contradictory dynamic. Working through two associations, the Institute of International Law and the Association for Reform and Codification of the Law of Nations, the jurists debated the boundaries of law, including who constituted the subjects of law.[83] They agreed that while international law would not be binding for non-European peoples, it would not obligate the Europeans to abide by such principles in their interaction with these peoples. They deemed that non-European states' laws and policies were too undeveloped to shape the affairs of European states, and that the former states were not fully sovereign or recognized as civilized.[84] By the same token, the gray-area countries, which included Japan, Siam, and the Ottoman Empire, were not considered fully civilized, since they only partly met the criterial standards of civilization. This was a surprising conclusion since these states' customs and laws were part of civilizations that stretched further back in history than European civilization. Yet Victorian lawyers chose to ignore this factor and to presume that the laws of modern Europe constituted the primary source of the standards of civilization. More than anything, this deliberate oversight reflected the ability of European states to dictate the application of these standards. As Martti Koskenniemi points out, "Negotiations had to be made through particular treaties or a case-by-case basis that were largely dictated by European states. . . . all of this gave the appearance of fair treatment and regular administration to what was simply a conjectural policy."[85]

Aside from political power, Evangelicalism played a vital role in determining how such standards were applied. In Britain's case, it assumed a particularly important role in helping the British to dismiss the cultural customs and beliefs of native peoples. By all accounts, Evangelicalism drove a conjectural policy of civilizing the natives by justifying a higher obligation or calling to save the souls of others.[86] Saving in this sense seemed to legitimize the severe ill-treatment in the name of Christ's work, by showing how "Christianity's universalist aspirations," as Gong puts it, "were easily transformed into notions of a universal civilization which could progress by adhering to scientific principles."[87] The idea was that "saving the savage" was necessary "so that the civilizing process of social order could be extended to all nations," writes Elias.[88] The standards of civilization thus restricted the extension of the natural order (and its natural rights) to British citizens, which meant that Evangelicalism, rather than mitigating the tension between naturalism and positivism and reasonableness and cultural pluralism, reinforced the exceptionalism of British moral propriety. In effect, British civilized manners and virtues had made the British the chosen rulers. The colonized people, in the eyes of the British, were, as Antony Anghie aptly points out, "devoid of social purposes and separated from the realities of social life."[89]

The question, then, was how the championing of civilization was inherently opposed to freedom. Did such championing of civilization impose the blind constraints that limited its potential for development and the narrow-sighted tendency to restrict freedom? In *Civilization and Its Discontents*, Sigmund Freud wrote that civilization was rooted in a desire for freedom that restricted its own extension in the world:

> The liberty of the individual is no gift of civilization. It was greatest before there was any civilization, though then, it is true, it had for the most part no value, since the individual was scarcely in a position to defend it. The development of civilization imposes restrictions on it, and justice demands that no one shall escape those restrictions. . . . The urge for freedom, therefore, is directed against particular forms and demands of civilization or against civilization altogether. It does not seem as though any influence could induce a man to change his nature into a termite's.[90]

Freud concluded that it was unclear whether any expedient accommodation could provide the happiness needed to resolve this tension between the individual's claim to freedom and the group's demands for preserving their values. The struggle of civilization was primarily concerned with how civilization's own restrictions had produced the pressures for expedient accommodation. For Britain, this expedient accommodation through educational development was the solution to reconciling these competing claims. But such accommodation, as we have seen, also reflected the degree to which these civilizational standards excluded the values and customs of other peoples and projected Western bias against these peoples.

It should also be noted that by the 1880s, Britain and much of Europe engineered many technological breakthroughs—including the multiple chamber gun, steam engine, and telegraph—that would reinforce the link between Evangelicalism and military power. As a result, there was less need to accommodate and more strategic desire to validate Europe's civilizational prowess. The technological gap between Europe and other parts of the world thus encouraged European states to further impose their military power and values on the native population.[91] While some African chiefs and natives resisted such hostile intervention in their way of life, many had already faced the reality of European invasion and their exclusion from British rule. In fact, most, if not all, Africans could not participate in treaty talks and negotiations, causing, as Anghie argues, "native resistance and opposition to be silenced by the positivist practice of reassessing a treaty with no regard to the violence and coercion which led to its formation."[92]

Victorian decency, in sum, represented an important feature of Britain's national identity and its global vision of moral progress. Not only did it arise at a time of great scientific progress but it also constituted a key moral driver of Britain's civic imperialism. But, in driving such imperialism, it also played a contradictory role in the Evangelical mission of civilizing native peoples. By reinforcing the national bias toward British manners and education, it became a political tool for oppressing non-European peoples. This, in turn, had the effect of betraying British decency and its emphasis on kindness, preserving the integrity of customs, and linking the capacity to choose with self-improvement. The effect, as we saw, grew out of the need to escape the social ills of rapid industrialization, which led Britain to project a self-serving global vision of moral progress. The rise of both methodological and legal positivism thus became the approach for confirming and championing this hypocrisy as well as justifying exclusionary civilizational standards. Victorian moral propriety in the end came to reinforce perceptions of the native peoples' own lack of civil propriety, which needed to be corrected through the forceful and hostile application of British decency.

The Duality of British Moral Propriety

The Berlin Conference (1884–85) marked the culminating event of this self-serving application of decency overseas. By annexing and acquiring colonial lands in Africa and instituting the sacred trust of civilization (where European states saw themselves as entrusted with a power to civilize or bring the natives into the civilized world), the leaders of Germany, England, Belgium, France, and Italy agreed to carve up Africa into colonial possessions among themselves. King Leopold II of Belgium, for instance, took control of the new puppet Congo Free State, while Britain assumed control over southern parts of Africa.[93] The leaders of the conference now took official license to rule over and impose their rules of propriety over natives. In exploiting the natural resources of these countries, European states assumed that native peoples lacked any mature sense of or capacity for decency and moral propriety. Britain seemed to be an exception in this case insofar as it took issue with the latter, or the capacity of the native peoples to abide by a higher moral propriety. As notable as this may have been, it also placed a strong moral burden on British administrators and leaders to uphold the universality of the standards of civilization. Beyond this, it suggested a disingenuous attempt to use the universality of these standards to forcibly reeducate the natives and to eliminate their cultural identity. As Koskenniemi points out about Britain's and other European states' policy: "In terms of dealing with otherness, [Europeans] had at least recognized the hypocrisy that was the flip side of universalism—the technique of including the non-European into European concepts by doing away with native identity."[94] With little or no sense of obligation to consult the natives or understand the worth of their customs, the Europeans reaffirmed their limited engagement with the native people by making it clear that the natives' ritualistic customs and beliefs could not, as Koskenniemi argues, "be logically reconciled with an alternative, pluralistic conception of state sovereignty."[95] In effect, Europe had managed, in the context of colonialism, to subordinate its view of natural rights and the natural order to its self-fulfilling and restrictive notion of the sovereign state.

Victorian decency, as I have argued, both shaped and was shaped by this growing alliance between positivism and self-serving naturalism. Politically, it had come to represent what we might call positivist morality, which could measure morality, that is, validate not only the boundaries of liberal constraint but also the superior morals and manners to determine the moral fitness of others' cultural customs. The same fear the British reserved for the effects of poverty was now marshalled against the natives and their differing beliefs. This, in turn, helped to invert the impartiality and other virtuous elements of British decency (self-improvement, respectability, and reasonability) at home by justifying a moral propriety overseas that could be applied to redress the natives' lack of propriety. This dual dimension of decency became central to understanding the operations of Britain's moral propriety, for it characterized "how," as Sandra den Otter states, "just, impartial and universal law could be given and . . . a legal reformation could inculcate the civic virtues essential to enjoying political liberty, notably individual rights to the security of property and freedom of contract."[96] In the context of colonialism, then, the rule of British law and legal codes represented a uniform set of rules that were used to legitimize British morality and to legislate it for the native peoples. Because British decency involved top-down constraints that forced it to steer clear of the stark cruelty shown by other European nations, such as Belgium and its ruler, King Leopold II, Britain seemed to possess a deeper commitment to moral propriety in the colonies. And yet, the colonial natives' subordinate place in this moral order represented a hidden, inner struggle to internalize such moral propriety as their own. Many non-white intellectuals saw such propriety not as a stabilizing force of the common good but as a source of conformist behavior or shallow loyalty to British customs.

In *Beyond a Boundary*, C. L. R. James claimed that in coming to England to play cricket, he had quickly learned how politics blunted and complicated the influence of British propriety:

> people educated as I had been could move rapidly from uncritical admiration of abstractions to an equally uncritical hostility to the complex reality. Some coloured well-to-do who had been well received in England used their experiences there as a weapon against the backwardness of the local masses, against the arrogance of the English in the colonies and the local whites. Political passion easily submits all other values to its purposes. Reactionaries would hold up the English as models far above us. The incipient nationalists armed themselves with bombs for debunking. In all the drumming and fifing done to England I could distinguish no order.[97]

The semblance of moral order spoke to the longstanding tradition of imposing European values (individual competition, liberty, and materialism) on colonial peoples. Marshalling these values against ancient civilizations presumed the moral prowess and development of modern civilization, while calling into question the moral fitness of ancient civilizations. In his letter to W. J. Wybergh, a member of the Indian Legislative Assembly, Mahatma Gandhi claimed that Britain's modern civilization could never instruct the Indians' struggle for liberation from Britain. "I cannot," he wrote, "help most strongly contest the idea that the Indian population requires to be roused by the lash of competition and the other material and sensuous, as well as intellectual stimuli. I cannot admit that these will add a single inch to its moral stature."[98] In advocating *satyagraha*, or the principle of nonviolence practiced by the common people (and its features of cooperation and civil resistance), Gandhi defended the ancient law of self-sacrifice and conscious suffering. The purpose, he argued, was to realize that "non-violence lies, dormant in the brute. . . . and the dignity of man requires obedience to the higher law—the strength of the spirit."[99] Obedience in this sense was the opposite of meek submission to the law(s) of the brute. To be conscious of *satyagraha*'s strengths, truth, and power was to confront and resist both the falseness and uselessness of arms and war as a means of achieving honor and strength. Gandhi thus recognized that the moral fitness of *satyagraha* was both the means and end of liberating humanity.

Still, in some African colonies, most native intellectuals chose the path of least resistance by embracing the values of material consumption and competition. Many upper-middle-class native bourgeoisie practiced these values, only to become the buffer against the native people's resistance to colonialism. They represented those who wished to fit in morally with Western lifestyles; but they remained divided against the intellectual discontents who resisted the moral duality (absence/presence) of colonization. The boundary between these two camps reflected the power of racial prejudice and class propriety in colonized societies. In *Congo: The Epic History of a People*, David Van Reybrouck describes how the upper-strata natives under Belgian control wished only to possess the same virtues and latest fashions of the colonizers.[100] The upper-strata natives were called *évolués* (evolved), whose sycophancy was unmatched for its development and refinement. The Belgians, as one might expect, welcomed the sycophants. And yet, as late as the eve of independence in 1960, the *évolués* were not allowed to integrate into society. Colonial politics, it seemed, relied on the moral propriety of the colonizer to simultaneously soften the edge of the brute's law and to suppress the revolutionary zeal of the natives.

For Frantz Fanon, writing in the context of the violence of the Algerian War (1954–62), this meant accepting the natives' innate moral impropriety. The idea that moral values could only be found in the developed countries of the colonizers, was, as he proclaims,

> not enough for the colonist to affirm that those values have disappeared from or still better never existed in the colonial world. The native is declared insensible to ethics; he represents not only the absence of values, but also the negation of values and in this sense he is the absolute evil. He is the corrosive element, destroying all that comes near him; he is the deforming element, disfiguring all that has to do with beauty and morality; he is the depository of maleficent powers, the unconscious and irretrievable instrument of blind forces.[101]

Here, Fanon argues that colonialism was based on the Manichean logic of black (evil) or white (goodness), in which blacks were treated as inherently evil and the white colonizers were naturally virtuous and as such entitled to inflict violence to repress this evil. Violent colonial rule permeated the natives' muscles, bodies, and minds, creating an inferior self-image. The only alternative, Fanon believed, was the absolute means of violence, or the uncompromising use of violence to bring about the totalizing awareness of one's oppression and lack of human development.[102] Unlike Gandhi, who claimed that the common people could consciously embrace self-sacrifice as their own law of resistance and salvation, Fanon insisted that any such law was merely the extension of this inferior self-image. In other words, any compromise with the colonizer, whether through decolonization or cooperation, would only reinforce the colonizer's political influence over the native and stymie the colonial natives' liberation and human development. Fanon's idea, then, was that a new humanism was only possible through a totalizing notion of armed resistance: that our understanding of this notion was rooted in the dialectical struggle between the colonized and colonizers.

Yet, "far from constituting an a priori universal," as Nigel Gibson points out, "Fanon's dialectic of individual and national armed struggle was a constantly developing process . . . and figured in immediate social relations, given the interrelationship between the intellectual and the armed movement."[103] To overcome the deep-seated effects of the dualism of civilized and uncivilized propriety in the colonies, it was necessary, as we shall see, to create a more open-ended moral propriety that stressed the urgency of meeting the basic needs of security and subsistence, as captured by the phrase that Karl Marx made famous: "from each according his ability, to each according to his needs." The liberal British state, in short, would have to find a better way to meet the basic social and cultural needs of the native peoples if it was ever to resolve the more pressing contradictions of this dualism.

Moral Pragmatism and the Dying Civilizing Mission?

By the early twentieth century, British and international authorities adopted a lego-pragmatic approach to address the issue of the native peoples' underdevelopment. Highlighting this approach was the League of Nations' (1919–39) international mandate system, which provided an economic system for managing and administering the self-governing units of backward societies and which sought to gather information on the native populations. The Permanent Mandates Commission, for instance, deployed new techniques and social programs, such as educational facilities and skilled transitioning strategies, which allowed officials to manage the social needs of natives and to transform cultural identities through participation and self-representation (e.g., Papua New Guinea and Cameroon).[104]

The mandate system thus marked an important shift from positivism to pragmatism in international law. Many hoped that its developed techniques of social engineering would broaden the remedial function of international law by granting native peoples the opportunity to adapt to the new international rules and laws and to govern their own cultural affairs. But in reality, it failed to deepen cultural diversity or promote cultural identity. For the most part, the mandate system required treating cultural difference as a deficiency or backward trait that could only be remediated with sophisticated techniques. Anghie, for instance, argues that the difference "operated with respect to the most intimate aspects of native life—his psychology, customs and health."[105] It was, as he points out, a "dynamic of cultural difference in which the science of objectifying the cultural differences of the peoples became a false effort at universalizing Western legal standards."[106] The dynamic stemmed from an optimistic faith in the neutrality of the mandate system's social programs, which informed not only the decision to replace "savage" with "backward" but signaled the introduction of new social rules and norms to manage the backward peoples' transition to civilized life. In short, the mandate system failed to ever advance a pragmatic shift that could, in practice, bridge the troubling gap between positivist and natural law. In symptomizing the deeper flaws of the League of Nations, such as weak enforcement (the U.S. Senate voted against ratifying the League of Nations Covenant in 1920) and high-minded idealism, it seemed to have the opposite effect of intensifying racist and nationalist sentiment against legal pluralism and moral idealism.

Nazi Germany and fascist Italy, for example, saw the League as a threat to their own national culture. But instead of dismissing the League, they manipulated it by using the League Covenant's principle of self-determination and its civilizing norms to marshal their plans of war and conquest.[107] In particular, Benito Mussolini invoked Article 22 of the Covenant, which stipulated that the "advanced nations were responsible for advancing the ideals of freedom," to launch his own brutal and hostile civilizing mission of the Abyssinian lands.[108] Fascism and Nazism in this respect came to represent the complete inversion of decency and pragmatic moral propriety at the League. By stressing how Jews were an alien race that threatened Germany's survival and German culture, the Nazis used the state to project their false sense of mistreatment or victimization by the Jews. The Nazis' rise to power seemed to expose the flaw of positivist law and its championing of state sovereignty over individual natural rights. By showing how the state's domination of nature applied to all other aspects of political and moral life, it proved that "in recognizing only the progress in the mastery over nature," wrote Walter Benjamin, a critical and literary theorist of the early twentieth century, "one loses sight of the retrogression of society and the technocratic elements found in Fascism; but more importantly how the exploitation of nature is intricately tied to the exploitation of labor."[109]

For Carl Schmitt, a political scientist of the Weimar and Nazi regimes, the League's civilizational standards contained a far more perplexing moral flaw, or what he saw as the ceaseless pursuit of the moral ideals of freedom and equality. Distinguishing between the liberal and ontological dimensions of friend versus foe, he argued that fighting for the humanitarian ideals of the League of Nations had managed to undo the ontological constraints of war.[110] Waging war in the name of human rights, in other words, was to engage in a conflict with no definable political goal. The only logical way of maintaining any of the structural constraints against war was to surrender one's individual freedom to a strong sovereign or decision maker, the one who, in his mind, could dissolve the constitution as a defining test of defending against foreign threat.[111]

Schmitt's authoritarian views seemed to capture the perils of preserving morality through a positivist framework of international law. If there was one true victim of positivism's dangerous implication of projecting state power as an end in itself, it was individual dignity. For example, Hersch Lauterpacht, a prominent international legal scholar of the twentieth century, argued that positivism's emphasis on the autonomy of the state had made it possible to abandon the rationalism of natural law and individual rights. Positivism, in his view, had enabled an aggressive nationalist impulse to go unchecked and to subvert the constraints of international law, thereby trumping the basic rights of people. In the end, Nazism forced many to question not only the shortcomings of liberal decency in international law but also the dangerous implications of inventing a new social order that (falsely) claimed to preserve the purity of manners and customary morals.

Still, Nazism did not mark the end of decency in international relations. In his writings, George Orwell celebrated decency by trying to understand the forces that worked against it. For him, war involved a group fixation on the common enemy—an ideology and group talk that Gustave Le Bon had diagnosed in the late nineteenth century,[112] and amounted to a total refusal to engage the powerful forces destroying Victorian liberalism's moral constraints. As Anthony Stewart puts it, Orwell's notion of decency represented "a dual sensibility that does not narrowly exclude others in the interest of self-personal gain, but instead acknowledges the interests of others in addition to its own."[113] It meant respecting and treating others humanely, while also remaining vigilant of the conditions producing both indignation and poverty. In *Down and Out in Paris and London*, Orwell wrote that "the evil of poverty is not so much that it makes a man suffer as that it rots him physically and spiritually. . . . No humiliation could do more damage to a man's self-respect."[114] His fascination with decency, it could be said, arose from his own self-awareness of the prejudice and bias that leaders and officials routinely exploited for political gain. This may be why he insisted on the need for a more inclusive policy of integration in Britain's colonies. In India, for instance, Orwell claimed that British colonial policy marked the wholesale abandonment of Victorian morality by not granting the same citizenship rights to Indians.[115] Orwell's idea, then, was that decency's decline was the result of weak moral commitments to individual rights: that in order to project decency for the good of humankind, it had to be treated as a universal human value and applied forcefully by committed nations to protect the most innocent and downtrodden people in society.

In sum, Britain's global vision of moral progress and decency, as I have argued, was predicated on a science of moral virtue that distinguished between British morals and other people's cultural customs, and that validated British prejudice against colonial natives as stateless, insensible, uncivilized subjects. Britain's moral propriety, it could be argued, was never truly (or voluntarily) shared. Nor did it provide the global basis of liberal decency. On the contrary, it had come to signify a self-serving benevolence and patriarchal attitude that supported the false application of the civilizational ideals of freedom and the rule of law. British decency, in short, was simply too ineffectual to manage the political tensions between these ideals and accommodation. It thus remained an unrealized idea of decency overseas, reflecting deep inconsistencies in constructing and maintaining a liberal global order.

American Decency and the International Liberal Order

After the end of the Second World War, the United States took much of the initiative in establishing the rules and standards of a new international liberal order. These standards included the codification of human rights, the principle of nondiscrimination, and the rules on free trade —all of which attested to its long-standing democratic tradition and written constitution with its bill of rights that derived from natural law theory. My aim in this final section is to discuss how American decency helped in part to furnish the practical basis of basic and liberal decency in international relations. American decency, I argue, partook of an individualism that stressed an independent spirit, industriousness, and courage. And unlike British decency, it remained more open-ended and forward looking in terms of advancing the needs and rights of the common(er) person and foreigner. There was also much less social decorum and class consciousness (throughout much of the early nineteenth and twentieth century) to reinforce the need for strict standards of moral conduct. American decency, it could be said, emphasized social mobility and private enterprise and was arguably less burdened by the social fears and prudishness that characterized British decency. And yet, as we shall see, American decency also consisted of a dark side that challenged its creedal function.

What makes the American moral character unique, then, is an individualist, enterprising trait that has long downplayed the need for proper manners and decorum (excluding the gilded class) and embodied a pioneering spirit and work ethic. The openness of this enterprising and civic spirit of America proved instrumental in effectuating the international standards of decency of the post–World War II order, which were based on a broad consensus. At the very least, it suggested that Great Britain relied a great deal on its national manners and customs to civilize others and that its reliance informed the partial or self-serving application of civilizing standards. This is not to say that American decency was any less conflicted by the prejudice and bias that characterized British decency, but rather that the enforcement of decorum and manners played a less pivotal role in its moral conduct at the international level. America, in other words, relied more on a pragmatic connection to the liberal and civic ideals of its national identity to define its leading role of erecting a new international order.

American decency thus seemed to contribute to a pragmatic vision of liberal international order. Much of this could be traced to the unique stress placed on individual opportunity/enterprise and egalitarianism. As Benet Davetian remarks, the U.S.'s founding leaders, in particular George Washington, laid the foundations for this informal sense of decency by embracing "an egalitarian courtesy that did away with aristocratic privilege entirely."[116] An American sense of decency in this respect seemed to project itself outward, so as to support a loosely, structured hierarchical society. In *Democracy in America*, for instance, Alexis de Tocqueville wrote that this dynamic of decency was interwoven with American democracy:

> Democracy does not give the people the most skillful government, but it produces what the ablest governments are frequently unable to create: namely an all pervading and restless activity, superabundant forces, and an energy which is inseparable from it and which may, however unfavorable circumstances may be, produce wonders.[117]

In the social milieu of small towns and the associations or local communities where every American seemed to have an opinion about issues, one learned to breathe the air of compromise and consensus in order to have one's opinion heard. Yet out of this dynamic, democratic experiment emerged a pragmatic ethos of respecting others' opinions, an ethos rooted in individual courage and deep religious sentiment.[118] The need for strict etiquette and niceties that had defined the class consciousness (even among the middle class) and existential fear of social disorder in Victorian England was tempered by an outgoing public spirit. Some of this spirit was captured by the metaphor of the rugged individual, whose sense of adventure meant treating others on an open plain of respect.[119] As Davetian further remarks, there was a "certain gentleness to tact, even a quality of pleading, that softens its edges of expansionism. America's navigating an uncharted territory required an adventurous, forceful American ethos that did not require tact and courtesy as much as it did raw courage and direct, quick, efficient interpersonal communication."[120] This interpersonal quality not only seemed to convey the ease and friendliness of American decency but also the public spirit of its morality.

The essence of this spirt derived from the Founding Father's efforts to project a public religion. Conscious of the sectarian divisions of religion inside America, they undertook the task of separating church and state, but not religion and politics.[121] Their deistic or providential sense of moral order led them to treat the natural rights of freedom and equality of the individual as an essential part of God's work. Nature's God, as Thomas Jefferson and Benjamin Franklin came to refer to God, would eternalize the truth of these rights, especially for those who were bound to contest it. As Jon Meacham writes,

> In securing freedom of religion—which is really the freedom of thought—freedom of speech, the Founding Fathers created a national milieu in which those who saw the right when others did had the liberty to bear witness to the truth as they understood it, in the hope that the rest of us might come to glimpse it, too.[122]

Such liberal sentiment expressed how Nature's God would best unify religious pluralism. In helping anchor the credo of America, or *E Pluribus Unum* ("one out of many"), it thus came to signify the deep commitment to the moral equality and freedom of all people. But such commitment also had to contend with the politics of interpreting the same God through scripture to carry out opposing political plans, or how, in this case, southern whites could draw on the same biblical source, Genesis, to support slavery. President Abraham Lincoln, though, recognized this political reality of drawing on scripture to advance opposing political interests. He understood that public religion as a moral truth required a complex mix of reason and revelation that would, in the end, prevail. He also realized that public religion, as Meacham argues "cannot only be a source of sunshine and comfort; it is also hard and demanding, for it requires us to do unto others as we would have them do unto us."[123] America's public religion remained, in this sense, rooted in the struggle to reconcile politics and religion. Yet in pitting liberal and conservative moral sentiments of decency, it embodied an important truth: that the eternal or essential natural rights would resolve the conflicts arising from the social consequences of maintaining and promoting these sentiments.

But many of these conflicts involved violent consequences that were difficult to resolve. The brutal treatment of blacks (particularly in the

South) and Native Americans stemmed from the moral conviction in the superiority of the white race. Throughout the South, after the period of Reconstruction (1863–77), moral propriety was about upholding the rules of racial separation (e.g., criminalizing miscegenation). This ushered in a long and dark period of severe abuse and discrimination, when Jim Crow laws essentially stripped African Americans of their dignity and when many invoked the Lost Cause (retelling the heroic story of the Confederacy) to celebrate the southern morals and customs of the Confederacy. By the same token, a persistent fear gripped many white southerners who feared that integration would threaten their southern identity and way of life. Externalizing this fear meant punishing and killing African Americans suspected of violating the moral codes of behavior (e.g., lynching). The civil rights movement would eventually help put a stop to these practices by publicly exposing the abusive effects of segregation and the Lost Cause features of southern propriety. It would also mark Martin Luther King's critical influence on the debate over America's public religion, which King came to see in terms of the fundamental precept of moral equality: that all people regardless of race were born with equal rights.[124] Still, the civil rights movement failed to resolve the tension between the sectarian and public spirit of decency in America and to fulfill the struggle for common decency.

For many religious proponents, uncommon decency in the United States continued to express the struggle to overcome the divisive effects of secular society. It reflected in this context the breakdown in Christian civility and the need to support the orthodox codes of conduct in Protestant and Catholic circles in America.[125] In the 1930s, for instance, the Catholics created the National Legion of Decency in order the uphold the values and practices of the Catholic Church in America. In combatting the offensive material in Hollywood films, they successfully pressured officials to censor the sexual content of these films.[126] More recently, the American Decency Association was established in the 1990s to censor pornography in both films and the media. The Association came to reflect the powerful influence of the Evangelical movement in American politics, which Jerry Falwell, the Baptist preacher, had helped to start by founding the Moral Majority in 1979. The Moral Majority's mission was to advance what Falwell called the "sectarian spirt" of moral truth.[127]

However, much like the conservative strand of southern decency, the religious idea of uncommon decency expressed an intolerance toward religious pluralism and the establishment clause in the U.S. Constitution (or the separation of church and state). It seemed to work against the essence of public religion, which was to treat natural rights as eternal, such that they could be used to properly interpret and deal with the challenges arising from changing social and political circumstances. The idea of American decency was based on this essence of public religion and, as such, represented the practical ability to resolve the tension between the conservative and liberal decency by recognizing the natural rights of all Americans, including those most affected and discriminated against (e.g., blacks, women, and minorities). But this also raised the issue of how basic decency could support America's civic identity. What, in other words, was basic decency's role in helping manage the consequences and effects of the tension between the conservative and liberal aspects of decency in American life? And did the government in this case have a special responsibility granted by God's providential design to protect citizens against severe harm, particularly in the workplace?

In the early twentieth century, the increasingly poor working conditions in factories came to symbolize the unprecedented power of corporate monopolies. America's large trusts had managed to profit from lax or nonexistent laws protecting the safety and lives of American workers. In recognizing the gap between the government and the needs of impoverished workers, President Franklin Roosevelt signed legislation (The Fair Labor Standards Act of 1938) that reduced the workday to eight hours and increased wages for many workers through a minimum wage. President Roosevelt's New Deal also included the Wagner Act (1935), which established the right to be represented by a union and the right to collective bargaining, and the Social Security Act (1935), which required employers to pay a federal tax to fund the retirement of their workers. By adopting such social legislation, President Roosevelt attempted to bridge the gap between the government's moral responsibility and individual rights. His New Deal legislation made basic decency an indelible strand of American decency and the progressive politics of navigating its tension between conservative and liberal decency.

Global Hegemony and Human Rights

American decency would also prove critical to understanding U.S. foreign policy overseas and its role in shaping the new post–World War II international liberal order. Here, the United States learned to apply its public religion and civic identity based on natural rights (while ignoring severe discrimination at home) to help reach sweeping agreements on international human rights. At the international negotiations leading up to the adoption of the Universal Declaration of Human Rights (1948) and the Commission of Human Rights, the United States—under the leadership of Eleanor Roosevelt—argued that human rights were natural and endowed in all people.[128] But its liberal view of rights ran up against collectivist interpretations of social rights, most notably the Soviet Bloc's insistence that rights could not be divorced from the economic planning of the state. From the Soviets' materialist perspective, rights were only to be equated with the social good of society or with the social and collective entitlements of free access to public goods. Their advocacy of collective rights, which derived from Karl Marx's theory that the bourgeois-controlled state had used individual rights and private property to divide and oppress the working masses, promulgated a universal right of all oppressed peoples to determine their own political fate. These starkly competitive views made it difficult, if not impossible, to devise a document that would encompass these opposing views of equality and human rights. More importantly, they tested the willingness of both sides to find common moral ground.

The challenge facing international policymakers was reconciling the formal protection of individual rights with the collectivist goal of remedying the social and economic needs of peoples. In wrestling with this tension between right and need, all parties had to learn to agree on what was basic to protecting rights and remedying social needs. Indeed, it had become clear in the early stages of the negotiations that neither a transcendent source of dignity nor God could determine the content and justifiability of human rights, meaning that a naturalist philosophy of rights could not serve as the universal source. As Jean Quataert writes of the tension at the UDHR negotiations, "While multivalent, the concept of dignity captured the change in consciousness that had underpinned the widespread resonance of universal human rights by the end of World War II."[129] In the end, though, it was agreed that dignity would refer to a common humanity, a value for all peoples, which encompassed collectivist or alternative critiques of naturalist philosophy on behalf of oppressed groups such as women and former colonial peoples. The language that would enable these practices to be advanced was contained in Charles Malik's compromise proposal, where the word "individual" was replaced by "person" to reflect how rights were constituted by social forces and identity.[130] In this way, Malik was able to secure the acceptance of all parties that had opposed the

Western conception of natural rights out of fear that it would lead to the imposition of Western values and individualism.

Under this compromise, then, human rights were considered a practice. Basic decency in this context was neither strictly individualist nor collectivist but seen as essential to both of these approaches at the international level. It served as a pragmatic idea for resolving the divisions between competing ideologies and the effects of discrimination and deep-seated prejudice, and for assuring that a broad international consensus would provide the basis of protections and constraints against suffering and exploitation. But for such an idea to work effectively, states also had to commit themselves to enforcing and upholding the basic principle of inherent dignity of all persons, as well as instituting the mechanisms that would monitor compliance with human rights norms. Although enforcement would always remain an issue, the framework of the human rights regime would rapidly emerge with the adoption of new conventions, protocols, and treaties that included the Four Protocols of the Geneva Convention (1949), the Convention Relating to the Status of Refugees (1951), the international tribunals for prosecuting human rights atrocities (the Nuremberg Trials, 1945–46), and the Genocide Convention (1948). These new mechanisms would reflect many of the new international standards of human decency and, to a more limited extent, the efforts to project the liberal values and normative constraints of decency.

Still, these new constraints did not end the ideological tensions that had initially hindered their formation. In fact, the Cold War, or the superpower rivalry between the United States and the Soviet Union, soon began to eclipse the broader impact and efficacy of these rules, norms, and standards, forcing the United States to largely exclude human rights considerations in its foreign policy. Moreover, it meant that the basic duties of all UN member states would be hampered by the power politics of the United Nations where the permanent members of the UN Security Council could use their permanent status to veto resolutions that threatened their political interests.[131] These emerging factors ultimately raised the question of how the new normative constraints of the international system could evolve in response to threats to international peace and collective security. How, in other words, would the idea of basic decency at the international level, which finally seemed to offer a framework for controlling the effects of ideological conflict and the tensions between liberal and conservative decency at the national level, furnish an evolving basis of moral conduct and the expanded normative constraints needed to reconcile these tensions?

The most promising answer seemed to lie in the unprecedented development of international criminal law, in particular the Nuremberg trails (and later the Tokyo trials). Leading up to the trials, the United States, Britain, and the Soviet Union met to discuss the moral accountability for Japanese and Nazi Germany perpetrators of serious international crimes. Winston Churchill, the prime minister of England, insisted on the summary executions of the Nazi leaders, while Stalin called for show trials.[132] President Roosevelt initially agreed with Churchill. But Henry Morgenthau, the secretary of state of the United States, managed to convince Roosevelt at a special meeting that a civil or legal option would allow civil restraint and justice to prevail over vengeance. The United States then managed to persuade both Britain and the Soviet Union on the need for a civil option, which led to the establishment of the Charter of the International Military Tribunal in Nuremberg and, later, in Tokyo.[133] In this case, the determination by international prosecutors of atrocities required new legal and moral constraints to deter other would-be perpetrators. In his opening remarks made at the Palace of Justice, Robert Jackson, the chief prosecutor of the International Military Tribunal, expressed

> That four great nations, flushed with victory and stung with injury stay the hand of vengeance and voluntarily submit their captive enemies to the judgment of the law is one of the most significant tributes that Power has ever paid to Reason.[134]

Jackson's hope was that the court would revitalize the strength of civilizational and liberal values and, in the process, define new rules, procedures, values, and norms of prosecuting criminal behavior across states, including new international impartiality standards that required clear-cut evidence to establish guilt and verify knowledge of serious international crimes. The political idea of setting up this new precedent in international law was that it could create a legal deterrent effect to future crimes. The losers in other words would finally be taught a political lesson for engaging in aggressive action or wars. But the lesson involved perils, for it constituted a politicized form of justice, or victors' justice, in which the victors were able to impose their own rules for who gets punished under international law. Victors' justice, it should be mentioned, still casts its shadow over today's adjudication of crimes at national war crimes courts. It is why (as I shall discuss in chapter 6) international criminal courts have assumed such an important role in advancing the impartiality standards of international criminal justice.

Nonetheless, a new international legal precedent was needed to constrain the behavior of other state leaders or extremist ideologues. As Jackson put it, "Civilization can afford no compromise with the social forces which would gain renewed strength if we deal ambiguously or indecisively with the men in whom those forces now precariously survive."[135] The hope was that the new legal moral propriety of the international military tribunals would reinforce the interests in international justice and create a permanent set of rules to prosecute not just the "frail human natures" of people but also their "illegal" acts and violations of accepted international criminal legal norms. As important as Jackson's idea of a new international criminal regime was, it also raised the issue of whether retribution could produce a credible deterrent effect to constrain unruly state behavior. States, after all, could still vainly ignore the demands or authority of international courts, something that still occurs on a routine basis at the ICC, as we shall see in chapter 6. On the other hand, this did not mean that the basic function of impartiality standards and the rule of law were improperly applied internationally; only that the idea of basic decency at the global level would have to confront the power politics that would hinder its transformation into a pluralistic, open-ended global moral propriety.[136]

In short, moral maturing in global politics is an imperfect process. It follows a zigzagging path in which, as Kant suggested, state power and competition can advance and retract the efforts to extend the rules and norms constituting proper moral conduct. For instance, the United States did manage to play an influential role in applying the broad principles of impartiality and nondiscrimination (also at home with the Civil Rights Act of 1964 and the Voting Rights Act of 1965) to punish South Africa and Rhodesia for their racial injustices.[137] For their part, Britain had proclaimed that "the regime" of Rhodesia was "illegal or in violation of the inalienable right of the African people of Zimbabwe to self-determination and independence."[138] Rhodesia, which once constituted a colonial territory of Britain before its declaration of independence from Britain in 1965, had a severely underrepresented black majority ruled by a tiny white minority.

The issue that this nondiscrimination standard raises, then, is whether its basic function is still being tested in ways that limit the liberal international order, or that expose the perils of overextending this order's rules to promote special cultural accommodation. It might at this point be helpful to imagine the hardening of decency constraints in terms of the pulling of a rubber band that quickly retracts to cause proportionately more pain and suffering. When we think of the protection of the U.S. tradition of decency in this manner, we are reminded of how the basic values and standards of decency can be extended through accommodation, only to be quickly pulled back by what we identified earlier as the cant of decency or the reflexes of moral exceptionalism.

As suggested earlier, one of the main effects of cant is the tendency to operate by a double standard on issues such as the opposition to the Mine Ban Treaty, which aims at banning antipersonnel landmines globally, and the ICC. It is here where moral exceptionalism betrays the basic idea of decency (or cultivating and fulfilling its humane sentiment) and creates its own political pressures (negative perceptions) that limit its capacity to evolve as a flexible liberal value capable of absorbing the effects of these pressures. For in turning standards of fairness and respect into politically self-serving weapons, exceptionalism can unduly limit the efficacy of any normative constraint against harm and prevent us from working toward Kant's implicit notion of moral maturity in international relations. But Kant, of course, was also a product of his time, whose liberal imagination was limited by his preference for ordered stability. His failure to confront the underlying political tensions between concept and reality meant that the only way to work toward a uniform set of constraints and rules was to have all states adopt liberal democratic constitutions and cosmopolitan right. And yet, the reason why contemporary liberal theorists opt for decency is because, not in spite, of the fallibility of individuals and states in politics. This, as we shall see in the next chapter, is what makes it possible to both to advance and delimit the possibilities of globalizing moral propriety.

The Pragmatic Challenge

By tracing the societal value of decency to the early Enlightenment period, we learned how the liberal and secular politics of decency represented ideas that had a transformative impact on European countries. However, the politics of decency also pitted materialist and sentimental notions of progress and equality, which seemed to complicate and work against embedding these ideas in practice. The sentimentalists or moderates, as we saw, believed that treating reason as a natural sentiment would help reform the injustices, corruption, and ignorance of past social orders. But it was this naturalism, or a sense of natural order, that failed to screen out the biases and prejudice that would hinder the idea of decency in global politics and further the pretenses of liberal empire in nineteenth-century Britain.

Decency, in other words, did not help to check the excesses of civic imperialism; rather, it justified such excesses through a moral exceptionalism and civilizing mission that reinforced the supremacy of British manners and education overseas. In the case of the United States, it exposed the contradictory yet dynamic forces of conservative and liberal strands of decency, whose tension not only revealed the hypocrisy of its race relations—or the false social opportunism/mobility driving the tolerance toward immigrants and its support for minorities in foreign lands—but also how America's public religion had created the possibilities of projecting basic and liberal decency at the international level. In effect, U.S. foreign policy in the mid-twentieth century reflected the first internationally based projection of basic and liberal decency, one in which the conservative and liberal elements of decency as a national value could no longer dictate the global vision of moral progress. Indeed, decency at this level revealed a diverse consensus about the common good.

With British decency, then, the effects of restricting the global scope of decency stemmed from the application of positivist law and the self-serving constraints of civilizational standards. This meant that no amount of legal pragmatism (e.g., the mandate system) could resolve such tension. Indeed, the pragmatic ideals of the League of Nations were symptomatic of an international moral propriety that embodied a cultural dynamic of indifference. In short, British imperialism came to represent the moral deficiency of Victorian decency in world politics, which would create a global gap between conservative and basic decency. Whether or not positivist law caused the rise of the extreme nationalist ideologies that stripped both the dignity and rights of people, it was clear that any nationally based moral propriety that sought to project itself globally would require the broad, practical, and legitimizing function of global consensus and inclusive participation at the international level. The human rights regime was a crucial centerpiece of this practical undertaking, but one that would reveal the mounting tensions between decency and liberal pluralism within the rapidly evolving parameters of post–Cold War global moral propriety.

CHAPTER THREE

Liberal Decency and the Global Challenge of Identity Politics

> This war in which I played so ineffectual a part, has left me with memories that are mostly evil, and yet I do not wish that I had missed it. When you have glimpse of such as this—and however it ends the Spanish war will have turn out to be an appalling disaster, quite part from the slaughter and physical suffering—the result of it is not necessarily disillusionment and cynicism. Curiously enough, the whole experience has left me with no less but more belief in the decency of human beings.
>
> —George Orwell, *Homage to Catalonia*

> There exists a vast abyss of sensibilities between the raw force that is nature, on the one hand, and the exertion of force by one human being in relation to another. I suggest that this has to do with yet another human possession, an attribute that is as much a social acquisition as it inherent in the human species—dignity.
>
> —Wole Soyinka, *Climate of Fear*

The post–World War II architecture, as we saw in the prior chapter, created the new practices, procedures, and rules that would bring together liberal and basic decency. While the Cold War rivalry between the United States and Soviet Union ended up restricting the scope of these new rules, the United Nations managed to adopt a series of documents and resolutions that sought to assist and protect the basic needs and dignity of all persons. The post–Cold War era, however, would mark a period in which liberal decency would be greatly expanded through the rapid spread of human rights and democracy as well as various broad-based UN initiatives that included the Millennium Development Goals, the Global Compact, the Responsibility to Protect, and the International Criminal Court (ICC). Such initiatives required not only deep moral commitments, decentralized capacity building, and broader participation but also the application of a uniform set of rules and procedures to govern the moral conduct of states, individuals, and groups. The simultaneous extension of basic and liberal decency to global politics amounted to a concerted effort to assist and protect the needs and rights of individuals as well as minority groups and communities. The idea, then, was to establish an open-ended moral propriety, which, in stressing voluntary cooperation and the new opportunities for participation, would provide the liberal basis for further moral cooperation and accommodation.

The trouble, however, was that the openness of the liberal system of moral propriety also increased the burden of accommodating individuals and minority groups. It created in this sense the conditions for resisting the global application of these rules and for politicizing the grievances that would complicate attempts to resolve the issues of the abuse of minority rights (of indigenous peoples in particular), refugee flows, acceptable working conditions (wages), environmental protection, genocide, and protecting innocent civilians at risk (the Responsibility to Protect). The question, therefore, was how the openness of this global project of moral governance could encourage those affected or excluded to see such openness as an unfair arrangement that failed to meet their basic needs and rights. One answer is that the application of liberal decency to identity politics helped expose many unforeseen tensions within liberalism itself. Another is that many liberal thinkers failed to adequately confront the political tensions of spreading liberal decency. Their failure it could be argued symptomized the propensity to overlook the retrogressive effect of liberal decency's rapid advancement in global politics, that is, the tendency to react against liberal decency by championing a past social order that offered better and fairer treatment of the people's basic needs. This might explain why many liberal thinkers have portrayed global populism as a tainted reaction to decency in general, when, in reality, it represents the most overt manifestation of the built-in tensions of decency—or the most intense political expression of the global propriety effect (political retrogression). The emergence of global populism, I argue, reflects this stark tension and growing political chasm between conservative and liberal decency (where the erosion of basic decency helps create the chasm). It is a tension that highlights the effects of the 2015 immigration crisis, which saw some states close off their borders to asylum seekers, resulting in the deaths of numerous migrants at refugee border camps.[1] By undermining the legitimacy of political liberal institutions and values (e.g., accommodation and equal respect),[2] such effects have forced liberalism into retreat and spurred attacks on intellectuals, cosmopolitans, immigrants, refugees, women, and black people.[3]

One of my aims in this chapter is to examine how this effect of retrogression has been overlooked in (normative) theory and in practice, particularly in terms of promoting basic rights and moral cooperation through the universal designs of a decent society and liberal multiculturalism (or group rights targeting). Both of these projects are based on the conventional idea of decency that authorities should provide assistance to meet the basic needs of all people, and that all persons, regardless of ethnicity, race, gender, and sex, should be treated with equal respect and dignity. However, both have become increasingly problematic in today's world, since they overlook the conflicting political biases toward fair treatment and dignity protection.[4] Instead of elaborating on the pressures destabilizing the standards of decency and their normative constraints on behavior, proponents of liberal decency continue to ignore the contradictions of global moral propriety and the forces driving the moral conflicts and possibilities of promoting dignity protection.

My other aim is to engage the efforts at reconfiguring these conflicts and possibilities. Here, I explore William Connolly's "deep pluralism" (or "new pluralism"), which seeks to reengage the possibilities of promoting cultural difference and representation in an increasingly borderless world.[5] His aim, as we saw in chapter 1, is to move beyond state territoriality and address the global political pressures—for example, open borders, rapid transmission of knowledge, and social media—that allow us to contest the deeply rooted (and restrictive) secular idea of separating religion and politics in liberal democratic states. But his deep pluralist approach also raises the question of how coupling religion and politics in the democratic global sphere can displace or weaken the normative constraints against nationalist violence and hatred. I argue that even deep pluralism cannot escape this problematic condition or propriety effect that is playing out in global politics.

The chapter has three parts. First, I address the basic rights to decency and the codification of the principle of human dignity and then explicate the concept of global moral propriety. Second, I analyze the limits and problems of normative theories of decency in international relations and how rapidly advancing liberal rules, principles, and norms intensified the global propriety effect. Finally, I examine how global pressures/challenges symptomize the instability of this effect, including the refugee crisis and the problematic constraints of enforcing freedom of movement.

An International Threshold of Decency

In chapter 2, I discussed the dark side to decency by addressing its role in the civilizing mission. I showed that the normative constraints of British decency precluded recognition of the colonial natives' customs and reinforced British imperialism and the mistreatment of native peoples. Victorian decency in this sense had become an important part of Britain's global idea of moral progress, but it also demonstrated how British morals and tradition were used to uphold a self-interested application of universal dignity. The new international human rights regime, as we saw, addressed this moral shortcoming by implementing a broad set of decency standards and normative constraints to govern the moral behavior of states. It thus marked a shift from Britain's restrictive application of decency to an internationalist framework of decency and human rights protection. Still, this internationalist framework would raise its own set of challenges regarding the relationship between basic and liberal decency in the discourse of human rights. For instance, it remained unclear how the claims to freedom and dignity, which sought to uphold laws protecting individuals against humiliation and degrading treatment, were logically connected to the basic protections of individual needs or entitlements to resources and security. Such a challenge required a conception of the basic claims to the adequate protection of needs for security and life to bridge this gap and reinforce the international application of decency standards.

In *Basic Rights* (1980), Henry Shue took up this challenge by defining a basic right as a right that was essential to the enjoyment of any other right. His argument was that depriving one of such a right would undermine the capacity to live or stay alive.[6] In his view, only the rights to security and subsistence constituted clear-cut basic rights, or rights whose denial functioned to deprive one of the capacity to enjoy any other right. Other putative basic rights, such as the freedom of movement, whose dimensions I shall address later in this chapter, failed to fully meet this essential criterion. As Shue makes clear, "Even in the absence of a right to freedom of physical movement, people can enjoy rights only as privileges, discretions, indulgences. . . . deprivation can occur as readily as provision, and this is not what enjoying a right means."[7] Subsistence and security in this sense constituted the necessary thresholds for justifying the claims to fair and adequate treatment of persons, without which one could not practically lay claim to the liberal protection of his or her dignity.

Shue's idea, then, was that in applying to all peoples, regardless of racial, ethnic, gender, and religious differences, basic rights functioned as rights that derived their substance (the necessary protection of individuals against the degrading effects of harm) from the basic treatment/protection of their social needs. What this essentially meant was that such rights addressed the threats to one's self-preservation insofar as they constituted the conditions under which one could practice and enjoy other rights. More importantly, basic rights suggested that the essential function of rights applied, in various ways, to both political and social rights, including the freedom of movement whose deprivation or denial, he reasoned, would amount to a serious hindrance to exercising other rights. Basic rights thus allowed us to see how basic and liberal decency were logically interconnected and constituted the normative threshold of proper moral conduct and dignity protection.

The threshold also exposes the intricate relationship between decency and dignity. Both concepts, it can be said, serve as principled values for protecting persons from harm and for respecting their claims to security and basic access to the resources required to live adequately. But they also differ in the way they represent the basic standards of human treatment, that is, while decency expresses the value placed on the proper moral conduct needed to uphold such standards, dignity can be thought of as the metaphysical value we assign to human existence or the inherent capacity of humans to feel and reason. For George Kateb, this means that dignity should be treated as an existential value and not simply as a moral one, since "the violation of dignity has existential weight that is independent of the suffering itself" and because "emphasis is not on the unique identity of the person but on the good character of the self."[8] The former reason explains why the basic right to life must always exist independently of the government's authority to determine this right's existence. The latter, however, suggests that human dignity is about more than simply the duty of protecting persons from cruelty or harm, but also about the potential for greatness or achieving some degree of stature of the species, whether this means becoming effective stewards of nature or sacrificing on behalf of others. Kateb's emphasis on the character of the self implies that identity and diversity play a far less defining role in projecting decency standards and dignity protection. Identity politics may even detract from this greatness by allowing other societies' customs to determine how the right to life should be pursued. This does not of course mean that Kateb downplays the normative constraints on violating dignity norms (e.g., torture and cruel forms of punishment as a means to extract information for national security purposes);[9] but it does reflect the tendency of some liberal theorists to downplay the problematic function of cultural identity in justifying a broader and diverse application of decency standards, as I shall explain below.

By diverse applications of decency, I am referring to how identity politics can and should inform these applications beyond the minimal threshold of decency mentioned above. The question is how diversifying decency conditions the possibility of enhancing the protection of equal dignity. How, in other words, do the multiple ways of practicing decency, or the variety of cultural proprieties, support the decency standards of protecting the inherent dignity of all persons? One answer is that like decency, universal dignity constitutes a plurality of ways in which human rights norms are practiced by peoples. It is to say that the norms of dignity are also constructed by different cultural understandings and practices of dignity, where dignity, as Karin Fierke argues, supports "a meaning that travels between the global and more local . . . and [is] translated into contextually specific uses that are buttressed by global shared understanding"[10] Dignity, in this sense, aligns itself with the core elements of decency, which, as Michael Rosen writes,

> is the status proper to human beings or an honor that is assigned to people for their achievements and what this, in a broader sense, brings in terms of a sense of responsibility for caring for others and/or ministering to their basic needs. It is also an intrinsic value or rather the inherent autonomous capacity to choose and not as a means to another's self-interested pursuit but as an end. Such capacity underscores the need for measured self-possessed behavior, or the self-control and restraint that counters aggressive and impulsive behavior.[11]

The capacity to counter impulsive behavior underscores both the willingness and ability to protect the dignity of all persons. The combination of willingness and ability, it could be argued, builds the capacity to enforce these protections and to erect global standards of decency that can regulate the moral conduct of individuals and states.

Globalizing Moral Propriety

During the Cold War, however, the superpower rivalry restricted this combined ability and willingness of states to apply such standards in any consistent manner. When the fall of the Soviet Union finally lifted this restriction, it allowed the United States to emerge as the single (moral) superpower, which, in turn, created the new conditions for liberal decency's projection in global politics. But, in aligning itself with the virtues of market forces (e.g., personal responsibility), or the neoliberal policies discussed in chapter 1, liberal decency could neither fully support the basic elements of decency, such as adequate housing and decent wages, nor the liberal ideals of freedom and equality. Its limitation in this respect might explain why many liberals elected to treat basic human rights as a right necessary for development and individual autonomy. But their efforts, as I will show, also called attention to the important challenge of expanding the liberal basis of decency in the new world order. What was needed were firm, voluntary moral commitments to help reinforce the liberal elements of these standards, such as freedom of choice and impartiality. The voluntary aspect of moral cooperation seemed to speak to a deeper desire to uphold these standards of regulating (and enabling) the moral conduct of states and individuals. Moral propriety, it could be said, expressed an openness for reshaping and extending the liberal values through moral cooperation, capacity building, participation, and dialogue. Global moral propriety represents how this openness shaped the way that decency was practiced within the growing network of global institutions. Yet, the rapid transformation also triggered a political effect or a retrogressive dynamic of combating the liberal and emotive features of this openness, including trust, fair treatment, empathy, and nondiscrimination. The resurgence of reactionary, conservative decency, in other words, helped justify, for many, the reversal of liberal decency's trajectory through these four domains of global moral propriety. Before I address this development, let us discuss in greater detail these domains and how their interaction (and overlap) enables us to understand this political effect and its intensification.

Cooperation of course has long defined the rules-based international order. Its function in global politics refers to the many moral commitments to uphold humanitarian norms and public goods. These commitments are part of a series of broad global initiatives to resolve or eradicate the global problem of human suffering. Such initiatives range from the adoption of the United Nations Global Compact (1999) to funding initiatives to end world poverty. These and other efforts have stressed the need for affordable, adequate shelter and clothing, access to water and food, access to education, freedom from persecution, limited hours of work, and the freedom to exit a state. With these efforts, the overall aim is not simply to preserve human life, but to enhance the basic qualities of a decent life, which, as Niko Roorda stresses, reflect "a minimum that would entail sufficient food, healthy food, clean drinking water, security from war . . . and, for most cultures, at least in modern times, a good education with a chance of finding suitable employment and . . . freedom, including the freedom of expression."[12]

Promoting a decent life continues to be about the standardization of a global threshold of dignity promotion. This is highlighted by the adoption of the UN's Millennium Development Goals (MDGs),[13] which has raised nearly $15 billion to fund its goals of ending severe poverty and promoting sustainability, and has recently extended its funding goals to 2030. In addition, the International Labour Organization (ILO) redesigned its "decent work" agenda to include the four pillars of employment creation, social protection, rights at work, and social dialogue.[14] The ILO's decent work agenda seeks, among other things, to facilitate and meet the funding targets and the MDGs of 2015 and 2030. On a similar scale, the UN Global Compact, which was established in 1999, aims to monitor and guide the conduct of multinational corporations operating in developing countries (with minimal standards), stressing the voluntary compliance with human rights, labor, and environmental principles. More recently, the European Commission (2013) published "A Decent Life for All by 2030," which laid out how the European Union would contribute to the Millennium Development Goals.[15]

What these practical commitments reflect is a substantive pledge or promise among individual actors to uphold moral objectives.[16] Marcel

Lieberman defines three priorities of substantive moral commitments at the individual and collective levels: (1) their stability over time and their capacity to be revised and reconsidered; (2) their guiding force; and (3) their relation to self-understanding and identity.[17] For him, stable commitments are largely based on independent-desire facts or facts that function independently of our desires and emotions and that help constrain and enable the influence of emotions and values. I will address the issue of agency or states as emotional and moral actors in chapter 4. For now, it is important to realize that the commitments of states can come under pressure and that such pressure is typically aimed at shaping the moral conduct of states. Inappropriate conduct can be understood as the deviation from accepted norms or rules. If a state, in other words, elects not to cooperate with international officials regarding human rights abuses, private and nongovernmental actors can apply the needed political pressure to compel them to cooperate. The naming and shaming campaigns of Amnesty International, for instance, publish a list of names of those who have been imprisoned unjustly in violation of their human rights in order to encourage states to cooperate with international human rights norms. As important as this action has been in pressuring state governments, it also reflects the difficult challenges of ensuring compliance with decency standards and achieving the national capacity building needed to promote global justice such as moral accountability.

Capacity building, as I mentioned earlier, underscores the efficient utilization of political and social resources to develop and fulfill certain responsibilities at the regional and local levels. It also points to the exercise and development of individual autonomy in which access to essential resources constitutes an inherent right to be protected from harm and humiliation. The conflict between national and individual capacity building, particularly in authoritarian countries (e.g., Singapore), exposes the many political tensions of advancing liberal decency in the global arena. One such tension involves the application of top-down rules or policies to regulate the behavior of actors. Many of these rules fail to address the root causes of conflict and the related obstacles to enforcing international human rights standards. Building capacity as a condition for meeting decency standards requires local and state agents to utilize their own political, social, and economic resources to comply with international human rights norms (e.g., the capacity-building measures of the Secretary-General's 2009 *Report on the Responsibility to Protect*, which adopted national capacity building as the second, streamlined pillar of the Responsibility to Protect),[18] that is, to show that they are respecting the people's basic human rights. Another such tension refers more broadly to actively developing individual autonomy to counter any state customs and rules that violate these standards and human rights norms. It involves equipping individuals with the resources to work beyond the effects of depriving anyone of their basic rights, such as the right to education. I shall address this remedial feature of promoting liberal decency, and its tension within liberalism in the following section, where I discuss minimalist and expanded notions of a decent society in international politics.

One of the conditions for building moral capacity and addressing these tensions is achieving effective cross-cultural communication. In recent years, this has led many to stress the role of intercultural dialogue in promoting resource utilization and human rights. Intercultural dialogue refers to the communication and respectful exchange of ideas among groups, organizations, and individuals. The European Institute for Comparative Cultural Research, for instance, defines intercultural dialogue as a process

> that goes beyond a mere "tolerance of the other" and can involve creative abilities that convert challenges and insights into innovation processes and into new forms of expression. The "shared space" in which such processes take place can be located outside of physical spaces, situated in the media or in a virtual environment.[19]

The goal of integrating minority groups around this process forms the basis of several of European Commission's initiatives, including "Creative Europe," which seeks "to establish linkages and common ground between different cultures, communities, and people, and promoting understanding and interaction."[20] In addition, intercultural dialogue represents the efforts of the United Nations Educational, Scientific and Cultural Organization (UNESCO) to end the exclusion of minorities and to prevent conflict though communication.[21] The idea is that in working beyond the legal constraints of the state, new channels of communication can be opened up among oppressed minorities to facilitate protection under the EU's nondiscrimination laws. As we shall see in chapter 7, the European Commission's agenda of intercultural dialogue has framed various strategies designed to promote the inclusion of the Roma in the European Union. One of the agenda's stated aims is to counteract racial and ethnic prejudice by integrating the Roma into society. In so doing, it seeks to complement rather than compete with affirmative action laws (or multicultural policies) that have tended to isolate cultural communities from each other, leaving them increasingly vulnerable to the effects of deep-seated prejudice. In short, intercultural dialogue is a broad-based attempt to increase interaction and understanding across cultures in order to counter negative public perception of discriminated groups and their cultural and moral values.

Lastly, participation, which remains an important feature of intercultural dialogue, reflects the efforts to institute global mechanisms that enable traditionally underrepresented groups and persons victimized by violence to shape the affairs of international organizations. The ICC, for example, recognizes the right of victims to participate in its legal proceedings, while the U.N. Security Council and the European Parliament have enabled civil society groups to participate at their meetings.[22] Also notable is the role played by the social media in allowing many to communicate and participate in discussions and forums sponsored by global political institutions. This has arguably helped forge new connections between leaders of groups while empowering individuals and groups to raise awareness of the application of global rules and principles, such as complementarity.

Together, then, these domains of global moral propriety constitute an open-ended project of advancing the opportunities for groups, individuals, and organizations to build capacity and to interact with each other. And yet, it is this very openness that exposes the embedded statist tension within the first two modes between the growing uniformity of rules and applications of such rules. The openness, in other words, raises expectations for fair governance as well as the need to act on and represent the expanded interests in global peace, security, and justice, When these two conflict, it results in hostile reactions against those expected to carry out the fairness of such rules, as we have seen with the ICC and the national backlashes against its targeting of African states, as well as the violent attempts to preserve national cultural values (e.g., Russia's opposition to LGBTQ rights). The open-ended dynamics of global moral propriety can thus create the political uncertainty that leads to the reaffirmation of existing national boundaries, customs, or identity—setting into motion reactionary pressures and effects that work against the institutionalization of a uniform set of rules and norms. The propriety effect represents this reactive or retrogressive tendency that is built into the open, processual modes of global moral propriety. It reflects, as I have argued, how the extension of liberal decency to identity politics in the global arena can create pressures that lead to the political perils of applying a uniform set of rules and decency standards.

In sum, globalizing moral propriety was never a transcendent event nor a sustained triumph of liberalism in international politics. Rather, it reflected a new set of pressures to conform with global actions and judgments that contradicted the idea of a fully inclusive global realm: where persons were free to adapt to the broad set of rules of moral conduct that could either complement or transform their loyalty to and identity with traditional proprieties. The contradiction seemed to defy any smooth progression toward a cosmopolitan order.[23] Indeed, the problem with global moral propriety is not simply that it creates political tensions and effects that it cannot fully govern, but that its rapid development through the spread of liberal decency requires a much deeper moral commitment to the common good to overcome the uncertainty and distrust of its openness. When we therefore speak of an expanding moral threshold of global moral propriety, we also need to see its efficacy in terms of the gradual cultivation of moral commitments and the capacity to overcome these pressures and tensions.

The Liberal Idea of a Decent Society

The idea of a decent international society was supposed to represent the concerted effort within liberalism to defend this moral threshold of justice. But instead, it came to reflect the varying degrees to which liberal thinkers sought to situate liberal decency in global politics. The disagreement largely pitted cosmopolitans[24] and liberal sovereigntists (or those liberals who upheld sovereign law against universal moral equality). While the latter theorized that decency involved tolerating others' different values and showing moral restraint, the cosmopolitans seemed to suggest that decency was an overarching standard of the common good. In their view, decency constituted an intrinsic moral end that supported the goal of transcending the constraints of sovereignty and advancing a global network of institutions, laws, norms, and actors. It thus highlighted the normative issue of whether the extension could be understood in terms of the transition from an international (or society of states)[25] to a world society that focused on the convergence of beliefs and interests around an evolving set of global norms and rules, including human rights and individual moral accountability. Transitioning to a world society required not simply a deeper trust in the legitimacy of global institutions but also getting more states to surrender their sovereignty to global institutions.[26] What simultaneously divided and tied together these differing liberal interpretations were two claims to upholding basic rights: namely, that a person be afforded minimal or adequate protection against the degrading effects of humiliation and the universal recognition and respect of one's autonomy and moral potential (or flourishing).

The first claim involved understanding the legal and policy constraints on humiliating others. A decent society, according to Avishai Margalit, must first ensure that there is equal access to the institutional resources (education and work), which means understanding how laws and actions can negatively affect an individual's well-being by restricting one's movement and degrading one's dignity (and not simply recognizing people's potential or positive entitlements to social harm prevention).[27] In Margalit's view, a decent society should at the very least be based on nondiscriminatory rules and laws that allow institutions to function in a "nonhumiliating" manner. At the personal level, he identifies three forms of degradation: (1) treating one as subhuman, or as a child; (2) rejection; (3) and acts intended to lead to a lack of self-control.[28] Each form reflects how biased and unfair treatment can diminish the self-worth of persons while diminishing the incentives to trust and participate in societal institutions.

But rather than emphasizing the irrational effects of humiliation, such as rage against the system, Margalit seems more concerned with rationalizing the debilitating effects of personal degradation. Here, he distinguishes between the "humiliated agent" from "humiliation situations" to analyze the nature of being humiliated rather than simply the "particularities of the humiliating agent."[29] "The paradox of humiliation," he insists, holds that when we define our sense of humiliation or injury to our self-esteem "through the eyes of others," we must also "respond from our own point of view."[30] In other words, humiliation may have less to do with the humiliator (or humiliating institution) than with the humiliated's sense of being wronged and repressed. From this perspective, systemic humiliation requires us to bracket—or set aside—the intention of the humiliating agent so that we can understand, as Margalit puts it, "why it is rational for victims of humiliation to consider themselves humiliated."[31] Part of feeling humiliated is knowing the source of the feeling—that certain tacit or explicit rules or norms were violated by the humiliator. When the humiliator fails to abide by constraints on harming others, it leaves the humiliated helpless and cynical, while forcing him or her to suspend his rage against the humiliator. This is why indecency, which represents the clear-cut and willful violation of civic norms and degradation, breeds the very worst forms of enmity and conflict.[32]

Nonetheless, laws can be considered nonhumiliating when they provide the internalized normative constraints on perpetrating harm or public humiliation (e.g., toleration). Margalit's point is that such constraints constitute a minimal threshold of dignity protection and trust-building. Without this, there are few assurances that anyone's claim to such protection will ever be properly carried out or respected. Still, it may be unrealistic to expect that those suffering the most from these effects will place their trust in authorities to truly abide by these normative constraints. A more realistic scenario is one in which such biases will continue to limit the application of these constraints. If this is true, then simply relying on these normative constraints alone is not enough; we also need to complement them by expanding the range of basic opportunities for participating in and shaping the affairs of governmental institutions. This means reconciling these constraints against the pressures of accommodating new claims to identity, especially at the international level. For example, at the negotiations leading up to the establishment of the International Criminal Court,[33] officials and negotiators at the preparatory meetings voted to allow national customs and laws on abortion to trump the crime of forced pregnancy.[34] The consensus reached on this issue allowed some Islamic countries to deny women an important right against forced pregnancy; however, it also humiliated many women's nongovernmental organizations and groups that had advocated for protection of women's basic rights.

Accommodating such harmful customs also raises the issue of whether additional basic human rights are required to uphold the normative constraints on harming others in a consistent and reliable manner. The issue forces us to grapple with the role played by basic human rights in building international human rights norms and in projecting liberal decency globally. How, in other words, does the remedial function of respect and autonomy allow us to understand the political challenge of spreading liberal decency in the global arena? The question involves more than simply investigating the sources of humiliation; it also entails a broader sensibility about basic human rights and how this allows us to theorize about individual capacity building. Perhaps more importantly, it means contending with the tension between the sovereign will of peoples and cultural pluralism.

Rawls's Law of Peoples and Cultural Pluralism

In *The Law of Peoples*, John Rawls argues that respect for other societies requires a minimal threshold of tolerance or acceptance of different political societies. His understanding of cultural pluralism suggests that societies often formulate their own genuine reasons for cooperating, reasons that derive from the importance of upholding their local customs and norms. For Rawls, accepting this reality means restricting the application of the cultural pluralist ideal in which freedom and equality are treated as conditions for achieving self-realization of the common good. In his conception of cultural pluralism, Rawls stresses the reasonableness or relative equality, or both, of peoples and legal orders, which for some cosmopolitans, as I have alluded to, amounts to an unacceptable trade-off between the basic freedoms of all individuals and state sovereignty.[35] Yet Rawls's idea of a decent society in international relations is not one in which liberal values fail to determine how one should value one's actions and ways of life; rather, it is one that says that what is basic to these values is a respect for life and dignity and the ability to cooperate and to live in peace.

A crucial feature of this idea is the willingness and capacity of peoples to consult and be consulted.[36] For Rawls, this means that all cultures consist of certain reasonable elements and that all decent or reasonable people should be provided with certain basic human rights, including protecting persons from slavery, freedom of conscience, freedom from torture, and freedom of movement. These are rights that derive from what he calls an overlapping consensus on principles of justice, whereby different comprehensive doctrines (political systems, religions, and so forth) can agree upon principles of justice such as relative distribution. This is the main reason why he stresses both the reasonability and the tolerance of others' political and religious values.

Rawls formulates three criteria to justify this reasonability or legitimacy of these basic human rights: (1) their fulfillment is a necessary condition of a decent society's political institutions and its legal order; (2) they are sufficient to exclude justified and forceful intervention by states; (3) and they presume the worth of pluralism, or differing political conceptions of freedom and relative equality.[37] His first and third criteria link decency with an open-ended notion of pluralism that supports the procedures for upholding the relative equality of peoples through asymmetrical degrees of equality among smaller and larger groups. For Rawls, decency is about tolerance and the trust one places in the person's capacity to adapt to and abide by acceptable norms and rules. This not only assumes that decent people are reasonable enough to abide by the normative constraints of the human rights regime but also that international authorities or the leaders of powerful states can and should show a restrained capacity to act on their "observation of non-intervention," as Rawls writes, as well as to abide by "the right of self-defense and the duty to assist other peoples, living under unfavorable conditions that prevent their having a just or decent political and social regime."[38] These are principles that constitute Rawls's "basic charter of the Law of Peoples," which forms as he puts it, "standards of fairness for trade and other cooperative institutions."[39]

Still, the application of these principles raises an important issue: whether underrepresented cultural groups can and should be recognized beyond the reasonability of what his basic criteria permit. While Rawls's list of basic human rights may seem understandably restrictive, it does raise the question of how these rights should be expanded to reflect a universal commitment to justice principles. Like Michael Walzer, Rawls argues that there are certain standards of fairness that determine how different groups communicate with one another to reach consensus and cooperation on issues. Walzer claims that commitments to human rights should reflect the shared desire to live by political rules that foster voluntary respect of communal values.[40] In his view, standards of fair and respectful treatment of others' values comprise a minimalist morality, in which rules, procedures, and principles (e.g., mutual respect and toleration) constitute the basis of obligations and duties of all peoples to assist (and not abuse) others.[41]

This is how, as I mentioned earlier, the internationalization of human rights reflects the acceptance of fairness standards, such as nondiscrimination and accountability. It also explains the reason for Rawls's decision to place restrictions on the broader application of liberal autonomy in international relations and, for that matter, the remedial function of liberal autonomy and our second level of capacity building. For ultimately Rawls's aim is to justify and preserve the political systems and cultural customs of peoples through a broad consensus on the principles necessary for achieving justice and peace across states. As he puts it:

> I think of decency as a normative idea of the same kind as reasonableness though weaker (that is, it covers less than reasonableness does). We give it meaning by how we use it. Thus, a decent society must honor the laws of peace; its system of law must be such as to respect human rights and to impose duties and obligations on all persons in its territory. Its system of law must follow a common good idea of justice that takes into account what it sees as the fundamental interests of everyone in society.[42]

Rawls's point is that the common good idea of justice is about the moral inclusion of all peoples, which does not "conflict with citizens' essential interests as formed and encouraged by their social arrangements."[43] For this reason, he downplays any strict conformity to democratic liberal principles as a precondition for reasonable conduct or accepting and tolerating all people's social and political arrangements. In minimizing decency, he thus seems to believe that toleration imposes its own normative constraints on intervention under international law; that any restrictive criteria for preserving basic decency (or its connection to liberal decency via basic human rights) must also govern the tension between liberal internationalism and cultural pluralism. But one could also argue that his restrictive list of basic human rights supports a strained notion of the common good insofar as it permits injustice overseas and works against instituting the needed normative constraints on serious harm. Are additional basic human rights necessary for remedying such unintended suffering and injustice along racial and gender lines and for reconciling the liberal ideas of autonomy and freedom with cultural pluralism?[44]

William Talbott's answer is that Rawls's restrictive criteria of a decent society (and its narrow subset of basic human rights) poses a problem of fairness for persons living in illiberal societies. This includes societies that still practice overt paternalism against sectors of its population, most notably, women in Islamic states (e.g., Saudi Arabia). Talbott argues that paternalism needs to be taken more seriously, since it is predicated on not allowing some people to exercise and develop their judgment properly. Reaching proper judgment on matters is for him a reasonable requirement, which involves self-awareness of prejudice—or the moral blind spots of injustice that often reinforce self-serving notions of justice and decency. More importantly, it discourages action that may be rooted in empathy for others. And yet, the empathy we feel for another's pain is what enables us to value the person's judgments and autonomy.[45] A standard of decency must be able to satisfy this requirement by protecting women from the effects of patriarchal norms, including the denial of their right to education. This is why Talbott justifies the right to education (not adopted by Rawls), as it allows us to confront the effects of these norms and to legitimize the democratically fair conditions of a decent society. In liberalizing Rawls's notion of decency, then, Talbott seeks to reinforce the standards of decency necessary for protecting the dignity of women in these countries and to remediate the effects of paternalism by preventing some illiberal societies from imposing their standards of unfairness on women or restricting women's autonomy. But Talbot's liberal decency also means that liberal autonomy constitutes the precondition for upholding the standards of decency. What remains unclear is whether there can be alternative conditions for promoting such standards, which is an issue that I take up later in this chapter.

In sum, liberalizing decency through an expanded set of basic human rights can be thought of as working beyond the limits of a minimalist notion of decency by consistently promoting standards of fairness and cooperation in all societies. As we have seen, the underlying idea of liberal decency is that human suffering should never be tolerated or justified in terms of an unfair trade-off between justice and the self-serving preservation of cultural customs.[46] Rather, it should always be about expanding global consensus on what counts as fairness and justice. All of this is not to say Rawls's weak or restrictive notion of liberal decency ignores this underlying idea, or the role played by empathy or compassion in upholding the basic principles of his charter of the Law of Peoples. After all, his list of basic human rights consists of the freedom of conscience and the right of persons to be protected from severe harm (e.g., torture). Instead, it suggests that emotions, if more properly engaged, can help to show how exercising proper moral judgment promotes the cultural pluralism that seems to restrict the expansion of rights (and their application) in his charter.

In Martha Nussbaum's view, this is the reason that Rawls's notion of a decent society remains undeveloped and weighted down by the tendency to champion the law of sovereignty. Her idea is that his notion of a decent society in international relations underestimates the important function of love in intensifying one's shared moral commitment to global justice.[47] Emotions are what forge the attachments that make it possible to realize a decent global society, where the love of principles, as she writes, can encircle a variety of cultural values and experiences:

> Real people are sometimes moved by the love of just principles . . . but the human mind is quirky and particularistic, more easily able to conceive a strong attachment if these principles are connected to a particular set of perceptions, memories, and symbols that have deep roots in the personality and in people's sense of their own history.[48]

Nussbaum considers compassion and love as forces that move us to embrace justice principles. They are not merely motivations or irrational desires but a set of feelings that "involve cognitive appraisals, forms of value-laden perception and/or thought directed at an object or objects."[49] Emotions, in other words, are judgments that measure and stabilize our commitment to values. Compassion and love register this commitment through action and proper moral conduct, which allows us to manage the effects of hostile emotions (e.g., alienation and exclusion), such as fear, anger, and shame. Love functions as a universal emotion that cultivates our social ties and bonds with others from other cultures. When anger constrains or disrupts these ties, it can also limit the potential to cooperate and work together to promote the common good. In this way, love becomes a way of transcending the hostile effects of the sovereign constraints that often prevent us, as we saw with Talbott, from universalizing standards of fairness.

Nussbaum's transcultural perspective on decency, then, emphasizes the need for universal principles of global justice (such as moral equality) to promote cooperation. But her cosmopolitan perspective also returns us to a familiar issue: whether extending and globalizing liberal decency unduly extends Rawls's limited threshold of decency. Does Nussbaum's effort to liberalize decency globally work against and destabilize this moral threshold by downplaying the intensity of political tensions between cultural pluralism and universal rights? What's important to stress is that Rawls's idea of decency is not about fusing together liberalism and a decent society in international relations, but about promoting an acceptable notion of toleration, cooperation, and standards of fairness. Rawls, as we have seen, downplays any strong or necessary link between decency and liberal societies, since this would assume that only liberal ideals could properly justify the application of decency standards.

For David Miller, a minimalist notion of decency in international relations needs to focus more on the intrinsic basic needs that make it possible to avoid harm and engage in core activities, such as working, raising families, and learning. These basic needs include adequate shelter, access to food and water, physical security, healthcare, and the resources to rear a family. Meeting these needs requires the state to properly distribute resources as well as to enforce appropriate decency standards that can enable all peoples to enjoy these activities and to adequately pursue their rights. As he puts it, "before a need can ground a right, we have to know that the proposed right would not impose obligations on others that would necessarily violate their own human rights."[50] Thus, while setting aside housing to protect the most disadvantaged people may be necessary in some cases, it might also mean putting others into destitution, leaving them homeless.

But Miller also acknowledges that a "minimally decent life is something less than a flourishing life."[51] Moreover, societies may have practices that fail to emphasize and fulfill these needs. To address this challenge, he distinguishes between basic and societal needs, with the latter referring to the needs determined by certain societal norms and values. The distinction allows him to argue that fulfilling these needs will depend on circumstances that vary from community to community. The idea is that there may be different social circumstances that determine how certain basic needs should serve as the grounds for justifying and exercising one's basic rights. For instance, in some societies, there may not be the social need for police officers to carry handguns to ensure the safety of its citizens; but in most other societies, officers must carry handguns to protect the basic right to security. What remains unclear, though, is if the distinction can address some of the more intractable moral conflicts arising from the gaps between conservative and liberal decency. In certain cases, fulfilling social needs may actually undermine the basic needs and rights of others. For instance, LGBTQ members living in a society with highly restrictive social norms against homosexuality may be forced to hide their identity to fulfill societal needs. But this of course would mean suppressing his or her identity and enduring the pain that diminishes the human flourishing that comes from meeting Miller's decency minimum. If LGBTQ members choose to make their identity public in a society where traditional decency standards demonize homosexual practices, then the government may punish them by stripping them of their basic rights. The question is what to do when a state acts on those reactionary decency standards to commission human rights abuses, or declares its moral commitment to preserve what it regards as the integrity of its national customs prohibiting homosexuality by enforcing its anti-gay laws that can carry the sentence of death by stoning for engaging in homosexual activity (e.g., Brunei)? Should we insist that people ignore their own social needs in order to ensure that the state upholds their basic human rights? Or should we refrain from judging other people's social customs and needs and allow reactionary or anti-gay sentiment of traditional decency to strip people of their basic rights? Whether we condemn or permit the social preference to suppress identity, anti-gay laws leave us with a political chasm between liberal and conservative decency as well conservative and basic decency.

In short, the prejudice that allows officials to use decency to suppress identity poses a challenge of coupling identity politics with minimal decency. The LGBTQ movement in this respect exposes a troubling gap between a global minimum of decency and the traditional moral propriety in some societies. And it is a gap that has widened over the years in many countries and become rooted in the conflict between the progressive and retrogressive tendencies of global moral propriety.

Cultural Accommodation and Its Pluralist Critics

For many moral cosmopolitans, decency's political tensions stem from the arbitrary suppression of basic rights and needs. Such tensions demonstrate the need to focus more on emotions to understand the problem of meeting minimal decency standards and situating identity politics within this minimalist framework. Having already explained this latter challenge facing liberal and basic decency in international relations, my aim in this section is to analyze two approaches that seek to meet this identity challenge: liberal cosmopolitanism, which attempts to work beyond, rather than extend Rawls's charter of the Law of Peoples; and liberal multiculturalism, which attempts to merge liberalism with the politics of diversity.

Liberal cosmopolitans, as I have mentioned, stress the importance of maintaining and upholding liberal ideals, such as freedom and moral equality. The goal is to treat these ideals as moral ends to which all individuals should aspire. These aspirations are what help to ground a rights-based approach, which treats human rights (including freedom of religion and the right to dissent against unjust laws and intolerant practices) as the means for fulfilling these ideals.[52] For many cosmopolitans, Rawls's Law of Peoples represents a betrayal of this cosmopolitan goal of safeguarding these ideals and the rights they embody. Rawls, it could be argued, creates a permissive environment in which the state can arbitrarily determine which members of groups can and should be protected or tolerated.[53]

What is more, decent consultative hierarchical societies provide little assurance that leaders will uphold the right to dissent of members belonging to repressed minority groups.[54] In Andrew Kuper's view, this is why this right must be defended as inviolable in all societies and why Rawls's idea of a decent society constitutes a weak notion of cultural pluralism, insofar as it fails to uphold basic democratic norms, such as the freedom from political persecution.[55]

With this issue of a permissive threshold of decency, we need to return to the case of LGBTQ discrimination, since it might enable us to understand how decency connects and disconnects us. In Uganda, national laws not only prohibit sodomy but also stipulate life sentences for repeated offenders. It took considerable outside foreign pressure to convince the Ugandan government to drop the death penalty for such violators. By comparison, the India Supreme Court ruled in 2014 that same-sex practices were unnatural (this was recently overturned in 2018).[56] Again, what these two cases highlight is the struggle to reconcile LGBTQ identity politics and the reactionary politics of moral propriety. By actively punishing the sexual practices of the individuals of the LGBTQ community, state nationalists have treated the practices of the LGBTQ community as both deviant and a threat to national customs or morality, while claiming that LGBTQ rights are yet another instance of Western liberal imperialism. Whether or not the latter is true, the emergence of a global human rights campaign for LGBTQ has led to increasing political tension between the moral propriety of nationalist identity politics and LGBTQ rights. This, in turn, has revealed the growing disconnections of global moral propriety, between moral cooperation and capacity building, as well as strained the role of participation and intercultural dialogue. With these tensions, the openness of such moral propriety confronts the closed off, bounded propriety of nationalists who use democratic norms to achieve the power to restrict rights. In effect, it is the very openness of global moral propriety that in these instances creates the pressures that can constrain the interaction and development of global moral propriety. The result is that in symptomizing the embedded nature of intolerance and fear, the nationalist challenge reflects the deeply fragile arrangement of tolerating difference in liberal and (some) illiberal societies.

Recent debates on toleration have helped to shed light on this fragility.[57] Derek Edyvane, for example, argues that in allowing psychological pressures to accumulate in the individual, toleration can produce an unbearable sense of guilt that both tests and conflicts with long-held beliefs.[58] In short, while toleration may be vital to supporting the decency conditions and standards in liberal societies, it also reveals the difficulties of advancing liberal decency in societies where the conflict between traditional customs and liberal norms can lead to the harm that undermines the basic needs and rights of individuals. Rather than advancing a global minimum of decency (or minimal decency standards that are uniformly applied) in all societies, the built-in tensions of global moral propriety can breed the intolerance and distrust that trumps the need to enforce basic decency standards and that ignores any sensitive claim to cultural identity. Some groups may well find the toleration of their different values as unacceptable to the extent that it requires them to be tolerated on a permanent basis (and prevented from actively shaping the institutions, policies, and laws that are supposed to uphold their claims to identity). If this is true, then toleration needs to be opened up or unmoored from some of the national and global institutional norms and customs that underpin it.

In summary, Rawls's restrictive criteria of a decent society and international toleration stress the importance of adopting a limited set of basic human rights. His idea, as we have seen, is that we need to adopt a narrow subset of these rights in order to minimize decency and to maintain the threshold of openness of toleration that supports the fragile balance between liberal internationalism and cultural pluralism. Cosmopolitans see this as an unnecessary restriction on rights and toleration. However, expanding the threshold of basic and liberal decency in the global arena also requires greater appreciation of the built-in racial prejudice and intolerance that can undermine cosmopolitan claims to global justice. The failure to confront the political reality of this liberal extension of decency—or the increasing tensions between basic and liberal decency—can lead to greater uncertainty regarding compliance with decency standards. The question we need to ask, then, is how the suppression of the basic rights of oppressed minority groups reflects the weak and volatile link between liberal decency and leftist identity politics (such as multiculturalism).

Liberal Multiculturalism and Populist Identity Politics

As one of the most well-known proponents of liberal multiculturalism, Will Kymlicka has done the most to advance its theoretical parameters and applications to global politics. In *Multicultural Odysseys*, Kymlicka argues that liberalism has become an integral part of cultural accommodation. In his view, liberal multiculturalism is no longer just an experiment of cultural accommodation in some European countries; rather, it has become a prominent policy rubric for accommodating cultural values and identities. Based on the idea that cultural beliefs and values are intrinsic features of citizenship, liberal multiculturalism addresses the complex political dynamics of preserving cultural values through a targeted set of group-differentiated rights—autonomy, polyethnic rights, and special representational rights, which are designed to empower minority groups.[59]

In justifying these rights, Kymlicka contends that the tendency up until the 1990s was to assume that robust human rights protection was not enough to promote diversity and security in many liberal democracies. But in the 1990s and 2000s, he concludes, there was a rapid shift from a procedural to a multicultural agenda in international politics (or the recognition of the cultural claims of minority groups to advance the human rights of these marginalized cultural groups, such as indigenous peoples). The shift marked the efforts by the United Nations (e.g., by UNESCO and the International Labour Organization) and the EU to contain rising levels of ethnic violence in the post–Cold War era. Through a series of policies aimed at accommodating the cultural needs and rights of indigenous and substate groups, these institutions began to focus on and institute various group-differentiated rights, such as special representational rights, which Kymlicka considers provisional rights that are advanced through measures of affirmative action and proportional representation, and the right to self-government that applies to national minorities or indigenous groups. Accordingly, liberal multiculturalism constituted an approach to liberal identity politics that sought to transform the cultural identity of subnational and indigenous minority groups.

Still, for Kymlicka, there was (and is) a "passive acquiescence" to the idea of multiculturalism's effectiveness in facilitating participation and diverse representation in institutions.[60] Indeed, his liberal identity politics approach depended on the willingness of the majority to move beyond a monocultural model that had relied on universal toleration to remedy racist stigmas and stereotypes. While Kymlicka admits that liberal multiculturalism is not perfect, he also maintains that it represents the most promising effort to address the global challenge of promoting cultural pluralism in liberal societies.[61] In fact, for him, the global challenge of diversity lies in overcoming an "us-versus-them" dichotomy, in which cultural empowerment insulates one from the institutional responsibility of changing the behavior of illiberal groups. Liberal multiculturalism, as he puts it, "has the same aspiration to link identities and interests. It not only recognizes particular minority identities, but seeks to transform the economic opportunities, political powers, and social status available to bearers of that identity."[62]

In assuming that group-differentiated rights transform cultural identities, then, he presumes that the majority of national groups will learn to adopt the policies and priorities of liberal multiculturalism, even if this means surrendering their own traditional values. Yet, as I have argued, liberal multiculturalism cannot escape the effects of working beyond national identity politics. In many ways, it remains a victim of these effects, insofar as it fails to guarantee that minority groups will not become isolated nor sufficiently integrated into society. It is always possible, in other words, that this policy-oriented liberal approach to identity politics may encourage nationalist groups to win the political power necessary for excluding minority groups from actively participating in the political process.[63] After all, the rise of right-wing populism and anti-immigration sentiment is not simply the result of illiberal forces capturing the liberal architecture. It is an effect of the openness of global moral propriety, which Kymlicka himself tacitly restricts, albeit in a progressive manner. To his credit, though, Kymlicka does seem to anticipate the global rise of right-wing populism by suggesting that multicultural models of accommodation had only managed to contain the hidden biases and stigmas driving nationalist politics and intolerance (e.g., England and the Netherlands) in Europe.[64] In replacing these models, liberal multiculturalism does not ensure that these reactive biases will disappear. As even Kymlicka puts it, "There is no guarantee that the infrastructure of multiculturalism will not be captured by illiberal forces intent on limiting civil liberties and individual autonomy."[65]

Now, this is not to say that liberal multicultural policies caused the rise of global populism. Rather, it is to argue that its attempt to extend liberal decency—or solidify its ties with basic decency through the transformative, substantive claim to cultural identity—was problematically based on transcending the anti-immigration sentiments or negative tendencies of conservative decency. In reality, it only inhibited and repressed such negative tendencies and allowed political leaders to stoke this negative sentiment by justifying the attacks on the rule of law and human rights, and by bolstering their nationalist agendas of restoring law and (a natural) order. For Jarosław Kaczyński, the leader of the Law and Justice Party in Poland, political propriety has meant returning to the basic rules and values, or, as he puts it, "Christian values, veneration to the Fatherland."[66] Other nationalist leaders, such as Geert Wilders, the Dutch politician and leader of the Party for Freedom, have exploited racial tensions to counteract the liberal bias toward migrants and their special protection, thus destabilizing the Netherland's once peaceful and tolerant society. Moreover, in Hungary, Viktor Orbán, the populist president, has politicized moral propriety by clamping down on the freedom of press and speech, the rule of law, and immigrant and refugee rights. The effect of his constitutional overhaul has placed unprecedented pressure on the European Union to devise a procedure for counteracting the reactionary nationalist policies that violate a member's commitment to meeting the EU's norms of democratic stability, human rights, and minority rights protection.[67] In this way, Orbán's populist campaign reflects the growing disconnection between basic and liberal decency and the increasing tensions between national capacity building and the individual autonomy of members belonging to targeted minority groups.

To summarize: the aim of liberal multiculturalism is to work beyond the normative constraints of tolerance by projecting liberal decency through the substantive claims to cultural identity that cut across individual and collective lines of representation. But in seeking to level the playing field for cultural groups by enhancing cultural participation, it also underestimates the problematic effect of extending liberal decency to identity politics, or how the reactionary elements of conservative decency can create disconnections between liberal and basic decency. A cultural pluralist politics must therefore do more than simply advance a basic claim to cultural identity. It also needs to reconfigure the politics of decency in order to meet the challenge of resolving the intense effects of identity politics.

Global Reconfiguration and Difference

The task of reconfiguration involves first and foremost moving beyond the statist constraints of decency. Extending liberal decency to cultural pluralist politics, as I have argued, intensifies the political retrogression of global moral propriety. As one of the primary examples of this retrogression, right-wing populism seems to show how the propriety effect of rapidly spreading liberal decency stems from the hostile nationalist sentiment that targets cultural pluralism. Reconfiguring a pluralist politics in the global arena, then, requires us to imagine the global spaces for reengaging or converting this pressure into political opportunities and representation. The critical task, in other words, is synergizing or recombining decency's basic, liberal, and conservative features through participation and open-ended, intercultural dialogue, that is, forging new global connections from the political tensions and disconnections between moral cooperation, capacity building, and participation.

Connolly's idea of deep pluralism is that pluralism is ultimately about challenging the deeply rooted secular idea of separating religion and politics in liberal democratic states. Contesting this idea (or treating it as agonistic) in global politics may actually be a desirable thing in terms of promoting dialogue, civic participation, and representation. Rather than simply drawing on preexisting moral beliefs to show who is right or wrong morally, we also need to politically engage these moral beliefs. Critical or deep pluralism, in this sense, is about "breaking open sociality"—or as Brain Massumi points out, "how we inhabit political uncertainty together"—while at the same time engaging the moral possibilities of freedom.[68] It means transgressing the constraints/limits of the state and realizing the moral possibilities of representing the different beliefs or faiths in the global arena.[69] For Connolly, this also requires critical knowledge of the relational ties of different sensibilities of justice and the moral possibilities of civic participation in global institutions.

There is not the space in this chapter to discuss the various strands of Connolly's deep pluralism, which date back to his work in the early 1970s. My aim is to elaborate upon the implications of two thematic objectives/global trajectories:[70] (1) the refiguration of the global political condition and its global political pressures, and (2) the dangers and new possibilities produced by the "globalization of contingency," or how global forces are shaping the meaning of events in unpredictable ways.[71] In this way, I will be addressing the "relational sensibility" and "relational modesty" underlying these themes, and refiguring moral constraints as the conditions of possibility and bodily freedom.

Connolly's relational pluralism involves a deep antagonism between a positive belief in transcendence and immanence. The former refers to the new and existing practices created by humanity's effort to institute higher, shared standards of justice and order; the latter to the practices that exist in nature. Both, it can be said, reflect an interlocking tension between transcendent (Rousseau, Kant, and Hegel) and deistic thinkers (Spinoza and Leibniz). Through the immanent tension between the liberal order/ideals and global pressures of social inequality, one becomes aware of his or her place in relation to another. He or she is able to extract the bits of truth about his or her political participation in democratic systems.

Connolly thus proposes an open-ended notion of public space situated within the tension between practice and beliefs: an agonistic space(s) mediated through a respect for others' different beliefs. Such a public space consists of the civic virtues of public accountability, self-discipline, and a commitment to justice, which enables one to negotiate or uphold democratic justice.[72] This pluralist ethos is "grounded," as he writes, "in the assumption that residing between a fundamental image of the world as either created or uncreated and a specific ethico-political stance resides a sensibility that colors how that creed is expressed and portrayed to others. The sensibility mixes into the creed, rotating its ethico-political compass in this way or that."[73] The notion of relational sensibility reflects the particular ways that individuals draw on their cultural beliefs to direct their thinking and actions in relation to other beliefs: where each faith or set of beliefs possesses a "chunk" of the truth that drives people to contest one another in the open-ended struggle for equality and justice.

Rawls's idea of cultural pluralism, as we saw, lumps these chunks into one commonsense conception of decency and justice. Relational sensibility, for Connolly, "transfigures the drive to reach a consensus on justice above contending faiths into the effort to negotiate a positive ethos of engagement between multiple constituencies who bring chunks and pieces of their faiths with them into the public realm."[74] So while Rawls focuses on an overlapping consensus, his minimal decency leaves the tension between the particular values and goods unresolved. Again, his idea of decency is that it should restrain us from unduly intervening in the affairs of peoples who cooperate with the principles of his charter of the Law of Peoples.

By comparison, Connolly's aim is to engage this tension by treating statist power and national capacity building as problematic constraints on pluralism. In other words, he seeks to decouple the two levels of capacity building (which have worked against open participation) by devising a pluralist ethos that will support a critical liberalism that shows, as he writes,

> an attentiveness to rights and constitutional protections in its extension of these concerns to forces that would encompass the dialectic of discipline and reactive disaffection to new corners of life, . . . against the hegemony of teleological and transcendental theories that conceal other people's voices and contestations about what counts as fair and respectful treatment.[75]

As this passage suggests, the hegemony of liberalism is logically tied to states' enforcement of universal rights. Liberal pluralism, as we have seen, depends on the state to enforce the rules of moral interaction and the principles of equal respect for one another (nondiscrimination). But it also presupposes a pre-constituted subject to direct and stabilize the application of these principles concerning representation and participation.

A global pluralist ethos problematizes this precondition. It concerns how justice involves not simply agreed-upon rules but the open-ended possibilities of interacting beyond these rules and their statist elements. As Connolly writes, "the possibility of multiple faiths negotiating with dignity on the same territory and where each faith minority amplifies awareness of the elements of rupture already simmering in it"[76] is what inscribes the effects of injuries, subjugations, and concealments into the global spaces of negotiation and dialogue.[77] In the end, it is how one develops an awareness of these effects and how global political pressures can inject a relational modesty into what Connolly states "is the ritual practice to amplify one side of its own faith—the injunction to practice hospitality toward other faiths coexisting with it—and to curtail pressures within it to repress or marginalize other faiths."[78] In this sense, intercultural dialogue can be thought of as an open-ended feature of this pluralist ethos in which people learn (sensibly) to manage the pressures by openly engaging each other through dialogue and participation. Its openness is based on communication and interaction that can be easily closed off or stymied by a nationalist agenda to preserve a cultural heritage.

But, in another sense, Connolly's pluralist ethos raises the question of how these global pressures come into existence in the first place. Do the political pressures to conform to a global set of uniform standards and rules create effects that work against the internalization of these rules, or that remain in excess (surplus) of what the global network of institutions can feasibly manage? In other words, if Connolly's global pluralism holds that democratic rules and virtues comprise the global political and civic spaces for engaging and learning to accept the contributions of each other's beliefs, then does this also require us to still deal with the effects and statist pressures of toleration? Another way of understanding this challenge is to say that just because global participation results in diverse representation, does not mean that it can sustain itself independently of the statist and individualist domains whose constraints brought it into and continue to shape its existence. The trouble with Connolly's pluralism is that it does not give us a good enough idea of how the domains of global moral propriety can create effects that feed back onto and intensify the conservative sentiments at the national level (which I shall address in the following chapter). Working effectively beyond statist constraints requires us to articulate the ever-present retrogressive tendency (and its political intensification) of moral cooperation and capacity building. This means that the moral possibilities of deep pluralism can be difficult to fully realize, precisely because they can never entirely escape the propriety effect of global moral propriety that continues to intensify and create the new conditions for disconnection.

Freedom of Movement and Exclusion

Before addressing this issue of political retrogression, it is important to recall that the global extension of basic decency in international relations was about expanding a liberal consensus through a uniform set of rules and normative constraints. This is what made it possible to undertake a vast new series of global moral initiatives and institutional building to integrate national and individual capacity building and promote participation, dialogue, and cultural pluralism. But this project also meant managing diversity largely from above, or from the state and global levels. This, I argued, led to a false sense of common decency in global politics, since it presumed that basic decency was already anchored in a liberal sensibility of the common good. The ideological gap between basic decency and liberal decency thus opened up opportunities for not only other local moral proprieties to challenge the effect of this imposition but also to mobilize negative sentiment toward immigrants. In this way, the uniform application of basic standards of decency has created a reverse, global effect of progressively extending and applying basic decency to promote cultural identity. Moral progression, in other words, turns into the political retrogression that seems to provisionally close down the potential to structure and diversify a sense of shared decency in the global arena. In short, the challenge we face is confronting the tension associated with extending both basic decency and liberal decency to the global realm, since, in stressing choice and freedom, liberal decency's extension (to identity politics) produces a conflict between it and the moral proprieties of cultural groups. The issue, then, is whether we can resolve this tension by learning to abide by something even more basic: namely, a self-acceptance of a common liberal bias that informs the way we use common decency. Or should we simply learn to confront this bias by recognizing a primary source of diversifying decency, or the effect of felt exclusion and insecurity and how this effect informs the way we respond to the openness of global moral propriety in terms of promoting security and well-being?

To begin with, we still need to better confront the complex political reality of diversifying decency. One way of doing this is accepting that the common essence of humanity is to come to terms with the suffering that makes us all human and shows that being humane will always remain a tenuous extension of being human. To be human, in other words, is to know your own sense of exclusion and insecurity in the world, while the latter means employing compassion and empathy to assist in and stop the suffering of others. In *We Are Already Migrants*, for example, Gregory Feldman argues that it is not this common essence of the former that defines our humanity; instead, it is that all humans share the common condition of atomization that makes individual differences "politically inconsequential."[79] Feldman's idea is that we are all ultimately migrants, since all of us are defined by our disempowerment and vulnerability. For him, the question is whether one matters and can or will contribute to society such that when we consider the migrant and refugee as a person unduly threatened (someone to be saved) we can also learn to treat him or her as fundamentally different from us, or as the object of our own insecurity. This is when we end up obscuring, as he puts it, "the shared conditions that undermine our political agency and theirs."[80]

For Georgio Agamben, the seemingly tenuous line between citizen and refugee is predicated on the idea of the sacred person losing his or her rights when the sovereign leader declares a security crisis.[81] The slippery slope from citizen to refugee means that while the state depends on the people's absence or silence as political subjects (who are not granted refugee status, for instance), it also requires their presence to assert its authority. This contradictory outcome reflects the moral tendency to dichotomize between stability and movement, which, in turn, represents how a shared awareness of exclusion and insecurity expresses an unconscious condition of seeking inclusion at the expense of others. The human condition thus encapsulates the uncertainty and fear of extending liberal decency to identity politics and suggests that there is a perilous tension between being human and being humane. Michel Foucault, for example, saw the effects of this uncertainty as the very reason for thinking about disciplinary power or the tools to discipline and control populations.[82] In essence, when one invokes decency, he or she is not simply expressing a sense of humanity but an intense feeling and belief in the idea of connecting with something more basic about humanity.

However, it is precisely this intense feeling that is routinely directed outward where it can be divorced from this inner shared awareness or any self-acceptance of common exclusion. For example, when President Trump chose to label the caravan of migrants fleeing the violence in their own countries as invaders and aliens, his decision had the effect of encouraging other groups on the margins (namely, militia groups) to take up arms against this perceived threat to the U.S. border.[83] It did not matter whether the threat was real or not, only that there were people ready to take up arms to defend the integrity of the U.S. border. In reacting to this flood of migrants, Trump and the militias stood up against America's prevailing custom of openness to the migrants' plights (asylum seeking), which, in this case, did not mean opening the borders. More importantly, the effect of closing off the borders involved separating parents from their children at the border. Confining and excluding the most vulnerable population violated the essential bond between children and parents. Not only did this policy reject the liberal decency of recognizing the migrants' rights of freedom from harmful treatment but it also undermined the basic conditions of decency or duty of providing proper treatment under the law and fair access to resources. By denying migrants their basic rights, the Trump administration managed to undermine the basic decency that informs America's liberal decency, as we saw in chapter 2. Such a restrictive or "get-tough" policy, however, was not simply the result of bigotry or overexaggerated fear: it was the retrogressive effect of the openness of accommodating migrants. The effect of this openness is that it cuts retrogressively and progressively through conservative and liberal sentiments that are built into the applications of global moral propriety. In this case, it demonstrates how closing off borders is never the exception to decency but the effect of recognizing the openness of moral propriety. This is another reason why it is impractical to speak of fully open borders, since it means doing away with the normative constraints that uphold an open-door policy or the open opportunities to seek refuge. In effect, decency can never be truly freed of the normative, institutional constraints determining its application, since such constraints, if promoted properly, enact the possibilities and opportunities for extending liberal decency or the increased freedom from improper and unfair treatment (e.g., green cards and full citizenship).

In much the same way, freedom of movement has been subject to a number of restrictions that seem to contradict its basic claim to decency.[84] In *Movement and the Ordering of Freedom*, Hagar Kotef argues that freedom of movement signifies how the state under liberalism has long constrained freedom: "movement was a given within many constraints and secured by many anchors that provided it with some stability. . . . it has been conceptualized and materialized within sets of material, racial, and gendered conditions in a way that allowed some subjects to be appear free when moving . . . but as oppressed when hindered."[85] Yet the idea of freedom of movement as a foundational principle in Europe was to enable the free flow of goods and people and, in the process, allow people to pursue a better, more stable way of life. This is why it lies at the core of the EU's identity as a liberal democratic polity—with de facto open borders among its member states—and why it remains a key part of the Amsterdam Treaty (1997), which incorporated the Schengen Agreement and its body of rules (or *acquis*), which provide for free movement of EU citizens.[86]

Still, the trouble is that freedom must invariably be predicated on the ability to manage the threats to this freedom. Managing these threats becomes the necessary condition of restricting the movement in terms of tracking suspected terrorists. The EU's Free Movement Directive (2004), for instance, provides for extensive surveillance and monitoring of internal borders, which enable states, in times of crisis, to trace the movement of suspected terrorists and to temporarily close down borders. In this way, increasing surveillance in the European Union becomes a necessary means of opening borders and exercising freedom and increasing the exchange of ideas. "Security," as Didier Bigo argues, "becomes not only about stopping [threats] but how opening can also be a 'security move.'"[87] This association between freedom and mobility thus results in the security measures used to defend the openness of liberal morality; it shows how the openness of liberal morality justifies the security mechanisms that restrict freedom of movement.

In terms of extending liberal decency, then, the openness of Europe's liberal morality is what in the end must be defended if migrants are to be treated fairly. And yet, it is this need for securing this defense that can also actualize the perceived threats to tradition and justify violently cracking down on protests at the borders. Indeed, the unprecedented flows of refugees from Syria into Europe has placed enormous pressure on European (and other) states. The total number of asylum claims to Europe in 2015, for instance, was 1,321,560, and approximately 3,770 migrants lost their lives at sea. In response, Hungary and Austria have (recently) elected to close their borders, while Germany and the European Union have implemented an aid package to Turkey to contain the flow of refugees. Much of this political pressure, it should be noted, stems from the Dublin Convention (2007), which required countries that received the asylum seekers to administer the asylum process and provide refuge for the accepted asylum-seekers. Not surprisingly, this has placed an undue and disproportionate burden on states such as Greece and Italy.

Violence at the borders nonetheless symptomizes the effect of Europe's own open-ended transnational moral propriety. The pressure to close state borders seems to confirm the state's continued ability to monopolize violence and to allow migrants and refugees to be unfairly treated and dehumanized.[88] Rather than treating all refugees as subjects of law, liberal democratic states (and the EU) have detained countless refugees at the border, where many have died from a lack of basic supplies.[89] And yet, popular anger directed at officials for implementing lax immigration policies has pressured state leaders to reinforce stricter codes of moral propriety as a means of bolstering border security. This is how populist reaction has reversed Europe's moral progress of accommodating migrant needs and rights.

Such reversal also raises the vexing issue of how stateless people should be treated as political subjects, especially when their brutal treatment opens up the gap between liberal and basic decency in world politics. Indeed, if the legalized areas situated in between state borders are the contested space where people are objectified and dehumanized, then deconstructing these areas in terms of the treatment of the stateless refugee (and not a refugee fleeing from a state) requires a deeper appreciation of the breakdown of basic decency in relation to the liberal aspects of global moral propriety.

In short, the question becomes this: How does this global pressure reflect the growing political uncertainty of promoting the openness of decency, or its moral potential of structuring conduct around a uniform set of liberal democratic rules? One answer is that liberal decency must be gradually applied to control the effects of populist anger and to ensure the basic rights of all persons, not just citizens.

But popular anger does not of course operate out of a vacuum; rather, as I have suggested, it stems from the biases and negative sentiment of being excluded. Extending liberal decency to remedy these biases can create a paradoxical effect of devaluing human potential. When, in other words, refugees are treated as if they are objects of compassion (or when they are viewed as bodies of pain or vulnerable human beings in need of protection and care), they also become the passive, subordinate recipients of charity. It is here where the negative, reactionary sentiments of conservative decency collude with the moral limits of liberalism to create division and instability in the global liberal order. But it is also here where decency has not only failed to support a liberalism that is critical of itself—as we have seen with Connolly—but has also become a common source of pressures and tensions that restricts the moral possibilities of intercultural dialogue, fair representation, and open participation in the global realm.

An Unconventional Idea of Liberal Decency

The conventional idea of a decent society is that all persons, regardless of ethnicity, race, gender, and sex, will be treated with equal respect and dignity. I argued that extending liberal decency to the global realm provided the basis of a global moral propriety (and its four interactive domains), which, at least initially, led to stronger moral commitments and the integration of national and individual capacity building. In time, though, this would give way to the contentiousness of identity politics. Yet, rather than reinterpreting decency in the face of these pressures, the tendency has been to reflexively defend it as a moral bulwark against populist attacks. My unconventional idea of decency in global politics, however, challenged this by showing how global moral propriety opened itself up to being shaped by the tensions and pressures of identity politics. But, in doing so, it also involved the possibilities and outcomes of the propriety effect in global politics. The advantage of treating decency in this way, or as a source of these tensions, was that it enabled us to critique liberalism and liberal identity politics and, perhaps more importantly, to engage its content pluralistically, that is, as an uncommon humane sentiment whose normative potential needed to be rooted in a wider self-acceptance of exclusion.

In one sense, then, global populist pressures test and even disable the liberal constraints of the international order. In another sense, they expose the conflict or lack of interaction of global moral propriety, creating a global propriety effect in which certain biases can politicize the openness of this multidimensional propriety to destabilize it. Decency, in other words, can become a victim of its own normative constraints, especially when it is invoked to support goals and causes that conflict with other uses of it. The feeling of exclusion thus becomes the political force fracturing and affecting the common bias against violence. Which can only mean one thing: that decency standards can never be freed from statist, legal constraints, since these restrictions are precisely how it manages and governs this propriety effect. The irony of course is that decency, which was supposed to project compassion, empathy, and regulate the effects of fear and ignorance, can also be used to project the latter. In short, decency's moral appeal may have less to do with the felt capacity to connect and understand others than with reinforcing a problematic transcultural moral perspective. This, at least, is how decency has become such a central part of the liberal imagination and why some, as we shall see in the next chapter, have turned to emotions and affect to champion the liberal ideals of a decent society.

CHAPTER FOUR

Affective Decency and Its Unstructured Potential

> Passion can't be explained, it can only be experienced. More exactly it has to be experienced from the inside before it can be understood from the outside.
>
> —J. M. Coetzee, *The Schooldays of Jesus*

> Politics cannot be defined on the basis of any pre-existing subject. The difference specific to politics, that which makes it possible to define its subject, must be sought in the form of its relation.
>
> —Jacques Rancière, *Dissensus*

Decency is shaped by a number of political pressures and contending forces. Much of today's right-wing populism, as we saw in the prior chapter, reflects the reactionary politics of conservative decency, in which political leaders have drawn on either anti-immigrant or anti-gay sentiment to angrily defend traditional values. Their actions, if anything, have helped show how anger and hatred are contributing to the growing rift between liberal and conservative decency. For proponents of liberal decency, the impulsive tendency to consciously deviate from decency standards only confirms the absence of many key virtuous elements of decency in populist movements, such as restraint and tolerance. More importantly, it suggests that more compassion, love, and empathy are needed to offset the debilitating effects of such hatred.

While this may be true, the need to cultivate these emotions also oversimplifies the forces shaping the politics of decency. Emotions, as we have seen, play a very complex role in connecting and disconnecting us in the struggle to protect the basic needs and rights of persons. Anger, in particular, can produce the political uncertainty that makes us wary about the need to uphold the standards of decency. Indeed, it can make being compassionate and trustworthy seem like a political liability. But in making us feel this way, it may also motivate us to treat it as an overlooked asset, that is, to take the moral high ground to defend liberal decency. Exactly what this moral high ground consists of is not entirely clear. Yet, however we choose to defend our sense of decency, political emotions seem to capture this variegated sense of decency and the ineluctable moral conflicts of defending the standards of decency. In many ways, such emotions can be thought of as ideological conveyers of decency (e.g., the promoters of conservative, liberal, or socialist values that justify dignity protection), which can connect and disconnect us in the struggle for decency. Ideology functions in this sense as a mode through which emotions motivate us to support the standards of decency. But it also says little about how the forces shaping decency can produce and intensify these emotions. As I have argued, whether it is the struggle to take the moral high ground or to defend the integrity of traditional customs along racial lines, the moral defense of decency tends to isolate itself from the identity politics that is shaping it. This is one way to emphasize the disconnections and gaps in the politics of decency. And it raises the question of how such conflicting emotions, which create these gaps, offer us an incomplete view of such politics. Why is there a persistent tendency to champion or hold up competing moral and emotive claims to decency? If the tacit political and emotive goal of promoting decency is to secure identity (and the basic needs and rights that come with this) in the world, then we need to better understand the underlying reality that structures or brings into existence this desired goal.

Confronting this political reality means understanding how decency functions ontologically or consists of primal forces that structure its existence in our experience and in society. It is through this ontological function, I argue, that we can learn more about the forces that produce the normative tendency of moral fixation (or permanently securing and elevating uniform moral constraints) and the hidden sources of political tension and disconnection that shape decency. As we saw earlier, emotions express the conscious feelings of being excluded, or of being unfairly treated. The primal desire of being decent resonates affect or an unfelt reality. Affect, as I shall define and use it, functions as an autonomous response that occurs "below the threshold of consciousness and cognition" and is rooted in the body.[1] It is neither directly connected to personal feelings nor to intense emotions but is an "unconscious experience of intensity" that expresses, as Nigel Thrift puts it, "a moment of unstructured potential."[2]

I shall deploy affect to configure the primal forces of tension that disconnect and connect us in the political struggle for decency. In doing so, I will distinguish between an ontological and normative concept of decency as well as between affect and emotion. Both, I claim, allow us to explain two issues: (1) why advancing liberal decency can be a perilous task of overcoming the hostile emotions in identity politics, (2) and why focusing on its ontological function via affect theory can enable us to understand the unstructured potential of decency and the mechanisms that modulate the effects of coupling decency and identity politics. While affect offers a more nuanced, but by no means perfect picture of today's politics of decency, it does allow us to conceptualize the problematic link between decency and identity politics, including the social gaps between top-down, liberal internationalist interventions and local interventions. In this way, I will critically examine the notion of intensity as it relates to an evolving, albeit politically fragile moral threshold of decency, which we discussed in chapter 3.[3]

My main objective in this chapter is to understand this intensity of affect in relation to the normative tendency of isolating decency from the volatile effects of identity politics, by first distinguishing between political emotions and political affect and then showing how the politics of affect reveals the hostile role of bias in the identity politics of decency. In the first section, I will critique value pluralism and political emotions, showing how the value intensity of emotions serves to deepen the problem and obscure the propriety effect of global moral propriety. I then move on to critically examine how affects circulate in between groups and institutions in global politics, and what this means for configuring the affective mechanism of complementarity and understanding the political stakes and constraints arising from the tensions between decency and difference.

Distinguishing Emotion and Affect

One of the ideas we addressed in chapters 2 and 3 was that decency as a value had evolved from small morals to a basic human value and that this change in its magnitude or normative structure involved an intensity or a new sense about the liberal features of promoting fair and reasonable treatment, such as impartiality, the rule of law, and individual freedom. The new secular quality of decency as fair and just treatment represented an intensity of this value, that is, it demonstrated how a value could be extended through reasoned sentiment and societal change to assume a universal and neutralizing function. In making a case for distinguishing between emotion and affect, then, we first need to explain how this liberal ontological approach to value intensity obscures the specific character of intensity, or, in this case, decency's inexhaustible character of structuring difference.

A value, it can be said, refers to the way we judge the worth of our actions and the qualities of an object or another person.[4] A political value in this sense reflects how individuals and groups evaluate and direct their actions in the world. It explains how we learn to justify the strategies and plans for action, while also signifying the different ways we feel about others' experiences. Liberal pluralism holds that there is no one overarching standard by which to evaluate the worth of other values (for instance, faith). Rather, the plurality of values such as justice, equality, autonomy, freedom, and tolerance, are in constant tension with one another. Their incommensurability means that they can never be fully reconciled. The only way to properly manage the effects of this tension is by reaching acceptable trade-offs between them (or between conflict and peace). Value incommensurability is thus a concept designed to avert the destructive outcomes of value monism, such as totalitarianism and the violent repression of humanity.[5] It signifies the importance of being rational or reasonable in terms of one's commitment to preserving humanity. For Isaiah Berlin, decency and dignity were two commensurable values with overlapping intrinsic qualities. Reasonable persons, he argued, learned to abide by humane ideals that could direct us toward the preservation and flourishing of human dignity.

Max Weber also claimed that value rationality was, as he put it, "determined by conscious belief in the value for its own sake of some ethical, aesthetic, religious or other form of behavior."[6] In distinguishing between value rationality and affectual action, Weber stressed how all values were inherently subjective; that even in science, one could not divorce values from scientific facts. Value rationality meant that values existed as an intrinsic part of one's subjective experience, or rather, as a vocational calling to act on one's intentions and beliefs. For Weber, modern science had emerged as the key source of value creation, having displaced the unified vision of monotheistic religion. But in deconstructing religion and other sources of value creation, it, too, had become dissipated in its capacity for value creation, leading, as Weber argues, to a fracturing of value systems. In other words, the disenchantment with religion, which gave way to the work ethic or vocational calling and science itself (in terms of the modern state and bureaucracy), expressed a continual divorce from the emotions and feelings that once supplied the energy of traditional worldviews.[7] The re-enchantment he spoke of was about affirming the plurality of these different value systems and the rational drive and instincts they embodied. It was an idea inspired by Friedrich Nietzsche's notion of the self-affirmation of a person's will to power, which held that the person, in being free from resentment (*resentiment*), was merely a "dupe" of linguistic habits. By distinguishing between good and evil, one learned to suppress and hide this resentment. "It was," as Nietzsche put it, "the pathos of distance that authorized [the high-minded] to create values and name them."[8]

For Nietzsche, such pathos characterized the affinity between the egotistic–altruism dichotomy and the herd instinct. With the decline of what he calls aristocratic values (those values that did not justify the affirmation of values in relation to a lower class), moral valuations could be easily reduced to this dichotomy within the emotion of rancor, for with "rancor," as he writes, "turning creative and giving birth to values. . . . the rancor of beings, who deprived of the direct outlet of action, compensate by an imaginary vengeance."[9] Value creation therefore was not simply about freeing or detaching morality from such emotion (as science had sought to little avail), but realizing that the person as the supreme sovereign was equal only to oneself. In his view, compassion, empathy, and love grew out of guilt or bad conscience, in which neither resentment nor compassion drove the desire to be good or the struggle against evil. These emotions were, instead, directed at the oppressed or the common man, in a way that treated these people as pitiable. Nietzsche thus inverted the normative meaning of liberal democratic society's constraints by claiming that moral duties stemmed from a moral detachment or cruel pleasure in punishing others. In short, the value creation of liberal democratic society was tethered to a compulsion to look outward and not inward: where 'no' is the creative act of engaging others.[10]

Nietzsche also suggested that the morality of custom, or what we've been referring to in terms of conservative decency, was an ascetic morality that, while not given to altruism, was perhaps the purer expression of egotism, albeit not one that was self-affirming of the will to power or mastery of one's instinct. But in engaging the value of ethics, Nietzsche had less if anything to say about the intrinsic value of commitments. Are they, for example, valued merely for the vitality they derive from a deep desire in preserving the life and dignity of all peoples? And do we value them merely for their stability and role in upholding the rules of the global system? For example, if I am committed to the liberation of an oppressed group of people, but then learn that their struggle was achieved through the systematic torture of their own people, should I revise my commitment to their cause given these new facts that no longer conform to my own belief in ending torture and fighting corruption? What this suggests is that some beliefs may be so deeply rooted that they cause us to not only react against novelty, or treat changing events as a threat to these beliefs, but also to become dispassionate in assisting others. Again, Nietzsche referred to this as the pathos of distance: a nonaltruistic and egotistical commitment (or reversion to traditional sentiment). For him, compassion, empathy, and love reinforced a slave ethic in which disengaging from our vengeance meant being ruled by these emotions and the values, customs, and rules that constituted the liberal qualities of decency.

The Limits of Political Emotions

In normative theory, value intensity reflects how feelings and emotions can change the quality of our behavior toward others. When, for instance, we value diversity in the work force or education, we also extend this quality of inclusion to these places; but even more importantly, we become aware of the drawbacks and costs of excluding people—with disadvantaged backgrounds—from participating in these public places. Nussbaum, as we saw earlier, sought to extend Rawls's notion of decency by showing how emotions structure our moral judgments and respect of others. She treated political emotions as measures of values and action, or as ways of appraising our actions to assist and treat others fairly and with respect. Hence, the idea of cultivating love and compassion is that it deepens our motivation to assist one another, while enriching our knowledge about the conditions for developing and protecting a person's dignity. As John Deigh points out, this idea shows how "the acquisition of knowledge is basic to one's learning to interpret the feelings constituting any specific value."[11] Our valued judgments, therefore, reflect the evolution of knowledge from the primitive knowledge of childhood to the acquisition of self-knowledge (reasoning).

The difference between primitive (early childlike impulses) and secondary emotions (learned emotive states) allows Nussbaum to claim that any extended quality of judgment or the appraisal of fair treatment must arise from a maturing sensibility about dignity protection. Thus, for example, shame can be interpreted as a powerful secondary emotion, since it reflects a judgment about a lack of self-worth and shows how punishment, if properly administered at the personal and societal levels, could have a necessary, beneficial effect of promoting the common good. This is demonstrated by Amnesty International's naming and shaming campaign, whose mission is to call media attention to human rights abuses and to force abusive leaders to recognize the political effects of their actions. While this does not mean that an abusive leader will necessarily feel compassion for victims' needs, it does suggest that all people are susceptible to feeling humiliated and that such humiliation can be used to redress human rights abuses.

Like shame, anger also tends to be misunderstood politically. Anger, one could argue, is not an inherently reactive emotion, but, as Robert Solomon points out, "a valued-rich phenomenon . . . or a complex process that proceeds through time and can last a very long time."[12] Solomon argues that anger is not simply a trigger or biological response to stimuli but part of a long-term strategy that reflects "years of practice and settled habits."[13] Anger (or the feeling of being wronged) can thus determine how our mistreatment by others tests our values and beliefs. Yet for Nussbaum, anger does not express a durable quality of decency in the political arena; rather, it shows just how unstructured and undeveloped compassion remains for gauging our altruistic actions. For compassion and love to structure the qualities of diversity or to extend decency in the public realm to all people, especially those with disadvantaged backgrounds, they need to reflect a felt obligation to treat all others as morally equal. Thus, they must nurture a shared sense about the importance of abiding by the normative constraints against injuring others' dignity—even if this defies the reality that civilians will be killed to stop the killing or severe harm.

Treating political emotions as appraisals of values, therefore, reinforces the idea that legal and normative constraints can also neutralize the reactionary politics of decency or the impulses to violate the laws and rules of dignity protection.[14] Love and compassion in this respect make it possible to extend the norms, standards, and rules of equal treatment in global politics, by contributing to an increasing moral threshold for dignity protection. By moral threshold, I am referring here to a value's intensity and how a magnitude of protection needs to be exceeded for a positive result (protecting the dignity of all people) to be manifested. Decency's threshold can be gauged by the magnitude of its norms and standards and the shared conviction in and commitment to justice. In effect, the political intensity of emotions attests to the force of these shared convictions to produce stable and desirable outcomes in global politics.

Political Constraint and Discerning Value Intensity

The idea of an expanding moral threshold, then, is that by tolerating and accommodating others, we can also build new and stronger attachments to others. But how do we know when we have crossed this shared moral threshold? One answer seems to lie in the positive feelings we acquire when we have become attached to others, whether through personal or professional responsibilities or an awareness of similar desires. It is a feeling that draws us closer to those who have assisted other persons in the same situation. However, the trouble with this idea, as Aaron Ben-Ze'ev points out, is that we often assume that "there are no two identical situations, but rather only situations similar in some respects and different in others. Hence, the moral task is to determine which differences are morally relevant."[15] Yet Nussbaum's transcultural view of political emotions presumes that all differences enjoy a morally equal status (moral equality) and that decency can and should be deepened to fulfill the conditions of realizing this and other ideals of global justice (such that every person possesses the equal capacity to discover his or her relation to the world). As she puts it, political emotions "have deep roots in the personality and in people's sense of their own history . . . and can be securely tethered to political ideals: which allows us to transcend problems and acquire a motivational power that bare abstractions could not possess."[16] But if, as she insists, "the political use of compassion is to create a stable structure that can extend compassion broadly,"[17] then the pressures of practicing and extending this compassion must be transcended. For ultimately the political pressures that threaten such policies—whether we are referring to expanded health care or environmental protection—must be conceived as threats to "appraising the world from the person's evolving conception of a worthwhile life," writes Nussbaum.[18]

Structuring compassion is a process of learning how to evaluate and neutralize the threats to justice. What it requires is placing the needed trust and faith in our emotions to move beyond the vices and effects of hostile emotions. Kant, as we saw earlier, tried to confront this reality by distinguishing between concept and reality and by advancing the notion of unsocial sociability, or the idea that although man wishes to live in concord with perfect or self-sufficient nature, it is his competitive self-interest in and need for recognition that determines his resistance to harmonious community.[19] But Nussbaum, I argue, seems to invert this Kantian idea by insisting that it is the inherent goodness of nature that resists the temptations to be vain; that in shaping the institutions and laws of a pluralist society, political emotions help us to understand how good intentions can structure the institutional values guarding against the excesses of vanity and their effects on promoting difference. Kant of course never spoke directly of the structures of emotion, certainly not in any way that would enable us to understand how liberal values such as decency could "best guarantee," as Nussbaum states, "the respect for diversity that is needed in a pluralist world."[20] Yet it remains unclear if Nussbaum's presumptive treatment of decency as a pragmatic ideal can either neutralize or transcend many of the effects of living in a pluralist world, such as competition and resource scarcity.

Value intensity, in other words, does not simply arise from a change in motivational belief in or compassion for others, but from the primal material forces that can exceed our immediate interest in something.[21] Finding perceptual common ground in this respect is about realistically forming a common interest in treating all others with equal respect. That is to say, it means adopting a generalizable common interest that can serve as a shared frame of reference for perceiving the unfairness of suffering (or unequal treatment) of others. From this normative standpoint, equal access to resources forms an important part of this common interest. Nussbaum's idea is that love and compassion require such material access to build greater awareness and solidarity around the principle of equal dignity and respect for the most disadvantaged. But the question that her liberal decency raises is how this awareness tends to generate the global pressures and contradictory demands on enforcing the new laws and policies designed to accommodate the needs of others. If anything,

Nussbaum's theory of emotion never truly engages the propriety effect of decency in which the openness of liberal decency, or the very freedom from its structured constraint, becomes the source of political uncertainty that fuels retrogression.

In extending the emotional boundaries of the common interest, then, Nussbaum suggests that positive emotions can also be treated as the measured intensity of liberal values and that articulating this association becomes a practical condition for treating all peoples with equal dignity. And yet, as David Panagia argues, Nussbaum's normative theory symptomizes "the compulsion to legislate judgment and to provide a common source of norms for appraisal that coincides with an instrumentalist urge to dictate the conditions of possibility for value that is subsequently deployed to direct political action."[22] Panagia draws on Gilles Deleuze's notion of "indistinction"—a condition in which the regimes of perception (such as creative or aesthetic interpretation) that structure one's appraisals are rendered indistinct from one another—to show how liberalism downplays these conditions of possibility.[23] For our purposes, though, it raises the question of how are we to reasonably decipher between justice and decency when both can be treated as intrinsic to the subject or as ends of judging the worth of action, and when both partake of a subject whose sense of worth depends on the implementation of certain normative principles. In other words, when we presume a preexisting individual subject, we also need to explain the ontological factors structuring the particular qualities of the subject's identity. Otherwise, the tendency is to collapse political and social differences into the intention of the subject: that is, to assume that all people regardless of difference possess the same capacity to access and contribute to the common good, and that such conditions exist beyond the perception of reality.

For Peter Goldie, the complex process of layering and projecting intention represents what he calls borrowed intentionality, or when the intentionality of our feelings is actually "towards the world beyond the body."[24] Here, he suggests the need to critically examine "the unity of emotional life" and to treat emotion as the "substantial event" that allows us to communicate the unconscious memories, reflexes, and habits of our experience. The felt intensity of this event, as I have suggested, is what it means to cross a threshold of bodily sensation, or to experience, for instance, a natural disaster firsthand: where emotions can reach an intensity that expresses the unconscious change from envy and shame to compassion and trust, at least in the immediate moments after the event has occurred. In this case, everyone has a different experience to tell, which is how such an event reflects the unconscious quality of affect, that is, how each person's felt unity with others structures the particular quality of this shared experience. In short, we can never fully escape the forces working against this moment of unity, or the built-in tendency to feel excluded or unfairly treated by authorities or officials. For such forces consist of the very biases and prejudices that can unduly restrict the potential of a common language of human dignity.[25] Emotions seem to form their own culture of action and modulated behavior, which Jon Elster refers to as an "emotion culture that acts as a modifier, whether it is as ameliorative, or as a brake."[26]

The point is that the universal structure of compassion and empathy tells us very little about structuring difference. The intensity of emotions, in other words, is not the same as the intensity of values, since emotions resonate an unspeakable or unconscious quality that cannot be reduced to cognitive appraisal. Trauma, for instance, can assume an intensity of bodily sensation that interrupts one's habitual day-to-day to life, forcing one to relive his or her past suffering.[27] By producing an intense feeling of political and social immobility, it also creates a dense mass of feelings and a fear that connects us with the instinctual tendency to repress the origins of this emotion. For Nietzsche, as we saw earlier, the suppression of rancor was how we learned to value the emotions of compassion and love that could repress such rancor. Compassion, it could be said, was a false means of claiming moral progress, since it masked the need to distance ourselves from the bad (conscience) origins of ethical values. If this is true, then contesting liberal decency is ultimately about exposing the effect of its elevation or idealization as a transcendent moral threshold, namely, the tendency to repress the hostility that gave rise to its modern existence. And yet, this does not mean that decency itself is a hollow concept, that it can only stand for either instability or a false notion of progress; rather, it is to say that its progressive character cannot be presumed to operate independently of its retrogressive tendency in politics. To acknowledge this dialectical tension is, in the end, to unmask decency's contradictory effects. Affect, as we shall see, is one way of confronting this reality, as it offers a window for understanding how the openness of liberal decency can create the conditions of what we have been calling the propriety effect of decency.

Configuring Decency and Affect

By distinguishing between emotion and affect, then, we come up against the ontological problem of universalizing decency or proclaiming the freedom of being protected against all forms of humiliation. No one disagrees that there should be such progressive standards or a shared sense of threshold for protecting peoples. Rather, the challenge is to understand how crossing this threshold at different levels with different types of identity claims can engender more political uncertainty, thereby making any uniform and concerted attempt to extend decency a perilous task of securing identity in the world. It is to ask whether the affective qualities of the unconsciousness allow us to engage and understand decency's dual, universal role of including and excluding identity claims. How, in other words, do we reconfigure the dense chunks of connective sensations, habits, and feelings, which work below the consciousness of dispositions, to probe this dual function of decency?

For William Connolly, the answer lies in the focus on affectivity, and not on activity. The latter, in his view, refers to the constant movement and disposition of thoughts that represent a sort of self-artistry, an experimentalness and playfulness of a reflective life. Such self-artistry, he claims, testifies to the power of consciousness, or how the layers of instincts require consciousness to be re-presented. Thought, as he puts it, is vested with affect that "bounces in magical bumps and charges across zones marked by differences of speed, capacity and intensity that is above all the dicey relations between the zones where the seeds of creativity are planted."[28] The power of consciousness, he goes on to write, "is changing your thinking on something fundamental to your identity . . . which often involves work on layers below consciousness . . . but to assess the effects of those experiments is to bring consciousness back into play."[29] This does not mean that the meaning and function of our conscious emotions should be reduced to specific parts of the brain, which neuroscientists do to show correlation between emotions and stimuli to the brain; instead, it suggests that affect, unlike the basic emotion that social psychologists have identified, may help to bridge the unconscious instinct (limbic system) and emotions as rational judgments.[30] For the unconsciousness, as Connolly puts it, "is itself preorganized and moved to some extent by modes of thinking below its reach."[31]

Still, for some social psychologists, it is not simply enough to treat basic emotions as essential qualities of the unconscious. We also need to pinpoint what makes these emotions basic per se by showing how affect brings emotions into existence through an unconscious, presocial mode of cognition. As Peter Ekman argues, affects are "non-conscious experience of intensity . . . with an unstructured potential that lies prior to consciousness and that is the body's way of preparing itself for action in a given circumstance."[32] On the other hand, treating affect as unstructured potential is not the same as structuring difference or understanding the diverse nature of emotions. Affect in this sense does not validate the universal quality of basic emotions, such as anger. Anna Wiersbicka, for example, points to the Ifaluk language in Micronesia, which does not have a word for anger. In her view, this explains why the Ifakuk people do not experience anger, but rather an emotion they call "fago," which characterizes an interpersonal kindness in the face of suffering.[33] The fact that this word means avoiding all feelings of anger suggests that the Ifaluk can be affected and moved in a profoundly different way.[34] As Robert Solomon argues, "differences in emotion will have much to do with the nature of the mode of engagement with the world that one or another group or culture embraces."[35] Certain emotions, in other words, manifest the particular quality of emotions and how different customs, habits, values, and rules can provide the particular experiences that shape these emotions. When these customs are threatened, they tend to register an inner, intensity of human emotion, an unconscious, moral instinct.

In the well-known trolley and bridge scenarios, this moral instinct plays out in an intriguing manner. Here, one is presented with two choices: to throw a large man over the side of a bridge to save five workers (working on the trolley tracks below) from an oncoming train, which they do not hear nor see (and the only way to save them is to throw the large man onto the tracks); or do nothing. Most people tend to choose the latter given the felt connection with the fat man, even if this would mean killing five people working on the track below. But such a preference suggests that a deeper moral force may be structuring our snap judgments. That is to say, treating emotions as moral judgments may have less to with reaching a rational decision on fairness than with the moral reflex of not directly harming others[36] And yet, if the intensity of compassion derives from the preference to not directly mistreat others, then our direct, felt interaction with others can be thought of as moral force constraining and directing our moral action and judgment.[37] Under some circumstances our compassion may involve a tradeoff between our immediate identification with others' pain or needs and a disengagement from the pain of others, especially those with very different cultural identities.

The idea is that one learns to accept and identify with the customs and rules of behavior at a young age when many of our emotions are either primal or nonexistent. This, in turn, underscores the problem of assuming any overarching standard of decency to measure the value of other proprieties, since it ignores how local customs of moral propriety structure one's identity claim to freedom and dignity protection. The task, then, is not simply to accommodate more peoples under this overarching liberal ideal of decency but to understand how this tension between this ideal and local proprieties works, and what this means for refiguring the intensity of interaction and the moral potential of structuring the interaction of a plurality of proprieties in world politics. All of this raises an important question: How should we engage decency's unstructured potential? As I have argued, understanding its unstructured potential requires us to work beyond the normative positions that assume that the predetermined subject can neutralize and structure difference. In short, we need to explore the open-ended political implications of confronting the affective ties between decency as a fixed ideal and the reality of exclusion. The aim of the next section is to address this idea of political affectivity.

The Politics of Affect

Up to this point, I have addressed how political emotions derive their intensity through the felt encounters with others. The intensity is predicated on autonomous individual judgment and the rule of consensus and cooperation. In questioning the unruly effects of applying decency in global politics, I have tried to conceive the intensity of these effects in terms of the failure to engage decency's ontological dimension as well as its complex ties to identity politics. My idea is that decency's broad. application in global politics has involved elevating decency as a liberal ideal (standard) of emotive justice (or privileging compassion and love). Doing so has exposed the gap between assuming and applying this overarching normative standard of fair and equal treatment and being inclusive of the various moral proprieties that structure one's cultural identity.

The challenge, then, is one of locating the political tensions and exclusionary effects of applying this normative idea of decency and imagining the affective mechanisms that can help us bridge this gap. But this also leaves us with the question of how have these effects of hostile emotion ended up isolating and disaffecting the very institutional mechanisms that were designed to promote global moral propriety. Political effect, as I have suggested, offers a critical tool to engage these effects and the interactive, moral potential of decency and difference. As Caroline Williams writes, political affect is "an inherently political concept," which "signals the enmeshing of the political with the corporeal and points to a dynamic process of production and circulation of forces and powers that create and mobilize political subjectivity."[38] For Williams, delinking affect from individual subjects is to think about affect as a movement among or in between bodies. The idea, she claims, is that affect "cannot simply be housed" by either body or mind and viewed as overwhelming the subject who experiences it. Rather, it "signals the degree of intensity moderating a body's motion and mode of communication with other bodies."[39]

Earlier in this chapter I showed how liberal decency was essentially about crossing a minimum moral threshold of fair and inclusive treatment. I argued that the advocates of liberal decency, in seeking to posit a transcultural notion of emotive justice, overlooked the particular quality of structuring difference as it related to bodily sensation. By coupling value and emotional intensity, liberal proponents of universal decency tended to overlook the bodily effects and intensities of mistreatment in the global system. One of the questions that Brian Massumi raises is whether the application of liberal ideals in the global system works at odds with the movement(s) of affect or affective potential of cultural interaction?[40] Is it more realistic, he asks, to assume that affect is not just about feeling a moment of heightened emotion in assisting others, but rather about the (political) uncertainty of a situation in which one's bodily sense of movement is always emerging in and intensifying the potential to connect with others and to advance mutual inclusion? His idea is that we are always moving toward and beyond thresholds; that the fluidity of today's global society means that power is not simply about establishing control over something or seeking liberation from constraint. Rather, it assumes that in having a definitive answer to present-day problems, such perspectives hinder the way we understand the affective dimension of today's changing political landscape: that reimagining such connectedness requires a deeper awareness of the effects of this openness in order to engage the creative conversion of constraints into freedom and to realize the meaning of affective limitation and surplus in value. Let us therefore examine each of these affective criteria by determining how affect helps us to understand the ontological and bodily dimension of decency.

Political Affect and Intensity

For Massumi, affect reflects the intensity of experience in two ways: through an open bodily sensation of being affected and the change this represents to one's capacity. Drawing on Spinoza's work, Massumi theorizes that when one affects something he or she also opens him or herself up to being affected in turn. The capacity to affect and be affected presupposes two interrelated bodily capacities or movements, the affect and the feeling of a transition. It is what Massumi calls doubling or how affect is about being redoubled by what he calls experience of experience or experiencing the depth of bodily movement (memories, habits, reflexes, and desire). "This doubling," he states, "gives the body's movements a kind of depth that stays with it across all its transitions—accumulating in memory, in habit, in reflex, in desire, in tendency."[41] Affect is never fixed nor purely subjective but is always about accumulating and making connections with others. It reflects the passage from one experiential state of the body to another, "implying" as he writes, "either an augmentation or diminution in that body's capacity to act, and not just to stimulate but to differentiate phenomenon and events in the world."[42] Political affect can in this way be thought of as the property of the active outcome of an encounter, which can take the form of an increase or decrease in the ability of the body and mind alike to act.[43] In other words, it is the variance between what the bodily sensations register and what the mind perceives that creates the gaps in experience. As John Protevi puts it, "openness is the differential relations of our autonomous reactions and their approving and or disproving reception by others form patterns of acculturation by which we are gendered and racialized."[44]

The second form of intensity concerns the way in which our bodies remain only faintly aware of the other's potentials or directly felt thoughts and memories.[45] Accessing the depth of experience is a process of sensing something larger than one's immediate capacity, or, as Massumi states, "a strong sense of embeddedness in larger field of life . . . a heightened sense of belonging with other people, in which one connects with others and to situations."[46] Affect thus signifies an encompassing event or the breadth and depth of "the experiencing of experiencing." It is different from emotion insofar as emotion reflects the depth of its intensity as a moment in time. Emotion, in other words, represents only a partial expression of affect, since it "draws," as Massumi points out, "on a limited selection of memories and only activates certain reflexes."[47] This is why emotions "are more or less disorienting . . . at the very point at which one is most in contact with oneself and one's vitality."[48] Thus, for example, in a politically partisan environment, angry populists and liberal cosmopolitans can both deploy decency to appeal to the angry or sympathetic sentiment of their followers.

In *The Cultural Politics of Emotions*, Sara Ahmed argues that this disorienting effect of emotion stems from a lack of self-awareness of feelings.[49] Emotions such as hate do not reside strictly within the individual subject, but rather bind human bodies together in groups. As such, they produce contradictory effects that intensify in partisan environments where political differences or identity politics can anchor themselves in hostile prejudice. For Ahmed, this reflects their tendency to latch onto other bodies, which is how they move in between and not strictly within the bodily sensations of hated or oppressed groups in society. Emotional effects do not simply work through judgment but in between bodies to produce adherence to an imagined subject. For example, when white nationalists racialized the notion of decency at the protests held in Charlottesville, Virginia, in 2017, they used terms like "fine people" or "unfair treatment" to amplify their feelings of exclusion and hate in their encounter with liberal progressives. Such an encounter helped affirm a shared, felt effect to the extent that it involved a positive bond or love of an imagined country or nation. As Ahmed puts it, "The passion of these negative attachments to others is redefined simultaneously as a positive attachment to the imagined subjects brought together through the repetition of the signifier 'white.'"[50] The moving effects of emotions thus diminish the actual awareness of the feelings of these subjects of others. Experiencing a virtual absence of self-presence is another way of saying that we have reached the heat of the moment/event or become lost in anger.

Such heated moments convey what Protevi calls the "dramatic episodes" of affect, which, as he states, "effectively desubjectivizes the body . . . a body left without a self-conscious agent."[51] In other words, the intensity of certain emotions can overwhelm our ability to judge and to constrain our action (e.g., rage). When they do, it is our bodily sensations and movements that capture our experience, which shows, in turn, how we are being moved by forces that we cannot explain. Bodily movements in this sense become the virtual markers of this heated activity, especially at political rallies where saluting and fist pumping give way to calls for violence. The desubjective program of affect is both retrogressive and progressive. It does not consciously discriminate among moral intentions or experiences of exclusion; instead, it is driven by the forces of exclusion. In this way, it highlights the perils of clinging to a preconstituted subject to defend the moral progress of the liberal order against the reactionary violence of nationalist identity politics. That is to say, there is no moral high ground that prevents the moral defense of liberal decency from becoming reactive or unstable itself. And yet, the tendency we have seen is to distance oneself from this political reality of decency by assuming that nationalist identity politics is the causal effect of liberal identity politics. But it is precisely this problematic tendency that offers us a limited and false vantage point by which to gauge the politics of decency.

The critical idea of political affect, then, is that nothing in politics can be predetermined or be assumed to exist independently (cognitively) of the forces that shape it. Gilles Deleuze and Felix Guattari, for instance, imagine affect as the ultimate expression of "human becoming," that is, as zones of indetermination or even beings whose validity lies deep within themselves.[52] Affects, they write, "are formless, non-reflective elements of behaviour that resonate what is unspeakable of past and present experience and that are composing, decomposing, and making the individual, correspond to intensities that shape the person."[53] They represent how different species connect instinctively through the layers of sensibility where bodily sensations resonate the memories and habits of experience. As such, they are not about expressing the thoughts and beliefs of the individual subject but about how the bodily effects that move in between individual subjects shape the tension between the progressive and retrogressive tendencies of decency in the political arena. The point is that the conflicting applications of decency in politics arise from a primal force of exclusion that operates at both the unconscious and conscious realms of experience. By engaging the latter at the expense of the former, however, we tend to adopt myopic views of decency. We begin, that is, to push its morality squarely into the foreground of our political imagination where we can consciously draw on our biases to apply it in the political arena. At the same time, we lose sight of its background role or unstructured potential in exposing the humane and inhumane effects of exclusion. Paradoxically, decency ends up becoming a tacit driver of political polarization. This, in turn, invites a far more destructive scenario: the brutal clamping down on identity politics altogether, which dissolves the normative constraints that hold in place this tension between the retrogressive and progressive tendencies of the politics of decency.

Consider, for example, the Egyptian Spring protests in January 2011 (which I will examine in depth in chapter 5). The protesters in this case had finally confronted and conquered their fear of torture and bodily harm by assembling in the streets in January 2011. But the confrontation with their fear and exclusion never furnished the credible, sustainable connection between the protesters—many of whom were liberal secularists—and Islamists. Rather, it led to another moment of intense confrontation with Islamists (who sought to use their power to erect an Islamic state), which ended up dividing these groups and resulting in stricter authoritarian rule. Indeed, the brutal government crackdown on Islamists and liberal dissent(ers) in the summer of 2013 marked not simply the violation of basic normative constraints but also the intensification of the retrogressive tendency of decency. By brutalizing both the Islamists and liberal protesters, in other words, the government had disengaged itself from the effects of decency's tensions as well as the possibilities of reengaging its political reality. In effect, it had substituted decency's political reality with a new one: that of the supreme strongman who could now manipulate the affective dimension of power by effectively modulating public feeling and suppressing any sensibility and trust in the constitution. The Egyptian case thus highlights the emergence of two oppressive conditions: the heightened, physical constraint on (and control over) bodily movement and the undoing of normative constraints on dignity violations. Both seem to suggest that the abandonment of decency standards stemmed from the resurgence of fear. But reducing the event to this factor of fear only seems to beg a more important question: how is saving the basic elements of decency so essential to cultivating its underlying political tensions into mutual trust?

Before addressing this question, it is important to stress the actual potential of mutual interaction among the contending political pressures, that is, harnessing the power of emotions and constraints to the actual tendency of connecting with others' bodily feelings, memories, and beliefs.

Massumi speaks of this actual tendency in terms of what he calls "enabled constraints" and creative interaction.[54] For him, there still is the need to address what he calls "differential attunement" among a multiplicity of bodily encounters.[55] The encounter among a plurality of bodies expresses how each is transitioning together and beyond existing thresholds of feeling and thought. Again, this is how affect signifies potential opening and not simply the extended quality of openness. The difference is that openness conveys freedom from constraint, or neutrality and nondiscrimination, while "opening" is about adapting our sensibility to these constraints, that is, showing an attunement to difference that requires us to hold such constraints together in the field of mutual inclusion. In this sense, enforcing such constraints raises not only the stakes of inclusion but also the effects of not attuning to such difference, or of applying decency outside this field of mutual inclusion. This aesthetic notion of affect returns us to a familiar issue: namely, whether intensity itself has value or if the value/defense of decency in this case is simply triggered by sharp or prolonged feelings of solidarity. Put differently, is extending decency to the global realm simply about how intensity is a value in itself, or about how structuring difference is an open-ended process of attuning to such difference?[56]

As we saw in chapter 3, cultural accommodation derived its intensity from working beyond liberalism's procedural constraints of neutrality. The change in focus from individual to collective rights reflected a specific application or extended affirmation of cultural beliefs. This suggested that there was a surplus of energy and power that accumulated in the value of accommodation or with applying collective rights broadly. The surplus explained how cultural elites and leaders could still appeal to national or subnational cultural beliefs and customs to oppress their own people. In effect, collective rights had to be targeted at groups' cultural needs if they were to transform cultural identities at the state and global institutional levels. But multiculturalism's politics would also become the target of populists who galvanized the support of excluded workers in the global economy. Paradoxically, it was multiculturalism's own targeted rights that seemed to close liberal identity politics off to these workers and that helped foment the anti-immigration sentiment aimed at the liberal global elites.

For Karl Marx, such inversion was the effect of an oppressive capitalist system. In his view, surplus value showed not only how money reified the value of labor and falsified the consciousness of the oppressor[57] but also how the effects of these oppressive practices accumulated over time through the objectivization of physical/bodily labor (the notion that oppression indicated how much unpaid work an owner of the means of production could extract from a worker). Marx's notion of surplus value symptomized the bourgeoisie's capacity to accumulate vast amounts of capital at the expense of the worker: the objective was not to free the workers from the capitalist constraints but to revolutionize or transform these constraints into new conditions of freedom.

Surplus thus expressed the idea that the political manipulation of values is what disconnected those in power from the social reality of exclusion and its oppressive effects. Confronting this reality meant not only championing the workers' sensibility but also, for our purposes, realizing the unstructured potential of affect, or what Massumi calls "a felt excess of potential over and above any particular state of being . . . that could stand quite well as a definition of aesthetic value."[58] The challenge here is imagining the felt excess of potential of redressing the effects of exclusion (e.g., where the many human laws and documents are rarely if ever consistently acted upon or enforced) over the myopic applications of decency. In short, to think of decency as functioning ontologically is to refigure it as an open-ended process of attuning to and structuring difference to the changing normative constraints in world politics. It is to this idea and the affective mechanisms it requires that I shall turn.

Global Political Affect and Consensus

To probe the notion of global political affect, I shall try to configure the affective potential of global moral propriety, something that Massumi speaks about but never fully develops in terms of a global context of political affect. But first let me summarize what I have argued up to this point. Affect theory helps call attention to an important limit in the political discourse of decency: namely, that the normative appeal of decency can fuel the very conflict it seeks to contain and govern. Decency's normative constraints become more precarious amid the myriad conflicting applications of them in the political arena. As we saw, using emotions to elevate or extend liberal decency makes it difficult gauge its perilous role in global politics. If anything, this only seems to contribute to the very moral dissonance that is undercutting its normative pull and structuring its potential.

My aim in this final section, then, is to critically examine the affective limitations and potential of two mechanisms in global politics: consensus and complementarity. The former is what validates the normative structure of constraints of the international system. By aligning beliefs and interests on matters related to peace, security, and human rights, consensus creates the conditions for both trust and a broad sense of moral propriety in global politics. By the same token, it is also a mechanism that remains fragile and prone to disruption—indeed, the source of much political tension. Complementarity was supposed to steer this mechanism beyond its own tension by offering a pragmatic means of extending these normative constraints to the global system and applying the uniform rules on moral accountability. Instead, it has exposed the undertheorized ontological dimension of its normative function, and the destabilizing effects of exclusion and the imposition of a uniform standard of rules.

Political exclusion, as I have suggested, determines the affective limitations of these mechanisms and their inclusiveness. Its role in the normative structure of decency symptomizes the tendency to champion an idea of a universal or overarching ideal of decency that marginalizes peoples and that can only be reliably enforced by hegemonic powers. It shows just how problematic decency can become in global politics, for it suggests that inclusion, rather than actually promoting diversity, ends up reinforcing the need for management from above. In this way, the virtual idea of diversifying decency (or pluralizing moral proprieties) restricts its affective potential or conditions of possibility.

To understand this contradiction is to realize that there are a multiplicity of forces and movements in the global realm. The tensions between these encounters are driven by intense emotion and the mobility of affects. As Ty Solomon points out, many of today's social movements testify to the "fluidity and mobility of the circulation of affects."[59] Such mobility signifies not only the effects of intense emotions but also the political uncertainties of dealing with threats.[60] The effects of emotions can tell us a great deal about movement and the tensions that drive global political conflict. Thomas Scheff, for example, argues that shame, which acts as a macro or master emotion in world politics, determines how the effects of conflict/war become embedded in the collective feelings of people (e.g., feelings of victimization and political grievances).[61] For others, knowing how emotions become political, or construct action, requires an understanding of their properties, which lie at intersection of macro and micro politics.[62] This means that global institutions can play an important role in curbing the fear on issues related to peace and security.[63] But it also requires distinguishing between emotion and affect to address the capacity of institutions to modulate the effects of emotion and the unconscious desires and needs that inform a person's sense of community.

The macropolitics of affect refers, in one sense, to how the power of global institutions has become affective in terms of actively redressing suffering; and, in another sense, how the top-down solutions to building mutual trust can lead to conflicting applications of decency standards and the volatile recognition of customs and memories. This programmatic effect of standardizing decency is supposed to suppress the reactionary strands of conservative decency by bringing together the thoughts, feelings, and beliefs of populations and groups (e.g., victims) through a formal set of rules and procedures (or the rule of consensus). But standardizing top-down solutions cannot itself capture the emergence and excess or surplus of micropolitics, since local interventions must in some way feed back up to the top; that is, the top and bottom can be thought of as mutually corrective, since the two meet each other in a way that transitions beyond the effects of their existing disengagement.[64]

The principle of complementarity expresses this formal idea of mutually corrective politics at both the international and local levels. It does so practically or institutionally through mutual assistance or mutual accommodation, or both. This, in turn, makes it possible to realize the creative intersection of local and international justice, something that I shall examine in greater context in chapter 6. Much of how we think about complementarity in international relations is conditioned by top-down accommodation and not local politics. There still seems to be too much political trepidation when it comes to exploring complementarity's permutations of international justice, peace, and security. Rather than engaging the political uncertainty created by complementarity's downward application, or whether it can accommodate local procedures of justice, we tend to see it as a pragmatic ideal of applying a uniform set of procedures and achieving consensus through dialogue and assistance. But the question is whether complementarity's application must solely reflect the dialogue of international and state authorities, and not that of the former local officials who may be most affected by its top-down application. The challenge here is one of converting, rather than expanding the normative constraints of administering justice (impartially), that is, seeing the affective potential of complementarity to the extent that we can treat the creative application of the mechanisms in terms of the felt degrees of freedom that accumulate with each encounter. As Massumi puts it, "the inflection of the tendency to accumulate from one encounter to the next leads somewhere new, a politics beyond self-interest, but not in any general interest."[65] The idea, in short, is that when complementarity is opened to being affected by multiple peoples or agents, it exposes the gaps and tensions between the different proprieties of justice. It reflects the moral dissonance that channels itself into the global practice of decency through the open interaction of the various legal customs and values of peoples. The dissonance ends up, in turn, representing the affective intensity of decency, or the creative potential of communicating and combining the diverse and experiential elements of such proprieties. This is also what it means to contest the need for a common moral ground to justify the tools or mechanisms for resolving deep-seated political conflicts.

Consider, for example, the comparable value of resilience in world politics. The concept refers broadly to the capacity to adapt to and manage the effects of political root causes of conflict, such as political corruption and the scarcity of resources (it has been instrumental in addressing the long-term threats and impacts of climate change, for example).[66] It involves the need for decentralizing responsibility to the local level and the capacity of local communities to manage threats to human dignity. Such local interventions of risk prevention, it could be argued, can be conceived as part of the unconscious experience of intensity concerning a community's exclusion from global policymaking. In this case, it requires converting the normative constraints imposed by the international community into the conditions of coordinating deeply felt responses to the effects of exclusion.[67]

But such creative conversion also reveals the difficulties of moving beyond the liberal subject. It is not clear, for instance, if this normative shift is creating new pressures from below, or if it is allowing us to work beyond the responsibility to protect's normative pressures and programmatic effects associated with UN planning.[68] Critics of the responsibility to protect (R2P) contend that this pragmatic shift has been anything but progressive, that most countries are still ill-prepared to manage such effects.[69] For others, the effect is diagrammatic or inherently disruptive of liberal norms by exposing the mounting tension/interplay of local and international interventionist politics of managing threats. As Kevin Grove and Peter Adey put it, the problematic of resiliency can be understood in terms of "the diagrammatic effects of affective relations. . . . effects that register what they call an aesthetic sensibility, which directs . . . the way that resilience addresses itself to insecurity . . . and why it is contingent and always open to being condemned."[70] Diagrammatic effects, in other words, signify the "commotion of interference."[71] The idea is that politics is no longer just about the rule of consensus but about disrupting this rule in order to understand the effect of promoting mutual inclusion. Resiliency politics in this sense becomes dissensual, to the extent that "it holds," as Massumi writes, "contrasting alternatives together without immediately demanding that one alternative eventuate and the other evaporate."[72]

This is where immanent critique aligns itself with our ontological-based analysis of consensus. For Jacques Rancière, dissensus reflects a condition in which treating the political subject as a preconstituted end is meant to control and suppress its relation to others—which is to say that it fails to realize its own difference or hidden relation to the truth (which disappears). From this perspective, consensus must create a detachable and fixed space by which to configure not simply the sum of the parts of societal relations but also how one should feel secure in this arrangement. In regard to conservative and basic decency, it represents the logical connection between power and moral propriety, or the moral capacity to determine what is and is not sensible or proper/acceptable behavior. The isolation of this affective dimension and its diagrammatic effects of local political proprieties thus suppresses the necessity for locally initiated interventions. It stands for a partition between what cannot be seen in terms of feelings and sensations of different proprieties and what can be seen. Rancière, for instance, distinguishes between police and politics to show how the former involves counting and categorizing the parts of something in order to dominate over what cannot be perceived. Politics is therefore about what can be seen or heard, while "consensus," in his view, "is the reduction of politics to police . . . and a return to the nonexistence of politics," by which he means that it ignores how politics is first brought into existence (as subjectivization) to contest and litigate any predisposition of the political subject.[73] The many proponents of R2P suggest that, while more consensus is needed, the UN Secretary-General's recent reports have helped streamline the implementation of R2P measures concerning the prevention of serious harm and atrocities.[74] The idea is that in diffusing responsibility to the regional and local levels, international states and local actors learn to coordinate their own affairs and to develop a mutual commitment to address the root causes of conflict.

In Rancière's view, the essence of politics does not lie in consensus or the political interest of cooperation; instead, it presupposes the condition of dissensus, which, as he puts it, is "not the confrontation between interests or opinions but the demonstration of a gap in the sensible itself."[75] This gap represents the partition of sensibilities, with one representing the exclusion of what can be seen, and the other with the possibility of what can be seen. It becomes a way of expressing the intensity of affect in regard to the accumulating pressures of constraints that can either disable or suppress the movement toward higher degrees of freedom. In other words, when normative constraints become the object of attack or when they nullify the necessity for the reciprocal intervention of macropolitics and micropolitics, as we saw with the nationalist attacks on the LGBTQ community, these reactionary pressures of national decency can also restrict the diagrammatic and programmatic effects of state propaganda. This nonetheless raises the stakes of maintaining an open, accommodative global political moral propriety, since it shows how participation and intercultural dialogue are already conditioned by the propriety effect and the political pressures arising from this effect.

Still, confrontation is not enough to revitalize the effects from below. We also need to engage the changing normative constraints that are reshaping the practical possibilities of mutual inclusion or the unstructured potential of representing the many competing moral proprieties. So, in one sense, the open-ended rule of consensus that brought the rules and uniform standards of basic decency into existence also produces its alter ego, dissensus. The problematic outcome of the polarizing politics of decency is thus the affective disinvestment of global populist movements and the gaps in moral and cultural sensibility. If this is true, then the critical project becomes one of occupying these gaps and demonstrating how the propriety effect forces us to further engage the tensions working against mutual inclusion.

Conclusion

In distinguishing between emotion and affect, this chapter examined the overlooked ontological status of decency. Normative theorists, we saw, focus on the cognitive potential of emotions, or how their intensity consists in one's attachment to others, and how this motivates us to treat others with fair and equal respect. But in light of the divisive effects of decency's reactionary politics, it is clear that more attention needs to be paid to the nuanced, political reality of decency. Ignoring this ontological dimension only raises the question of how to overcome the divisive politics of decency. The unmet task, then, is to understand how the political reality of decency functions and arises from the political forces of exclusion. Political affect, as I argued, furnishes us with an important yet difficult conceptual tool to realize this challenge. By enabling us to configure the tension between decency's retrogressive and progressive tendencies, it demonstrated the possibilities of structuring difference and converting its normative constraints into higher degrees of freedom. Perhaps more importantly, it allowed us to understand the implications of decency's politically fragile state: namely, the dissolution of its tensions and what this means for imposing strict authoritarian rule.

In short, affect steers our understanding of the gaps between our different strands of decency and their divisive emotional effects. Within these gaps lies significant political uncertainty that we need to occupy and that requires a more creative understanding of reactionary identity politics and the volatile effects of global moral propriety. This is one way that we can begin to realize the creative conversion of these constraints and the possibilities of modulating difference through the reciprocal interaction of affective mechanisms such as complementarity. Indeed, because global moral propriety creates its own political uncertainty, it also requires actual demonstration of the gap between normative and ontological thinking about decency. The following chapters, as we shall see, will contextualize these gaps and the pressure to undo or escape the constraints of the liberal international order.

CHAPTER FIVE

Islamism and Egyptian Politics

Pride and dignity would belong to women if only we left them alone.
—Egyptian proverb

We have appointed a law and practice for every one of you. Had God willed it he would have made you a single community but he wanted to test you regarding what has come to you. So compete with one another in doing good. Every one of you will return to God and he will inform you regarding the things you differed about.
—Surat al-Ma'ida

Since its violent crackdown on the Muslim Brotherhood in the summer of 2013, the Egyptian government has gone on to impose strict controls on dissent and to conduct a systematic campaign of human rights abuses and torture. The government's current and past repression of its citizens' basic rights grows out of a long struggle to contain the threat of militant Islam. In chapter 3, we discussed how recognizing certain basic human rights of Muslim women in Arab states required a deeper application of individual autonomy to overcome the constraints on their development. But in the case of Egypt's brief experiment with democracy, deepening such autonomy has created significant political and social effects that the government seems unwilling to address.

The question I take up in this chapter is how the deep-seated tension between liberal decency and Islamism in Egyptian politics created the conditions for political distrust and instability. I argue that the pressures to accommodate and address the demands of Islamists reveal gaps not just within Islamic moral propriety but also between Islamism and basic decency. The former, as we shall see, involve disparities between moderate and radical strands of Islamism inside the Brotherhood. In particular, Sayyid Qutb's militant Islamism, in constituting the intellectual source of today's global jihad, highlights the intense propriety effect of Islam in the political arena. One of my aims, then, is to show how these effects contradicted core elements of decency, which the Brotherhood's leadership sought to control through its pragmatic approach to politics. My other aim is to focus on the gap between liberal decency and the piety practices of Egyptian women, by analyzing the difference between liberal and Islamist identity politics, or, in this case, the politics of piety that highlighted the tension between liberal, secular, and religious norms and practices in Egyptian society.

Accordingly, I shall first examine the ideological tensions between Islamism and liberalism, which have shaped Egyptian politics and society, as well as the competing degrees and strands of moral propriety of the Islamist movement in Egypt. I then move on to analyze how the rigid moral propriety of the Salafist movement became further intertwined with and reinforced many of the moderate political proprieties of Islamism inside the Muslim Brotherhood. In the final section, I turn attention to the issue of the gender gap between Islamism and liberalism, by examining the women's piety movement in the 1990s—or the Cairo Women's Mosque Movement—and the contradictory relationship between liberal feminist politics and the Egyptian state.

Egyptian Liberalism: Modernization and Its Discontents

In chapter 2 we briefly discussed how the mandate system of the League of Nations (1918–39) reinforced a cultural dynamic of difference. This dynamic grew out of the League's attempts to educate and manage populations and was part of an ambitious plan to reshape world order. But the League's idealistic vision of a new liberal international order contained flaws. The absence of U.S. leadership, for example (the United States voted to withdraw from the treaty in 1920), meant that the League lacked an important source of enforcement. In addition, the League's decision to impose harsh reparations on Germany helped destabilize the country and allow the Nazis to rise to power. The result was a severely weakened League that had to rely on a set of culturally sensitive civilizational standards to carry out its flawed vision of international peace and security.

The trouble, then, was that the League's vision of world order failed to provide opportunities for non-Europeans to control their political destiny. This was especially true in Egypt where secular liberal values had met with considerable resistance by Islamic leaders and officials who saw individual freedom and equality as threats to their cultural customs and practices. Their concern was that secular liberalism could not effectively regulate the moral conduct of persons in accordance with Islamic principles. Egypt, which had declared its independence from Britain in 1923, required an Islamic vision of modern Egyptian society, one that was neither a dismissal of liberalism nor an endorsement of its secular basis, but rather reflected its larger struggle to (re-)merge Egyptian values with liberalism. Egyptian liberalism would thus proceed on a basis in which it would gradually bring together the liberal secular values of the West and the Islamic values of the Egyptian people.

But the process of merging these opposing ideas remained complex and tense. Many of the problems could be traced to Britain's failure to practice its democratic ideals fairly during a time when Egypt was an autonomous vassal state of the Ottoman Empire (1867–82). Britain's unwillingness to respect the Egyptian people and their values paved the way for the occupation of Egypt in 1882 and the installment of a new puppet leader. The British controlled the economy and suppressed the Egyptian people. However, their ill-treatment of the Egyptian people became a source of deep political grievance. National uprisings and popular discontent would eventually lead to nominal Egyptian independence and a more limited role for the British in Egypt in 1922. In the end, Britain had underestimated the resolve of the Egyptian people and showed little willingness to reconcile its secular views with the Islamic values of the Egyptian people.[1]

Still, British colonialism had helped shaped the struggle between Western-educated Egyptians (those trained at British universities) and indigenous Egyptian intellectuals (many of whom were liberals) who sought to reconcile Islam and secular liberalism. In stressing the need to adapt Islam to liberal democracy, Egyptian intellectuals pressed for a modern Islamic society that they hoped would forge the basis of a progressive national identity. But their efforts also exposed competing strands of thinking: one that stressed the revival of Islamic values and education to counter Western secular influence; the other that focused on the values of tolerance and pluralism and their ties to civilizational and material progress.[2] The latter emphasized science and technology to bridge the gap between scientific rationality and Islam, which many attributed to the ulema's (the Islamic class of scholars) particular form of interpretation or reasoning by imitation.

British decency, it could be argued, widened this gap by either excluding or deprioritizing the teaching of Islamic history and customs in the school curriculum. As we saw in chapter 2, Britain and other European states believed that Islam as a civilization did not measure up to Europe's liberal, moral standards. This had the unintended effect of motivating Islamic scholars to reassess the independent moral structure of Islamic values, in particular, the concept of *ijma* (consensus), which they reinterpreted in connection to the doctrine of reasoning by imitation (*Taqlid*).[3] While the centrists endorsed human fallibility, the revivalists remained opposed to adapting Islam to liberal morality, stressing instead a more formal and generalized interpretation of the Sunnah and Quran texts, and the verbal tradition (Hadith). The centrists, in embracing the open flexibility of *ijtihad* (interpretation), rejected the traditional power of the ulema to determine how Egyptian Muslims could effectively modernize society. *Ijtihad*, for them, served as the principal means of reconciling liberal principles to Islamic customs and values.

However, for the revivalists, Islam had to be more strictly interpreted from within to understand the threat posed by Western liberalism and positivist legalism. From their perspective, colonialism had undermined any possibility of a concerted Islamic response. Not only did it divide the Islamic community in Egypt (Ummah) and its seventy-three different sects along Sunni and Shia lines but it also permitted Britain's schooling system to determine the parameters of instruction. Despite these problems, some came to see the liberal curriculum as an opportunity to adopt a new national identity rooted in Islam. The Islamic scholar Muhammad Abduh, for instance, argued that nationalism could furnish a new vision of an Islamic Egypt. But for this to happen, Britain would have to learn to tolerate Egyptian customs and manners, which, in turn, meant that British decency could no longer be imposed on the Egyptians. Instead, it would have to coexist with national customs and morals and overcome its own moral duality between respect and disrespect. For the centrists, though, this would mean removing a key moral obstacle to their idea that Egypt's Islamic heritage and Western liberalism were mutually constitutive.[4]

The Rule of Which Law? Sharia and the State

Egyptian liberalism, then, was as much a progressive ideology as it was a mixed effort to respond to revivalist calls for Islamicizing society—or for Islamic values to permeate the governing, political institutions. In the early period of Egypt's statehood (1922–55), there was growing sentiment and demand for establishing an Islamic state based on a strict reading of the Quran. The demand was in response to Muslim thinkers' attempts to defend the merits of the separation of state and religion. Among the most prominent was Faraj Fuda, who believed that Islam should remain a moral, not a political doctrine of the state (other thinkers included Said al-Ashmawi and Husayn Ahmad Amin).

The liberal, secular perspective of these thinkers was both pragmatic and substantive. For in seeking to work beyond the rigid application of sharia (Islamic law), they insisted that sharia was based on the false precept that religion and politics were inseparable. Al-Ashmawi, for instance, claimed that even the prophet Mohammed had to exercise judgment when deciding how best to resolve and apply the principles of justice and compassion to society. Sharia, in other words, was not a fixed or static principle, but rather, as Al-Ashmawi puts it, "a scheme of redressing and adapting to a changing environment."[5] His idea was that Mohammed had his own reasons for promoting principles on a pragmatic basis: that the conditions of the time shaped the very application of Islamic principles. Al-Ashmawi thus argued that sharia's adaptation was necessary for promoting progress and development, and that there was a need to clarify the political contexts of the principles of *shura* (consultation) and *ijtihad.* He and other liberal Islamic thinkers saw sharia as an evolving pillar of societal justice and compassion. For them, *shura* and *ijtihad* could be readapted to the liberal principles of autonomy and individual political freedom in order to help direct the will of the people against the caliphate.[6]

However, for Fuda, sharia, rather than offering a clear path toward salvation, made governing difficult in the twentieth century. It was more the product of utopian thinking put forth by the caliph than a special, sacred form of moral propriety. The challenge lay in preserving its sacredness and practical value within and not against secular liberalism. In his *Before the Fall*, Fuda proposed that sharia could be best preserved through its relation to liberalism.[7] But this idea required a leap of faith of sorts, since it meant revising the ruling feature of its propriety, or the inseparability of politics and religion, in order to create the political space for Egyptians to promote democratic human rights, including equal protection under the law and freedom of choice. What is more, it was unclear whether the caliph would ever be willing to uphold the rights of people against violence. The failure to question this guarantee led, as he writes, "to the dispute with regard to the nature of the *shura:* does the *shura* obligate the ruler, which is the majority opinion, or not obligate him, which is the majority opinion?"[8] To recall, Rawls argued that in decent, hierarchically ordered societies, the people not only learned the value of cooperation but were consulted (either directly or indirectly) on decisions and matters related to governance. This was how he expressed his own limited faith in the decency and capacity of peoples to tolerate cultural difference. Like Rawls, Fuda saw the caliph's rule as an obstacle to social cooperation and consensus-building in Islamic society. Only Allah could determine through his omniscience when the people did or did not count. In short, for the people to enact and exercise their will, they needed to feel free to express their faith and to form a collective national interest grounded in the protection of the basic rights of Muslims.

Fuda's idea of marrying democracy and nationalism in Muslim societies was thus intended to synthesize Egyptian values in the Sufist tradition and Western liberalism. But its emphasis on the national interest would inspire later nationalists, such as the pan-socialist Arabist Gamal Abdel Nasser in the 1950s,[9] to unite Egyptian Muslims around a common political platform of Arab identity.[10] In particular, Nasser adopted Fuda's secularist approach to restrict U.S. influence in Egyptian affairs, while at the same time containing and eventually suppressing the influence of sharia through the secular rule of law.[11] Arab nationalism, which had managed to mobilize mass support among the Muslims, thus highlighted the difficulties of steering beyond the tension between Islamic law and liberal secularism. The question was how could such a broad cultural, top-down movement adopt the constraints and standards of basic decency (e.g., against cruel and unusual punishment) when sharia represented the preservation of strict practices and codes of punishment that seemed to defy these constraints? Centrists had to find a way of reconciling secularized constraints with dogmatic sharia codes of the Islamic faith.

Islamic scholars such as Muhammed al-Ghazali and Muhammad Imara argued that the solution lay in a flexible approach to Islam, one stressing a creative combination of *shura* (or consulting all Muslims on particular social issues, e.g., women's freedom) and *ijtihad.* This meant broadening *ijtihad* or adopting a less restrictive application of sharia by the ulema and consulting with more sectors of the population to expand this interpretation, all in hopes of helping spur Islam's evolution in the modern world.[12]

But getting the ulema to adopt a more open-ended interpretation would not be easy. Imara, it seemed, underestimated the ulema's strong and abiding commitment to uphold past Islamic customs, and in so doing, may have reinforced the need to preserve Islam's traditional customs.[13]

Still, it was difficult to detect any clear-cut dividing line between this centrist and liberal approach. Neither appeared to produce the sort of flexible sharia-based model that could manage or accommodate the orthodox, demands of purist Muslims. If anything, such uncertainty raised the more troubling question of how to resolve the increasing conflict between liberal decency and the rigid, conservative decency associated with Islamic orthodoxy. Could, in other words, the synthesis of sharia and Western liberal principles produce its own set of reactionary and normative pressures? And would these pressures destabilize the common political ground between Islamism and liberalism and the notion of a shared, common decency? The concern of course was that secular liberal freedom, not the Quran, would largely determine how this synthesis would be achieved. In effect, there was still a social gap between Islamism and liberalism that would intensify the ideological divisions between the reactionaries and the progressives.

The Muslim Brotherhood and Islamist Pluralism

As Egypt's largest, most successful Islamic organization, the Muslim Brotherhood (or the "Brotherhood") sought to bridge the gap between democracy and Islamism. By making sharia politically appealing as a source of political inclusion in Egypt, it aimed to make Islam broadly constitutive of the normative constraints of liberalism. But it soon became clear that their efforts to harness the political power of these above pressures would fail to staunch the tide of reactionary, fundamentalist sentiment inside its organization.[14] As we shall see, the issue was no longer about adopting a synthesis of liberal and Islamic moral propriety, but rather about containing radical Islamism and the threat it posed to secular order inside and beyond Egypt.

Centrism and Religious Pluralism

The Muslim Brotherhood was founded by Hassan al-Banna in 1928. In seeking to build an Islamic movement, the Brotherhood focused on establishing an Islamist government that would serve as an updated caliphate in

Egypt—one in which Islamic values could coexist and function together with democratic principles.[15] To this end, it was neither an inflexible nor static organization, but a broad-based movement that aimed to adapt itself to British liberalism and Arab nationalism (which held that all Arabs belonged to one Arab homeland, a principle that would be adopted by the Arab League). The Brotherhood thus attempted to position itself as an agent capable of mediating the conflict between the secular liberal forces of the new state of Egypt and traditional customs of Islam. But it confronted an obstacle in the latter, namely, the doctrinal rules of behavior, which Islamists applied to counter the growing threat of modernity. This made the Brotherhood's pragmatic task of navigating the tension between liberalism and Islamism all the more difficult.

Even so, the Brotherhood enjoyed tacit and often sporadic support by the Egyptian government, which saw its pragmatic tendencies to govern as a politically expedient opportunity to suppress Islamic radicalism inside Egypt. The Brotherhood's pragmatism in this respect allowed it to form a tense, albeit working relationship with the government. Predicated on the doctrine of *wasatiyyah* (Islamic moderation), it constituted a centrist approach that enabled the Brotherhood to seize a middle ground in Egypt's Islamic politics. *Wasatiyyah*'s application arose out of the long-standing efforts to balance the Brotherhood's commitment to Islam against its political ambition for power. Marc Lynch writes that the doctrine "stemmed from a series of critical junctures shaped by Egypt's Sadat-era political and economic opening and the emergence of violent competitors, which encouraged the Muslim Brotherhood to embrace political participation and gradualism."[16] Even so, the Brotherhood's efforts to stake out a middle ground proved difficult. There was simply too much distrust of the Brotherhood, beginning with the Brotherhood's attempts to organize militarily against the government in the early 1940s.

In addressing this threat, the Egyptian government resorted to drastic measures. In 1946, it had al-Banna assassinated, which was soon followed by the arrest of numerous Brotherhood officials and the closing down of many of its operations. Still, the government failed to break up or significantly weaken the Brotherhood. Rather, its actions led to a growing cycle of distrust and violence that would reach its apex in the summer of 1952, when the Brotherhood was accused of staging a coup d'etat against the government, a charge the Brotherhood vehemently denied. In July 1954, the Brotherhood retaliated by attempting to assassinate Nasser, prompting Nasser to violently crackdown on the organization. Nasser's actions seemed to have a pronounced effect on many of the Muslim Brotherhood's most prominent pragmatists at the time, including Sayyid Qutb, who soon became one of the harshest critics of the Nasser regime. Qutb contended that the regime was complicit in facilitating Western occupation of Arab lands, which had helped spread apostasy throughout Egypt and the Arab world. Western modernity required a new, militant form of jihad to defend Muslim lands.[17] Qutb proposed an agenda that advocated violence against all Muslim apostates, particularly Muslims who abided by Western values and lifestyles, despite the Quran's forbiddance of the killing of a Muslim by another Muslim. Qutb, it could be said, embraced a totalizing approach to counter Western liberalism and materialism and to end the complicity with Western materialism that had corrupted Islamic principles of justice and social welfare. Jihad, in his view, had to be an all-out, proactive defense of Islam against Western secular influence, one which was capable of purging the effects of Western materialism on Muslims.

Nasser would soon have Qutb arrested on the charge of inciting violence against the government. In 1966, the Egyptian government executed Qutb. The decision would turn Qutb into a martyr and help pave the way for his wide-ranging influence on today's global jihadist movements, including Al-Qaeda and Daesh (the Islamic State), which have come to champion the negative impact of *jahiliyyah*, which refers to the period of ignorance that preceded the divine prophet and Allah (the emergence of the Ummah either eliminated or diminished such ignorance). While *jahiliyyah* may reflect the ignorance of non-Muslims or the domination of humans over humans under secular modernity, it also continues to occupy an important place in the minds of Muslims practicing Islam. It does this by virtue of the accepted Islamic practices and principles that allow knowledge of Allah's will to continue to prevail over the ignorance of non-Muslims. *Jahiliyyah*, in this sense, structures the moral propriety of many Islamic societies by motivating Muslims to adhere to Islamic law and the rules and practices of religious devotion. The role of Jihad, as invoked by Muslim groups and Jihadists, is to oppose *jahiliyyah* and any idea that calls on Muslims to find common cause with liberal, secular morality. For these groups, any such interaction taints the purity of Quran and Sunnah texts and justifies the uncompromising need to root out the infidels, or those who have deviated from strict adherence to the Quran.[18] For many, then, *jahiliyyah*'s existence reinforces the traditional distinction between *dar al-Islam*, which refers to the land occupied by Muslims, and *dar al-harb*, which defines land occupied by non-Muslims by delegitimizing the physical or geographical nature of the threat to Islamic society.[19] Taken to its extreme (interpretation), *jahiliyyah* represents the controversial tendency of militant Islamic groups to attack and kill other Muslims who they believe have been deluded by liberal secularism.[20] Although the Salafists belonging to the Brotherhood never embraced this extreme form, their embrace of *jahiliyyah* would force the moderates of the Brotherhood to become more pragmatic and accommodating of this and other rigid, sectarian moral proprieties.

Intolerance and the Problem of Gradualism

After Nasser's death in September 1970, Anwar al-Sadat was appointed as the third president of Egypt. Sadat did away with many of Nasser's repressive tactics of the Brotherhood, helping facilitate the Islamic movement inside Egypt that led to the adoption of an amendment to the constitution that declared sharia an official source of legislation. Despite Sadat's tolerance of the Brotherhood, many inside the Brotherhood distrusted Sadat. The distrust would soon turn into rage after Sadat agreed to turn over Arab land to Israel under the Camp David Accords (1979), and lead to Sadat's assassination by an Islamic extremist in 1981.[21]

Sadat's successor, Hosni Mubarak, adopted a different strategy for appeasing the Brotherhood. Instead of allowing the radical fringe to grow inside the Brotherhood, he decided to support the moderate forces' efforts to be more inclusive of the radicals. This, in turn, encouraged the radicals to focus more of their attention on their political strategies and less on attacking the government. For Umar Tilmisani, the new supreme leader of the Brotherhood,[22] this meant assuming a more pragmatic role of watchman or guardian of Islam and the founding tenets of the Brotherhood, which included the establishment of an Islamic government as opposed to an Islamist state. Mubarak's approach also inspired the Brotherhood to exercise patience when it came to forming its own political party and making sharia the official source of law in Egypt.

Still, many religious radicals remained wary of this pragmatic approach. Believing that it would dilute the significance of Islamic principles, such as social justice and welfare, they feared that it would corrupt the organization. The feeling among many Salafists was that Mubarak's government was manipulating the moderate, pragmatic Islamist forces. On the other hand, non-Muslim minorities remained concerned that it would legitimize the Islamicization of the state. For instance, the Coptic Christians were worried that a stronger, more well-organized Brotherhood would deprive them of their basic rights.[23] But Mubarak addressed this concern by proving adept at containing the Brotherhood's rising political influence within the government. After the Brotherhood won nearly thirty seats in the parliament in the 2005 elections, Mubarak had several Brotherhood members arrested.[24] The repression had the effect of instilling discipline and moderation in the Brotherhood, rather than dividing the moderates and radicals.

With their increased discipline, they were able to contain much of the factionalization inside their orgnaization. This meant, among other things, striking the needed balance between government repression and political ambition. It was not, as Sumita Pahwig writes, "a sign of dissimulation or lack of ideological evolution. Instead, it had its roots in a thirty-year process of adapting to democratic and secular ideas by reframing them in religious terms."[25] Political moderation, it could be said, imposed its own constraints on the Brotherhood, which were tethered more to a faith in its political potential and less, if at all, to secular moral principles.

Nevertheless, the Brotherhood found itself caught between the need to apply a pragmatic set of rules of behavior and to accommodate the Salafists' rigid moral propriety. Steering between and beyond these pressures required the restraint to realize its goals of political empowerment and party pluralism. The Brotherhood's collective sense of political restraint, it seemed, was driven not so much by the shared desire to appease the Salafists, but by the appearance of securing the needed political power to achieve these goals. But was it, one might ask, this calculated restraint that contributed to its lack of readiness to merge its pragmatic goals with upholding the basic rights and needs of all peoples in Egypt? Could this fragile sense of moderation also explain the reason for the Brotherhood's rapid rise and downfall in the Arab protests, in which instituting decency standards suddenly became the subject of transitioning beyond a repressive regime to a nascent democratic system that seemed ill-prepared to uphold any normative constraints against violent force?

The answer remains unclear. The wave of protests and demonstrations that swept through Egypt in the spring of 2011 took everyone by surprise, including the Salafists. Sparked by Tunisian street vendor's decision to light himself on fire to protest the Tunisian government's decision to raise food prices (the vendor spent several days in the hospital before finally succumbing to his burns a few weeks later), the Arab Spring protests represented deep discontent with the corruption, brutality, and dictatorial power of Arab rulers. Not only did the protests reflect the democratic and collective struggle for a common Arab identity, it also meant that powerful liberal democracies, which had once backed military dictators like Mubarak, now lent their support to the protestors' demands for upholding human rights protection. The United States, for instance, pledged nearly $1 billion annually in military aid to the Mubarak regime; but its tacit support of the protests eventually contributed to the rapid downfall of Mubarak.[26] It could also be said that the Egyptian people's embrace of Western democracy was a long time in coming. As F. Gregory Gause points out, "The common enemy of the 2011 Arab revolts is not colonialism, U.S. power or Israel, but the Arabs' own rulers."[27]

With Mubarak ousted and Egypt now committed to holding democratic elections, the Brotherhood took advantage of the new political system by forming its own political party, the Freedom and Justice Party (FJP). The Democratic Alliance led by the FJP received 37.5 percent of the votes, and the FJP won 213 of the 498 parliamentary seats in the 2012 elections.[28] Yet its political success also created the challenge of bringing together the liberal decency of new elections (or democratic rights) and the religious-based, conservative moral propriety that it had cultivated through its years of pragmatism under the Mubarak regime. The reactionary strand of conservative decency focused on the maintenance of customs in accordance with traditional rules and practices of the Quran. One of these customs, as I shall discuss below, involved the exclusion of women from public affairs, which not only placed the Brotherhood's sense of moral propriety at odds with the secular freedoms of liberal decency but also characterized the difficulty of managing the tensions within the movement, in particular the powerful role of the Salafists in driving this tension.

The need to accommodate the Salafists would prove fateful, however. Mohamed Morsi, the newly elected president, faced the challenge of placating both the demands of the radical Islamists and the secularists in order to carry out his presidential duties while also holding together the FJP. The Salafists applied considerable pressure on Morsi to work toward an Islamic state, which led Morsi to announce his intention of adopting sharia as the primary source of constitutional or public law. The move triggered an immediate and hostile response by the democratic secularists, forcing Morsi to back down. The FJP's suspect commitment to democracy not only indicated its inability to manage the effects of this political tension but also how its Islamist policies seemed to drive this tension. It was not simply an issue of desiring too much too fast. It was the failure to coordinate the intensity of anger that by the summer of 2013 had fractured the alliance between secular liberals and the FJP into secular and religious factions. As we saw in chapter 4, when such pressures intensify emotions, they can also lead to an affective disinvestment in the political ideals and normative constraints of the democratic system and for that matter, liberal decency.

Accordingly, Morsi could ill ignore the FJP's tacit goal of Islamicizing the country. And while he sought to reassure the secularists that the implementation of sharia would not in any way conflict with the freedom of religion, his faint reassurances only served to stoke fear and anger in the people who believed that his ultimate plan was to establish an Islamic state. This had the effect of calling attention to an outside or neutral mechanism to suppress the effects of this political conflict: the military. But it was this mechanism that would also repress the main drivers of this tension—namely, the Brotherhood and later, the liberal protesters—and reverse the efforts to work beyond the effects of the tension. In forcibly ousting Morsi from power, Abdel Fattah el-Sisi, the commander of the army, suspended the democratic process.[29] Sisi's takeover initiated a violent crackdown of the Brotherhood, leading Steven Cook, a foreign affairs scholar, to write that "Sisi's war on the Brothers has made a mockery of the calls for unity, decency, and tolerance."[30] Since 2015, Sisi's government has gone on to sentence 600 former government officials to death and to suppress all political dissent against the regime.[31] In targeting the liberals, he has made it a crime to commemorate the January 25 anniversary of the Egyptian uprising and also clamped down on the freedom to assembly, detaining thousands of protesters.[32] Because of these actions, seventeen Egyptian NGOs have accused Sisi of committing gross human rights violations.[33]

Sisi's violent crackdown has become part of a larger campaign to combat global terrorism. But it also poses a new threat to both basic decency and the process of balancing Egypt's liberal values against the traditional customs of its Islamic identity. By violating the principles and rights of the people stipulated in the 2014 constitution, Sisi has managed to undermine the normative constraints of basic decency standards and Islamist moral propriety, which has widened the gap between basic decency and Islamism. On the other hand, Sisi has remained somewhat sympathetic to the issue of gender inequality, even though his human rights abuses have created considerable ambivalence toward his commitment to gender equality.

Freedom and Gender Identity

The Social Gender Gap

The Brotherhood's centrist position, as we have seen, played both an ambiguous and uncertain role in managing the political tensions between extremism and the authoritarian state. The conflict between the Brotherhood and basic decency in Egyptian politics suggests that liberal democratic norms will continue to assume a destabilizing function in Egyptian politics. But an even more important question is how the complex perceptions of gender reflects the longstanding gap between liberal decency (and its extension) and religious propriety. The gender gap in Egypt underscores the long tradition of feminist piety, whose modern roots can be traced to the mid to late nineteenth century, when an increasing number of Egyptian women became educated and entered the middle class. As early as the late 1890s, in fact, Egyptian feminists called increasing attention to the discrimination against women. The Egyptian feminist Zaynab Fawwaz, for example, insisted that Islamic law did not prohibit women "from involvement in occupations of men."[34]

But the issue was not simply whether women remained oppressed in Islamic societies. It was also about how women's sentimental affirmation of piety could test and even undermine the political ideal of individual freedom. As the symbol of female piety, the veil represented a practice of covering most of the face and all of women's adornments below the shoulders.[35] "Veiling," as Juan Cole writes, was "a new response made by educated young women to contemporary problems in a postcolonial setting."[36] Cole argues that in addition to serving as a protective symbol of a Muslim woman's identity, the veil provides a modern source of strategic resistance to Western colonial rule and Western values. But many critics of the veil point out that it continues to symbolize male patriarchy and the traditional restrictions from participating in public affairs in Islamic societies. As we saw in chapter 3, such restrictions represent the paternalistic values and practices of Islamic state governments that deny women basic rights and privileges, such as the right to an equal education. Still, ambivalence toward the veil raises the issue of whether promoting the autonomy of veiled women in patriarchal societies can help reconcile their freedom and moral propriety. Does such autonomous capacity building transform their sense of propriety or threaten the piety that defines the Muslim woman's identity in Islamic societies?

Some contend that the answer lies in reconstructing gender identity from both modern and traditional cultural perspectives.[37] The idea here is that gender expresses the diverse inner feelings and sentiments that have been shaped by cultural norms and customs. Yet gender norms, as one might expect, vary from culture to culture and signify the various political tensions between countries. For instance, the gender equality that exists in many Western liberal democracies constitutes a sexual freedom that many Islamic societies with strict codes of behavior (e.g., Saudi Arabia) reject. Gender and sex can in this sense remain in stark tension in these societies where gender norms exclude or repress women's social roles. The tensions may be less intense in Islamic societies, where women have always been forced to internalize these socialized roles or become habituated to the restrictions placed on them in public life. However, the tensions suggest that gender identity remains, on the one hand, a diverse phenomenon and that customary restrictions remain integral to how many Muslim women practice their faith and learn to affirm their identity.[38] On the other hand, the repressive nature of these restrictions forces us to confront the male bias that structures these practices and the legitimacy of rules against allowing women to participate in public affairs. Of course, the role of identity politics assumes a very different function here, as does the propriety effect I discussed in chapter 3. The difference being that many Muslim women treat Islamic practices and folklore as both a source of identity and freedom. In liberal democracies, this can take the form of a woman's choice and right to wear the veil in public. When a liberal democratic state restricts this right, as we saw in France, it also imposes a dual constraint on both this freedom and right that have shaped her identity. But in Islamic state societies that lack any protections of freedom, moral propriety dictates the underlying bias of this constraint on removing the veil.[39] This is not to say that liberal democracy upholds a more robust notion of decency, but rather that the difference reflects a gap between traditional and liberal decency in politics. It is a gap that we can hardly expect to bridge by simply spreading liberal decency to Islamic state societies, particularly when some liberal democracies have imposed repressive constraints on women. But it is a gap that we should understand as an unmet challenge to reconcile liberal decency with a Muslim woman's piety.

For the women who took part in the Egyptian Women's Mosque Movement of the 1990s—a pietistic revival movement—the challenge seems to reveal the Western misunderstanding of their pietistic experience. From their perspective, the veil occupies a deeply personal, private space and represents more than a symbolic constraint on women in public. Saba Mahmood, who interviewed and surveyed numerous Islamic women of the movement, claims that the veil frees these women from the secular customs and laws that often objectify their devotion and limit their felt connection to Islam. As Mahmood writes,

> The practices of the women's mosque movement have not emerged as a result of an abstract tendency toward objectification, but are provoked by a specific problem, namely, the concern for learning to organize one's daily life according to Islamic standards of virtuous conduct in a world increasingly ordered by a logic of secular rationality that is inimical to the sustenance of these virtues.[40]

Mahmood's point here is that the veil is not simply a custom but a practice that is essential to living in accordance with the religious standards of moral conduct. The problem with liberal decency is that it often involves the imposition of the liberal ideals of equality and freedom on these moral standards of Islamic societies. For many Muslim women, this downplays the particular role played by certain emotions and feelings in anchoring their piety, including shyness and modesty, which Mahmood interprets as virtues embodied in the performative acts of wearing the hijab. For Mahmood, wearing the veil can also be construed as a "deliberate choice," since it enables women to preserve and protect their religious piety against secular forces of rapid modernization.[41] However, the private value of shyness is routinely overlooked in Western societies, where it represents for many, a weak personality trait and impediment to public participation (the lack of self-confidence that prevents one from acting accordingly). This cultural and political difference in sensibilities is what sets apart much of Islamic moral propriety from liberalism.

Consider the case of Morocco. Like Egypt, it is another place where the hijab has become part of what Leila Hessini calls a "sexual ethics." Here, women can assert that they are clean or pure insofar as they align their conduct with the oral teachings (hadith) and the texts of Islam (the Quran).[42] Veiling, contrary to Western perceptions that reduce the meaning of the veil to the man's control over a woman's body, requires both men and women to control their sexual feelings. Shyness, in this sense, can be interpreted as the inflected self-desire to resist the glorification of fashion symbols and the nudity that objectifies the female body in the public realm.

This is not to downplay the oppressive function of the veil, especially in the former Taliban-controlled Afghanistan where women were forced to wear the niqab and were severely punished for walking (without it) in public during the daytime. Rather, it is to emphasize the difficulties that arise when we assume that liberal ideals should ipso facto take priority in determining how one preserves and practices one's beliefs and identity. As I have argued, moral proprieties are rules of behavior that are rooted in traditional customs and habits. In most cases, they involve strict boundaries and impose legal constraints on persons. Our global dimension of moral propriety, which I discussed in chapters 1 and 3, allows us to understand the possibilities of opening up these boundaries through the interaction and dialogue of these proprieties. Global moral propriety in this context becomes a way of sizing up the political obstacles to reconciling liberal and traditional decency in Muslim countries (with rigid patriarchal norms).

For Muhammad Said Ashmawi, a prominent liberal critic in Egypt, reconciling these decencies entails the public recognition of a secular ethic of decency in Egyptian politics. As he puts it, "The veil is already a preordained virtue designed to guard against excessive lust and reinforce a decent ethic or the virtue of modesty."[43] For him, decency should stem from a secular belief in the efficacy of impartiality and its role in upholding the rule of law and neutralizing the political effects of gender empowerment. The question, however, is how does the veil maintain the beliefs and private virtues that enable women to make a choice? Is there something more that is driving the pressure to conform or that testifies to how the veil is valued in itself as a tool to express Muslim women's faith? As Mahmood claims, the veil represents "a modest bodily form (or the veiled body) that did not simply express the self's interiority but the means by which it was acquired."[44] It is the means employed by Muslim women to gain awareness of their inner selves.

For Western feminists this presents a troubling case of gender politics. Judith Butler, for instance, argues that patriarchal norms can still dictate the means by which one seeks to escape their oppressive effects. She argues that symbols such as the veil are performative acts of the body that continually construct gender and a woman's identity. Such acts are part of what she calls "performance," which refers to how they are constituted historically by accepted customs and norms.[45] They come to express the sedimented acts that have accumulated over time and reified gender or made it concrete in practice and custom. Gender, in this sense, becomes naturalized through the "performance acts" of bodies, that is, it is habituated through the way women carry out their daily duties—whether this refers to their domestic chores or putting on the veil to hide one's identity in public. That women learn to accept these bodily acts as culturally given belies the fact that gender is historically constructed. For Butler, this means that the body remains distinct from the cultural beliefs and mores that constitute it.[46] Through this separation between body and culture, we learn how to critique the natural facts that constitute gender and to break down and disrupt naturalized gender norms. The veil is the product of this inseparability of culture and body; it remains a socially constructed reality. Thus, to employ this discursive strategy of destabilizing one's role in society is to deploy the means of becoming aware of the effects of the patriarchal structure on gender identity.

But this radical strategy also raises the issue of whether destabilizing norms and practices is a Westernized means of attaining liberation. Does Butler's discursive strategy end up placing unintended normative pressure on the mosque women to adopt a different self-conception of the good? For Mahmood, it is not clear whether the strategic need to destabilize norms overlooks the different cultural space occupied by these women. As she writes,

> Any attempt to destabilize the normative structure must also take into account the specificity of embodied practices and virtues and the kind of work they perform on the self, recognizing that any transformation of their meaning requires an engagement with the technical and embodied armature through which these practices are attached to the self.[47]

The veil does not symbolize an absolute constraint on the women's bodies—as if women were material property; rather, it is a distinct marker of a Muslim woman's self-directed sense of bodily movement. That is to say, the veil becomes central to the Muslim woman's interior self and her modesty or shyness (*al-haya*). In effect, she is learning to convert these material constraints on her public participation into an increasing degree of devotion and solidarity.

One could thus argue that the veil is in fact deeply symbolic of her self-conception of the good and an unconscious form of resistance to liberal norms and ideals.[48] Wearing the hijab is how the mosque women come to inhabit norms that construct their gender identity.[49] Veiling, as Mahmood argues, is a way of expressing genuine desires and emotions:

> If we think of agency not simply as a synonym for resistance to social norms but as a modality of action, then this conversation raises some interesting questions about the kind of relationship established between the subject and the norm between performative behavior and inward disposition. To begin with, what is striking here is that instead of innate human desires eliciting outward forms of conduct, it is the sequence of practices and actions one is engaged in that determines one's desires and emotions. In other words, action does not issue forth from natural feelings but creates them.[50]

Mahmood's point is that in determining the desires and emotions of women, the arranged practices of piety enable women to act. But critics of this point claim that practice must at some point be detached from action, particularly if practicing piety reinforces patriarchal norms and gets in the way of promoting social public goods, such as ending poverty and oppression. Lila Abu-Lughod, for example, contends that learning to act on one's emotion can also be about breaking away from the practices that repress these emotions. The practice of piety need not divorce a Muslim woman's religious faith from her public duty to improve society.[51] As I suggested in chapter 4, when the practical surplus of piety becomes a condition for desiring further political protection against harm, then the freedom of desire can be said to (co-)constitute these practices. The gap between free and repressed desire, in other words, is what conditions the dogmatic separation of conservative and liberal decency in Islamic societies. In some cases, the gap can involve the most overt forms of violence against women (or the reactionary politics of piety), such as brutal and barbaric codes of honor practiced by tribal leaders in many parts of the Middle East and Africa.[52] Here, upholding tribal honor means subjecting women to brutal treatment that violates the very core meaning of decency, that is, of protecting the basic needs and rights of the most marginalized against extreme violence. Navi Pillay, the former UN High Commissioner for Human Rights, echoed this sentiment when she stated that "I do not even wish to use the phrase 'honor killing' . . . since . . . there is not the faintest vestige of honor in killing a woman in this way."[53] As this statement suggests, when honor becomes detached from the core sentiment of nonkilling, it represents the political chasm between conservative and liberal decency; that is, it shows how the absence of basic decency can cause a deep fissure to open up, in which the freedom to harm, shame, and humiliate eliminates any need for normative constraint.[54] The absence of such normative constraints should remind us that basic decency standards at the international level remain fragile, and that understanding the obligation to enforce them is predicated on better reconciling conservative and liberal decency.

Of course, shoring up liberal decency will not always allow us to bridge this divide in moral propriety. Recall, for instance, the French National Assembly's passage in 2008 of a law restricting the right of Muslim women to wear the hijab in public. The reversal of their freedom amounted to a habituated attack on their faith. What is more, it suggested that the veil had become as much a tool for fighting against the suppression of faith as it was for suppressing women's rights.[55] If this tells us anything, it is that the separability of moral propriety norms symptomizes the undertheorized complementary notions of liberal and conservative decency in Egyptian politics.

Affective Activism in Egypt's Gendered Politics

Egyptian liberalism, as we have seen, seeks to balance two fundamentally differing beliefs systems, often against one another. But liberalism and Islamism can intersect in ways that involve the broader interpretation of consensus (*ijma*) and consultation (*shura*). The political difference between these two is what generates the contradictory and debilitating outcomes in Egyptian politics, including the advancement of women's status and rights in a society that represses its liberal protestors. This gender gap, I argue, exposes a deep-seated tendency to exploit traditional, religious sentiments for political purposes. A narrow political propriety isolates our second mode of global moral propriety from the other modes, and is driven almost exclusively by blind political ambition for stability and security and a strict political expediency of empowering women in Egyptian politics.

The political empowerment of Egyptian women (and their rights) dates back to the 1956 constitution, which granted women the right to vote. Mubarak's rule (1981–2011) managed to usher in many top-down solutions that helped advance women's rights in Egypt and bring them into conformity with the Convention on the Elimination of All Forms of Discrimination against Women (CEDAW).[56] The initiative came to be known as the First Lady Phenomenon, which referred to how the first lady helped reinforce Egyptian rules and propriety in accordance with international norms. This included Law 1 of 2000, which recognized a woman's right to file divorce from her husband without his consent, as well as the Child Law of 2008, which raised the minimum legal age of marriage from fifteen to eighteen.[57] These remained limited gains, however. As Miwa Kato puts it, "The effort was tainted by perceptions held by some that an authoritarian regime that suppressed freedom and social justice was instrumentalizing women's rights in the name of modernization as well as to gain regime acceptance from Western partners and the international community at large."[58] Hosni Mubarak, in fact, had become adept at playing off social movements, including the Brotherhood.

The 2011 Egyptian Spring uprising tested this modernization in both negative and positive ways. Initially, Mubarak sought to shut down public access to the Internet. But this had a counterproductive effect: it compelled people to take to the streets to continue their exchanges and to build solidarity, in person. More important, the killings of their fellow protesters would incite the rage of the people and motivate them to overcome the fear of arrest and torture that the Mubarak regime had used to control the people. Yet, while the first few days were relatively peaceful, the subsequent days were marked by violence and what would come to be known as the blue bra incident, in which a veiled woman was assaulted and dragged through Tahir Square in only her blue underwear. In all, there were nearly twenty-five sexual assaults against women from January to March 2011. And the Supreme Council of Armed Forces did little to redress the situation. Not only did the government fail to condemn the attacks, but it ended up appointing no women to its subcommittees and governing councils. Unsurprisingly, when Mohamed Morsi won the presidency in 2012, he allowed the traditional status of women as domestic servants to take precedence over the basic rights of women. Of the sixty-four items on Morsi's agenda, there was no mention of women; their complete absence amounted to not only their public humiliation but also to a virtual political abyss between liberal and conservative decency.

However, el-Sisi's coup d'etat and subsequent crackdown on the Muslim Brotherhood quickly reversed these policies. The 2014 constitution, which replaced the 2012 constitution (which had removed equality for women from the earlier constitution), granted sweeping rights to women, including the right to hold higher office. In the 2015 parliamentary elections, women won several seats in parliament, bringing their total level of representation to 14.9 percent of the parliament, the highest ever in Egyptian history. These political gains showed just how much gender activism had affected Egyptian society. As Kato writes:

> Looking back on the turbulent years since 2011, there is a silver lining for women's rights: the fight against regression brought activism to a new level of intensity, which in turn enabled the cause to become more deeply rooted in the minds of Egyptians throughout the country. Ultimate success will depend on whether women's empowerment becomes a movement owned by the people and supported by the state, rather than the other way around.[59]

The intensity of women's activism also came at a time when the state brutally clamped down on the rights of liberal advocates. By helping empower women, the state was able to employ an effective strategy for combatting Islamic terrorism and the threat of Islamic fundamentalism. For a powerful women's bloc was, on the one hand, treated as a buffer against the implementation of sharia. On the other hand, it was an event that forced many to confront the politically expedient use of state power to clamp down on Islamism and political dissent.

Which returns us to the issue of the veil, or the political difference between freed desire and norm-constituted desire. Earlier I had argued that the politics of piety was defined by its opposition to the constitutive role of desire and the secular constraints of Western liberalism. Yet the politics of the women's struggle in Egypt came to reject the expedient use of state power to repress the action of Islamists. The reassertion of women, in other words, placed increasing pressure on the normative constraints of secular politics, which ended up dividing rather than connecting liberalism and the basic rights of women. Such a contradictory result can be thought of as an affective disinvestment in democratic politics to the extent that it demonstrates how the heated emotions of political movements can produce effects that fail to support any meaningful political change.

To sum up: the tension between Islamism and gender in Egyptian politics highlights the complex link between decency and Egyptian liberalism. While it could be said that some of the feminist movements suppress the conditions of possibility for freedom (for women) and that many of the state's recent concessions to women have not paved the way for any substantive notion of gender equality, both of these claims tend to raise the question of what decency should mean for Muslim Egyptian women. As we saw with the Cairo Women's Mosque Movement, gender identity in Egypt seems to consist of an inner sense of moral propriety that still needs to be better reconciled with liberal and basic decency.

Conclusion

The specter of sharia's implementation doomed the Brotherhood and its moderate and tenuous embrace of liberal ideals. Since its inception in the 1920s, the Brotherhood in Egypt has sought to strategically adopt and apply the centrist doctrine of *wasatiyyah*. But the Brotherhood's rapid fall also testified to the acute tension between Islam's traditional moral propriety and basic decency. The many years of palliating Mubarak's government (and acting as the buffer between them and the Islamic radicals) could hardly prepare it for dealing with the effects of this tension. Despite its strategy of political restraint and cooperation, the Brotherhood found itself caught up in the politics of fear. Its struggle, while dealing with conflicting moral proprieties, eventually gave way to a highly expedient political propriety that has done far more to undermine liberal and basic decency standards in Egypt than to support these standards.

Nonetheless, this tension has also come to reflect the important social and gender gaps in Egyptian politics that expose the reactionary, conformist, and normative pressures contributing to the growing political chasm between liberal and conservative decency. If anything, it shows just how political manipulation of liberal principles can lead to the conditions of fear and threat perception that fuel the deep divisions between traditional and progressive sentiments of decency. The idea I explore in the following chapter is how this stark divide reflects the challenge of accommodating difference to advance the global rule of law.

CHAPTER SIX

Global and Local Justice in Northern Uganda

> The common sense of mankind demands that law shall not stop with the punishment of petty crimes by little people. It must also reach men who possess themselves of great power and make deliberate and concerted use of it to set in motion evils which leave no home in the world untouched. It is a cause of that magnitude that the United Nations will lay before Your Honors.
>
> —Robert Jackson, "Opening Statement before the International Military Tribunal," 1945

> A tremendous passion is this longing that our memory may be rescued, if it's possible, from the oblivion which overtakes it.
>
> —Miguel de Unamuno, *Tragic Sense of Life*, 1954

Since becoming fully operational in 2002, the International Criminal Court (ICC) has provided a uniform set of rules of procedure and impartiality standards for trying many of the worst perpetrators of serious international crimes. Today, it plays a central role in an expanding network of global justice that consists of regional courts, international criminal tribunals, hybrid courts, and truth commissions. In many ways, it has become an example of global moral propriety by representing a global commitment to advancing moral accountability, the capacity of national judiciaries, and victim participation in the legal process. As I mentioned in chapter 4, it promotes these features through its complementarity principle, which stipulates the conditions for assisting state officials and promoting dialogue between these officials and the Office of the Prosecutor (OTP).

The idea of the complementarity principle is to facilitate state cooperation and enable ICC officials to work out conflicts that may arise between it and state officials.[1] But in recent years, the tensions between state and ICC officials have increased in Kenya, Uganda, and Libya and have reflected the difficulties of reaching mutual accommodation.

In this chapter, I will address what these political difficulties mean for developing global moral propriety through the affective qualities of complementarity. As we shall see, there has been considerable attention devoted to the politics of selective justice or the conflicts surrounding the Office of the Prosecutor's selection of investigations.[2] In fact, many African states have angrily accused the ICC of intentionally targeting African states and their leaders. This, in turn, has led to growing distrust inside the African Union of the ICC and exposed the limits of several states' moral commitments to the ICC.[3] Perhaps more importantly, it has pointed to the troubling prospects of cooperating through complementarity (e.g., dialogue and assistance) and of merging local procedures of justice and the ICC's standards (e.g., evidential standards and the protection of victims' needs and rights). Proponents of local justice claim that its role remains an important part of building global civil society.[4] However, critics contend that the informal customs of local justice constitute an unrealistic task of reconciling local with international justice, especially in terms of promoting victims' needs and rights.[5] I argue that the skepticism toward reconciling these dueling standards of justice exposes a critical bias against local justice, which seems to restrict more than reinforce complementarity as an affective mechanism of international justice. By having to impose uniform decency standards to fulfill the interests of international justice, the ICC has had to confront political opposition by restricting the application of its complementarity principle. The imposition has thus created many political effects and conflicts that it cannot adequately address much less govern, including the political opposition of powerful states. Such effects raise the issue of whether the ICC is effectively promoting the interests of international justice or if it needs to do more to serve these interests.

The idea that complementarity can be used to accommodate local differences or interests in local justice reveals the challenge of diversifying the sources of these interests in global justice, that is, creating the conditions for the mutual justification of formal and informal procedures of restorative justice (or restoring victims' rights and remediating their needs). However, I claim that this mutual justification enables us to understand the interactive potential of local and global morality propriety in politics. My aim in the chapter, then, is to analyze this interactive potential by first exploring the perceived limits of local justice and then discussing the relational proprieties of local and international justice—that is, showing how local justice can be understood as an informal mechanism capable of shaping the ICC's complementarity and the application of its decency standards (such as fair and equal treatment under the law). These two forms of justice, as I shall show, signify a procedural difference in global justice, which tends to be downplayed in the application of international justice and complementarity. To contextualize my analysis of complementarity, I will examine the ICC's situation in Uganda, specifically how the Acholi people's local justice allows us to engage the (moving) relational effects of justice and the constraints of a top-down approach or solution to injustice, or both.

The Legal and Political Gap

The establishment of the ICC in July 1998 marked an important step in bridging the long-standing accountability gap between international and national law. With its rules of procedure for administering justice, the ICC provides lofty evidential standards for investigating and prosecuting perpetrators of atrocities. But while the ICC represents the world's first standing criminal court, it can only prosecute in states that are party to its statute (or the Rome Statute) or where the UN Security Council refers a situation to the OTP. Beyond this, it has to rely on the voluntary cooperation of states to enforce its arrest warrants. Having therefore come to embody many of the key features of liberal decency or the standards of impartiality and nondiscrimination, it has had to confront political pressures to defend these standards. The challenge of course has been recognizing that such standards are not wholly independent of the politics that shape them: that when their application conflicts with other rules, they can produce pressure on ICC officials to impose them on recalcitrant states. But there is more to this idea of justice than simply states electing not to cooperate. As I have suggested, there may be substantial conflicts between the proprieties of justice, or proper ways of administering justice according to national and local customs and norms. The ICC's complementarity principle is supposed to work out these conflicts, but the problem with taking over investigations, or accommodating states, is that state leaders may have an interest in manipulating these national rules to gain political advantage.

This is an issue that has received considerable attention over the years.[6] Less studied is the difference between local and international justice and how the latter might intervene and complement the former. In the early 2000s, international and local officials began to study the general parameters of this issue by examining the various ways in which local procedures of justice could inform international criminal norms. A focal point of their study was the traditional procedure of Mato Oput practiced by the Acholi people in northern Uganda.[7] The creative task in this case was to accommodate the virtues and legitimacy of local justice; that is, to understand how informal justice could complement, not replace, the Court's standards of fairness in prosecuting the commanders of the Lord's Resistance Army (LRA), a rebel group based in the northern region of Uganda, which had fought against the government in the civil war. Bringing justice and accountability to this region thus involved a multilayered process of accommodation capable of remedying the traumatic effects of the civil war and regional instability (especially since many of the LRA members appear to have fled either to the southern part of South Sudan and the northeastern part of the Democratic Republic of the Congo). However, it was a process that seemed to pit, in the minds of some, the opposing sources of legitimacy, in particular, the international standards of impartiality and the local customs and procedures of ceremonial justice.[8]

Nonetheless, ICC officials feared that in surrendering jurisdictional control to local authorities (and their customs), the ICC risked losing its own credibility and legitimacy. But Mato Oput was never meant to challenge the ICC's credibility. Rather, it was to spur both dialogue and understanding of connecting local and international justice procedures.[9] The ICC's high legal standards of impartiality, in other words, represented opportunities for accommodating these local procedures and enabling local officials to adapt their own legal customs to the ICC.[10] Accommodation via the complementarity principle meant that the local peoples needed to fit their informal local procedures into the ICC's global framework. And yet, this understanding of accommodation already assumed the need to reconcile two differing systems of rules that enjoyed "incontestable legitimacy."[11] The idea, then, was that local authorities would need to meet the ICC's lofty legal standards and legal constraints in order to administer their local procedures, while the ICC would only administer justice to the top brass, which in this case, included Joseph Kony and his top commanders (two of whom are now dead). In short, many presumed that there was an irreconcilable difference between the ICC and local justice, that if these two were to be united in the struggle for global justice, the ICC's standards would need to determine the conditions for administering local justice to the LRA members. Let us therefore turn our attention to these standards and their application by ICC officials.

The Politics of the ICC

Mission and Structure

Part of the ICC's mission is to serve as a court of last resort for investigating, prosecuting, and punishing individuals for the crimes of genocide, crimes against humanity, and war crimes. Under its statute, states are accorded prima facie recognition to investigate and prosecute the perpetrators of these crimes. Thus, where national governments once could adopt immunity laws designed to shield the perpetrators from international prosecution (e.g., Chilean dictator Augusto Pinochet's immunity for life as a senator), the ICC's automatic jurisdiction ensures that such laws will no longer obstruct the prosecution of such crimes.[12]

One of the issues discussed at the Rome Conference that established the ICC on July 17, 1998—with 120 participating states voting to approve the Rome Statute—was whether either the UN Security Council or the ICC prosecutor should be able to determine when acts of aggression had occurred. Here the negotiators failed to reach agreement on a solution or compromise to this issue. They elected instead to hold open-ended sessions or meetings to discuss the future elements and comprehensive definition of the crime of aggression and the role of the prosecutor. ICC officials and state delegates nonetheless agreed that the OTP would reserve the right to initiate an investigation (*proprio motu*). This would prove important for two reasons. First, it provided the prosecutor with an added measure of independence and, second, it encouraged the prosecutor to assume a potentially assertive role in pressuring states to hand over suspected perpetrators. It is worth mentioning that Luis Moreno-Ocampo, the first chief prosecutor of the ICC, had already issued arrest warrants for rebel leaders in Uganda and the Congo, including Thomas Lubanga (the first person to stand trial and be punished by the ICC), Joseph Kony, and two heads of state, Muammar Qaddafi and Omar Hassan al-Bashir.[13] Moreno-Ocampo's successor, Fatou Bensouda, has since conducted in-depth preliminary reviews of the gravity of violence in the Palestinian Occupied Territories and Georgia, and opened investigations in Georgia and Afghanistan.

Still, the ICC has had to deal with the political fallout of accusations by African states, such as South Africa and Burundi, which have claimed that the ICC is a politicized mechanism that discriminates against the less powerful states (where the powerful states lack any strategic interests).[14] These political pressures have challenged the ICC's rules of procedure and complementarity principle by suggesting that the ICC places the political interests of the most powerful states above those of African states. For example, South Africa announced its decision to withdraw from the ICC, after having refused to comply with the court's request to surrender Bashir, who had visited the country in June 2015 to attend a high-level meeting of the African Union.[15]

Jurisdiction and the Normative Issue of Complementarity

The complementarity principle, as stated above, holds that states will be allowed prima facie to investigate and prosecute, but that the ICC prosecutor may intervene in the national judiciary's affairs should the state prove unwilling or unable to investigate or prosecute, or both. It was largely seen as a compromise between those who wished the ICC to exercise universal jurisdiction and those who wished to subordinate the ICC's jurisdictional and discretionary powers to the sovereignty of the state.[16] But when the officials and leaders agreed to adopt the term at the preparatory meetings leading up to the establishment of the ICC, they began the difficult task of determining the parameters of its jurisdiction.[17]

One of the issues that dominated discussion of the changing parameters was how the complementarity principle could help build mutual trust between the ICC and state officials. Much of the discussion focused on the proactive ways of meeting states' needs, including empowering and advancing the equality of national judiciaries through legal and technical assistance and dialogue. In the 2006 OTP Report, for example, the prosecutor, in referring to this type of complementarity as "positive," stressed the importance of deference to national authorities and the need to participate in a system of international cooperation. In commenting on this development, Carsten Stahn argued that "positive complementarity can be essentially understood as a constructive relationship, based on partnership and dialogue with states."[18] From this perspective, the ICC could play an active role in national capacity building and promoting the global rule of law, especially in developing countries.

But this proactive approach also raised concerns about meeting the legal standards of the ICC. Since it depended on the ICC's ability to assist state officials and its willingness to enter into dialogue to resolve conflicts between state and ICC officials, it was feared such an approach would complicate the legal process: that in framing the dialogue in terms of what these latter officials must do to satisfy the ICC's legal criteria, the ICC and local officials had to ultimately find a way of reconciling their differences. In short, the court would end up encouraging two unequal standards of the rule of law/justice, creating even further uncertainty concerning the uniform application of legal rules and standards.[19]

The concern, then, was that in pressuring state and local peoples to adjust to its standards, the ICC could force state officials to place pressure on the ICC to stop imposing justice on their state. What was partly overlooked was how the local peoples could begin to pressure the state itself to recognize the application of its own local procedures to promote reconciliation. This first type of pressure was negatively linked to the second (conformist), since it involved the goal of building trust and voluntarily cooperating with ICC officials; while the second had more to do with the state's reactionary response. However, the third constituted a very different source of pressure: namely, the need to focus on the creative possibilities of reconciling local and international justice norms and customs. The emergence of this pressure from below underscored the prospects of working beyond the difficulties of state (non)cooperation at the ICC. Yet, for many, it was a new scenario that remained largely, if not wholly, symbolic.

Still, it is this symbolic nexus of international and local justice that matters. For it allows us to confront the formal limits of the ICC's selection process in terms of the diverse (reality of) international interests of justice. If complementarity is supposed to engage or actively accommodate other procedures of justice through dialogue, then the values and emotions underpinning these local procedures must play a role in extending complementarity. This affective dimension of complementarity thus raises considerable uncertainty about upholding the ICC's impartial application of its rules of procedure. In particular, it challenges us to test the limits of this impartiality and to determine how complementarity's extended application can create new cultural preferences for merging local norms and rules with those of the ICC. My aim in the following section, then, is to understand the local/international justice nexus in northern Uganda and what it means for extending the ICC's legal constraints (its formal impartiality) through informal mechanisms and for exposing the possibilities of converting these constraints into the conditions of increased interaction between different moral and legal proprieties. In effect, I will be charting a mutual complementarity, which unlike a proactive and positive approach that only stresses the ICC's role in producing mutually desirable outcomes, will be about connecting and integrating the symbols, feelings, and norms of local and international justice.

Traditional Justice in Northern Uganda

To understand the cultural legal dimension of local propriety and how it relates to the legal dimension of moral propriety—or how the ICC seeks to govern the moral conduct of parties through the application of its rules of procedures—we need to address the informal justice practiced by the Acholi people in northern Uganda. Much of my analysis will focus on Mato Oput, an intertribal procedure practiced by the Acholi people in northern Uganda. Its underlying aim is to resolve disputes and promote reconciliation among the different clans. Other local rituals in Northern Uganda include Kayo Cuk, Tolu Kakwa, and Moyo Pliny (there are four or five different tribes in northern Uganda and about fifty in all of Uganda).[20] In particular, Mato Oput involves the sacrifice of livestock and healing through ritual: the consumption of the bitter tasting oput root (*mato oput* literally refers to the "bitter root"). When mixed with a local brew, *kwete*, consisting of the blood of sacrificed lambs or goats, it becomes a viscous, bitter substance. Both the perpetrators and victims are required to drink it at a tribal ceremony—to taste the bitterness of the vengeance of their victims—symbolizing the act of moving beyond hatred, distrust, and hostility.[21]

In this context, reconciliation is achieved through truth-telling, symbolic/ritual bodily acts, compensation, and tribal well-being. And unlike criminal courts that hold trials to punish and isolate the perpetrator's guilt,

Mato Oput remains an informal procedure of justice, which encourages goodwill and mutual trust among the members of the tribal community. The voluntary nature of the process is designed to encourage confessions or truth telling, or both, by diminishing the perpetrator's fear of reprisal by members of the group. Placing faith in the community's willingness to forgive is thus the first step of what is called "cooling the hearts," or the coming to terms with one's guilt.

The clan leaders or elders who comprise the Ker Kwaro Acholi, the local institution of the Acholi, oversee the second step of determining the amount of compensation (or the number and size of goats and lambs to be sacrificed). In doing so, they help conduct negotiations between the victims' families and perpetrators and, under the leadership of a paramount chief, serve as a trusted mediator in conflicts involving the killing of a family member (although disputes can also involve lesser offenses). As the leader of the council of elders, the chief determines what amount of compensation is adequate to commence, performs the healing process, oversees the rituals or symbolic acts,[22] and ensures that confessions are neither pressured nor coerced. In acting as judge of the motives and guilt of perpetrators, the Ker Kwaro Acholi enjoys the highest level of trust and legitimacy.

Such legitimacy is based on extensive knowledge of local custom and law as well as the chief's exclusive authority to intervene in the ceremony through improvisational acts and bodily movements. These movements may assume an elaborate and unique role in bringing together the different parties. As one observer explains: "Both clans eat the exchanged food separately, and after [they finish] both start approaching the other holding sticks as if they want to fight and the Ker Kwaro chief calms them down as they hit the mediators' stick as a barrier preventing them from reaching the other side."[23]

The Ker Kwaro, then, offers the source of timely and creative intervention in the Mato Oput ceremony and determines the symbolic power of the ritual in relation to other traditional forms of local justice. For example, in the intertribal ritual Gomo Tong (or "the bending of spears"), both sides place their bent spears beside the fire to express their shared commitment to peace. Like Gomo Tong, Mato Oput varies in its application from clan to clan. Its public ceremonies feature the mixing of goat's blood with the oput herb to produce the bitter taste of Mato Oput. Others, however, take place at private residences and use different items, as one report details:

> They do the mato oput at the home of the victim, and do not use Kwete or oput herb. All they do is prepare a kind of sorghum grain called Lawera. Its husk is removed, and the grain ground to flour, and it's that flour that the mediator with his finger scoops and puts in the mouth of everyone at the ceremony of reconciliation, and the husk is sniffed by everyone.[24]

Since all community members eat this grain, the ritual becomes a holistic, communal event, in which each community member learns to associate the bitter taste with the painful feelings of vengeance and hate. All parties are able, in one extended bodily act, to confront their vengeance and guilt. In this case, the perpetrators and family members and formerly conscripted child soldiers of the LRA—especially those who elected to voluntarily return to their villages—use this bodily ritual to reconcile their differences and to affirm the Acholi's communal identity of forgiveness. In short, Mato Oput tests and confirms the Acholi's identity by allowing the people to come to terms with the traumatic effects of the civil war.

Still, it is hard, on the one hand, to think how this communal event could be properly scaled up to address the atrocities perpetrated by the commanders of the LRA.[25] On the other hand, this is not what Mato Oput seeks to achieve; rather, it is about bringing people back into the community. In this respect, Mato Oput and the ICC's standards constitute two very different ways or legal proprieties of dealing with guilt, in spite of some overlapping, common goals between them, as I shall address in the next section. Whereas the ICC's lego-political objective is to isolate guilt within the community, or focus on the individual and the specific elements of his or her crimes, informal justice is about engaging the shared guilt of the community. The latter constitutes a communal process of healing, or, as alluded to above, a shared effort to root out the desire for vengeance and its divisive effects on the community as a whole. Unlike the latter, though, the ICC is equipped with the resources to prosecute the most serious international crimes. But its mission, as already mentioned, is only to investigate and prosecute the worst of the worst perpetrators of international crimes. If authorities wish to prosecute lesser crimes, then they must do so at the state or local level. The International Criminal Tribunal in Rwanda (ICTR), for instance, faced the daunting, if not impossible, task of trying thousands of perpetrators. Yet, in relying on the Rwandan state (and its implementation of Gacaca courts or local traditional courts) to try the thousands of lesser perpetrators, the ICTR was allowed to focus on only high-profile perpetrators. In this way, the Rwandan state complemented the ICTR's efforts of bringing justice to the victims.

But the Gacaca courts also exonerated thousands of accused perpetrators. Moreover, critics argue that it engaged in victor's justice by electing not to try many leaders of the Tutsi-led Rwanda Patriotic Front.[26] Whether or not this was true, the Gacaca courts were forced to make difficult tradeoffs in order to promote reconciliation. The same predicament applies to Mato Oput and its ability to complement the ICC's work. In fact, many remain highly skeptical of Mato Oput, arguing that it poses a metaphysical threat to justice.[27] Evangelical Christian groups living in the Acholi region, for instance, have labeled Mato Oput as a form of devil worship. These are the same groups that have supported the Ugandan parliament's passage of the anti-homosexual laws mentioned in chapter 3. Yet their hostility to difference raises the question of how the condemnation of the relational aspects of local justice works against the need for diversifying the interests of international justice that informs the application of decency standards, such as fair and equal treatment under international law? Are we not undercutting this sense by presuming the ICC's inability to accommodate informal justice and to be accommodated in turn? The problem with the moral bias against local justice is that it presumes that local justice procedures cannot interact with international justice, since the two are based on different and incommensurable standards of legitimacy. And yet, to assume this is to reinforce the prevailing preference for international law while suppressing the very difference between the ICC's and Mato Oput's legal and moral proprieties. As Sverker Finnström puts it, "The preference for traditional justice should reflect a greater understanding of the social contexts and acts, and not simply the concepts of forgiveness and reconciliation that Westerners and Christian groups like to invoke."[28]

When international justice is imposed on other peoples, it reinforces the affective limitation of the ICC's complementarity, or its restriction on remedying the trauma that informs the needs and rights of victims, by failing to assist efforts to administer local justice (and its bodily rituals). Beyond this, it denies the possibilities of linking traditional justice to the larger network of global justice and truth and reconciliation commissions.[29] As Martha Minow writes,

> Such reconciliation would assist stability and democracy, but it also would require other measures: restoring dignity to victims would be part of this process, but so would dealing respectively with those who assisted or were complicit with the violence. Otherwise, new rifts and resentments are likely to emerge and grow.[30]

The issue, then, is whether biased sentiment against local justice limits the affective potential of justice, that is, the mutual interaction and accommodation of formal and informal procedures of justice. Moral preference or partiality toward international justice, as I have suggested, creates the political perceptions of either foreign legalism (legal procedures that do not represent local and national customs) or selective justice. The problem is that the ICC's impartiality standards cannot protect it from the political effects of this preference. Complementarity, in other words, cannot simply be applied from the top down; it also must involve some bottom-up approach to diversify the interests of justice that it serves.

The Political Sentiments and Affective Limitation: Mato Oput, National Trials, and Local Custom

To realize this diversity goal, we need to understand the moral and cultural propriety of local justice. In Gulu, Uganda (2007–8), there were mass ceremonies of Mato Oput witnessed and observed by not only families but also outside observers. Critics of Mato Oput's revival have claimed that the mass application of Mato Oput will only undermine its traditional purpose of healing the Acholi community. The issue here is whether Mato Oput can deal with the unprecedented effects of years of conflict and violence in the northern region of Uganda. Local officials or proponents of the Mato Oput project are careful to stress the implications of these effects for regional peace. "For most," writes one proponent, "the adaptive ideas of assistance with compensation and promoting reconciliation through a mass Mato Oput ceremony lie beneath the threshold of change that is acceptable for pragmatic purposes of applying Mato Oput to conflict."[31] Nearly 66 percent of the victims in northern Uganda, it should be noted, indicated that they would prefer punishment or retribution for the worst perpetrators, while only 22 percent preferred a traditional or nonpunitive option for these perpetrators.[32] Many locals based their preference on the need for balancing the formal standards of the ICC against the local procedures of justice and practice.

Forgiveness, as I mentioned earlier, expresses this integrity of Acholi identity by serving as a means of gaining trust (trust building) and protecting the community from further harm and potential division. Legally, this means that conditional amnesty can impose an undue threat on this identity; that without blanket forgiveness, the voluntary admission of guilt may come to naught. In short, Mato Oput can only proceed when such admission is followed by the affected family members and victim's willingness to forgive. In this way, Mato Oput requires that forgiveness not be "commanded." As the Justice and Reconciliation Project notes, "forgiveness comes before *Mato Oput. Mato Oput* is a ceremony that marks an end to every kind of anger that exists among the affected people. For the sake of this war, I think you should forgive so that the abducted children can come home."[33] Mato Oput is nonetheless designed to address only single murders or stealing, not the wide-scale killings committed in times of war. Its affective potential depends in this sense on the willingness of the perpetrators of these former crimes to confess their guilt, so that the community can participate in the process of forgiveness and healing (in terms of shared guilt). However, when the Ugandan national legislature passed a 2000 amnesty law (despite President Yoweri Museveni's staunch opposition) to encourage the LRA commanders to put down their arms in exchange for confessing their crimes, it was hoped that such confessions would forge the basis of healing.[34]

But many came to view the confessions as nothing more than politically expedient measures to end the war. While the national government possessed the resources to compensate the victims, they refused to use state funds to aid the victims, insisting that to do so would be bearing financial responsibility for the crimes committed by the LRA and not by them.[35] By granting blanket amnesty to the top commanders of the LRA, therefore, the government felt that it was doing a service to promote peace in the country. In reality, though, it introduced strict, new legal constraints on justice and accountability and placed peace before justice. These constraints have in turn led to considerable tension between the Ugandan government and the ICC, particularly over the issue of whether peace can proceed without justice. Under the Juba peace talks (2006–8), for instance, the Ugandan government established its International Crimes Division of the High Court of Uganda to try the worst perpetrators for war crimes.

The second agreement sought to deal with the conflicting aims of the triangulated relationship of ICC action, national criminal proceedings, and traditional processes. The national war crimes court, as stipulated under the Juba peace agreement (2008), was intended to provide an alternative to the ICC. The hope was that the LRA commanders would voluntarily cooperate with the proposed national war crimes court. The commanders, however, insisted on a key condition: that the ICC drop its arrest warrants. When ICC officials refused to rescind its warrants for Kony and his commanders, the LRA leaders stated that they would not attend the peace talks. This eventually led to a breakdown in the talks and prompted the Ugandan government to criticize the ICC for its refusal to drop its indictments of the LRA's top brass in exchange for setting up the national war crimes court. But dropping its indictments would have placed the ICC's own credibility at risk, something that it could ill afford, especially given its nascency at the time. Beyond this, there was its moral commitment to the victims of the LRA commanders' crimes. With so much at stake, many lost sight of the effects of these tensions between the ICC and the state, including how the Acholi people's felt demands for justice were being ignored. The looming issue was not simply whether the Acholi would ever benefit from the national war crimes court, whose commitment to prosecute in a genuine manner remained in doubt, but also how the Acholi people could apply their own justice procedures to complement the national government's and ICC's efforts.

The question of local cultural intervention thus demanded more attention. To meet this demand, various local scholars and officials recognized the local opportunities to remedy these effects. Together they initiated a project to appeal more directly and openly to the role of traditional justice in addressing the limits of international justice and healing. Their Justice and Reconciliation Project required that

> traditional justice processes require a face-to-face interaction between perpetrators and victims and their communities, and this provision may not be sustainable in the case of senior LRA or government commanders whose victims would identify directly with their suffering. In supporting traditional justice, the government believes that a modular form of traditional justice application can offer redress to war crimes.[36]

It was not entirely clear how this modularity would take shape, that is, whether the local elders would have to change their practices to meet the ICC's standards of prosecuting gender crimes and its extensive list of gender-related war crimes, most notably, forced rape.[37] At the very least, the discrepancy between local and international justice would require the local people to change their attitudes toward women and to take more seriously the impact of the crime of rape on the community. Both events thus signified the difficult conditions of reorienting the practices of confession and compensation. The elders, for instance, could ask for more compensation (e.g., goats) in recognition of the effects of rape on the community. But since no woman could sit as an elder, this seemed unlikely to happen. In addition, many of the rape crimes have been committed by national government soldiers. The fact that few soldiers had taken responsibility for their actions only seemed to reinforce the need for outside assistance to help end the culture of impunity.

Museveni's government was also unwilling to take the necessary steps to end the culture of impunity. Its strategy all along was to try to deflect attention away from its responsibility to investigate and prosecute rape crimes. And it extended as far back as the creation of the Commission of Inquiry into Violations of Human Rights in 1986, which Yoweri Museveni, the new president of Uganda, had established to investigate the past abuses from 1962 to 1986. Rather than adopting a broad remit for investigating past crimes, Museveni restricted the scope of the commission to atrocities committed during the prior regime. Critics argued that the decision was a deliberate attempt to prevent investigation of the actions of his government.[38] As Joanna Quinn put it, "The public at large, which had for so long been disenfranchised, seemed reluctant to talk about what happened and sensed that their participation in the work of the commission could lead to renewed retribution."[39] By discouraging the people from participating, the government believed that people would opt for peace over accountability. They seemed to assume that peace could be achieved without accountability: that people would simply learn to forget about the past, and that it was probably better not to reopen old wounds. In reality, though, people do not learn to forget their grievances nor to ignore the traumatic effects of war, but come to rely on accountability mechanisms to redress these wounds and to work toward peace. Peace and justice, in other words, are not mutually exclusive; instead, they can work together to promote reconciliation. The purpose of accountability mechanisms is to facilitate such reconciliation through restorative justice or a combination of restorative and retributive justice.

The ICC represents the latter approach. In punishing the very worst perpetrators, it seeks to deter would-be perpetrators by creating a credible global threat of prosecution of state leaders. But much of this credibility depends, as I have mentioned, on the national government's willingness to cooperate with the ICC and to carry out fair and impartial justice. Whether or not it has fulfilled this objective is not altogether clear. Yet in the case of the Commission of Inquiry into Violations of Human Rights, Ugandan state leaders showed a strong inclination to investigate only its enemies. Their intentions were largely to remain immune from justice. This is one reason for considering more deeply heterodox or local justice to promote reconciliation and to complement the ICC's efforts to enforce its standards of accountability. At the very least, it suggests the need to address the limits of administering formal justice by converting these formal constraints into opportunities for cultivating peace and local justice.

The way to imagine this conversion is to think of the local effects of imposing a uniform set of rules of procedure. This means understanding the local people's emotional disconnection from the ICC's application of justice. The idea is that this disconnection arises from the imposition of international justice and the overlooked role played by local identity in potentially complementing the ICC's work. In other words, the gap between the Acholi's communal identity and the ICC's legalism involves a rift between peace and justice at the local level. By failing to construct the emotional bonds needed to redress the effects of trauma, the ICC allows these effects to potentially hinder its legitimacy in the area. Its failure reveals how retributive justice relies on fear to build cooperation. And yet, fear, as we have seen, is not what enables people to move beyond these effects, or to learn to forgive; rather, it is how one practices forgiveness that matters. By affective practice, I am referring to the customs and procedures that are designed to connect people through feelings of trust and empathy. Such practices correspond to the ritualistic mechanisms of Mato Oput (e.g., Ker Kwaro Acholi) that complement the retributive dimension of the ICC's complementarity by merging peace and justice through the positive emotional bonds established under local justice.[40]

Still, the issue is whether this type of hybrid complementarity can positively affect the Uganda government's role in promoting peace and justice. Must, for instance, national laws on immunity continue to serve as a principal means of building such trust when doing so only conflicts with and obstructs the legal constraints of impartiality and the due process of the ICC? How, then, do we begin to get beyond the effects of fear and distrust driving the affective disinvestment in the legal and moral process of administering justice?[41]The question brings us to the next challenge of affective complementarity with the ICC: namely, aligning the ICC's formal restorative dimension with Mato Oput.

Emotions and the Mutual Complementarity of Victims' Justice

Complementarity represents the growing political stakes of extending the ICC's procedures to local justice. The extension is not a top-down but a bottom-up event. The affective dimension of complementarity I want to develop in this last section involves the unstructured potential of aligning the ICC's formal modes of justice and Mato Oput's informal procedures of victims' justice.[42] Having already described the legal and moral propriety of both—or how individuals, states, and communities conduct themselves in accordance with the rules of procedure—it is important to address two features of this dimension: first, how Mato Oput's informal procedures of justice can be properly attuned to the ICC's impartiality and legal standards; and, second, how Mato Oput can be construed as converting the legal constraints of the ICC into extended opportunities for affecting outcomes in victims' justice.

Earlier I showed how the ICC's impartiality standards grew out of the rapid evolution of international criminal accountability norms. The implementation of these procedures represents more than simply putting away the worst of the worst perpetrators but the practical attempt to promote universal decency or an overarching ideal of decency to measure compliance and cooperation with a uniform set of international decency standards. This idea of promoting universal decency, however, sets into motion the conflict between our two strands of liberal and conservative decency, by exposing the tension between impartiality and the partiality associated with preserving the integrity of local customs of justice. More important, it reveals the tacit bias against local justice and its capacity to prevent harm and provide legal remedy to the victims who have been most disadvantaged/affected by or excluded from the legal process.[43] The task of diversifying decency in this context, therefore, is to creatively bring together the formal and informal modes of restorative justice in the most realistic manner—that is, to show how best to diversify the interests in international justice.

The ICC's Restorative Dimension

The ICC consists of several formal mechanisms of victims' justice. This includes the Victims' Trust Fund, which is a body with a separate legal personality. The fund has two mandates: (1) reparations in which the court orders the perpetrators to pay for reparations; (2) and general assistance, which consists of voluntary contributions from donors to offer material support and physical rehabilitation for victims and families in the ICC's situations.[44] The overall aim, as Uri Rosenthal, the Netherlands minister of foreign affairs, states, "is to positively contribute to the lives and dignity of victims within the jurisdiction of the ICC."[45] The most important constraint of the court in this respect is determining how much and to whom should be paid pursuant to Article 75 (1) of the Rome Statute, which holds that "ICC authorities either upon request or on its own motion, in exceptional circumstances, shall determine the scope and extent of the damage, loss and injury to, or in respect of, victims, and will state the principles on which it is acting." Additionally, the victims identified by the ICC cannot initiate the proceedings or recommend the dollar amounts to be paid; only the court can do this.[46] The Rome Statute, it should also be noted, spells out the procedures for offering redress and for determining how and when the victims will receive information and monetary compensation.

Still, the ICC's compensation mechanism has raised concern. William Schabas, for instance, argues that "the concept of international compensation is seductive, but it is not without many practical obstacles. . . . The irony is that these people are the very people who are widely believed to have looted the countries where they once ruled. It may simply be unrealistic to expect the new Court to be able to locate and seize substantial assets of its prisoners."[47] Moreover, under the Victims' Trust Fund, compensation will be based on lost income/wages and the emotional distress caused by trauma (medical costs, for instance). This difference between the individual and community reflects an important and long-standing issue of whether reparations should be devoted to communal reconstruction or be distributed directly to the individuals affected by war in order to best redress their basic needs. The South African Truth and Reconciliation Commission grappled with this issue and settled on the latter. The ICC thus faces the same predicament of placing individual interest above the community and potentially compromising societal healing and rebuilding.[48]

At the local level in northern Uganda, this predicament remains a legitimate concern for officials and the elders who fear that monetary compensation for individuals will weaken the symbolic power of communal compensation. As discussed earlier, tribal justice is a symbolic process involving the bodily capacity to heal. Mato Oput compensation in this sense forms an important part of the communal experience (with both victim and perpetrator participating) of tasting/feeling the resentment and hatred that divides the community. When victims and perpetrators drink the Mato Oput in a public ceremony, they are forced not only to confront their vengeance and guilt but also to feel the effects of isolation caused by these emotions. This experience instils them with a collective desire to reconnect with the community. Yet the experience contrasts markedly with the ICC's mission of isolating the guilt of perpetrators from the community. The goal of mutual complementarity is to bring these two procedures together by locating their points of intersection, before using these points to imagine the combined, positive benefit for the victims. In other words, the task is to show how both can play a mutual role in enabling the victims to overcome their distrust and resentment.

Thus, for example, while the ICC's monetary compensation signifies material remediation of pain suffered by individuals during war, Mato Oput's symbolic power is directly tied to rebuilding social capital or the trust of the community. Neither, it could be said, are themselves adequate to promote a shared sensibility of justice. But both come to rely on one another to actualize the social trust and legitimacy that enable monetary compensation to achieve its effect psychologically and communally (the money can go back into the community). It is this idea of local intervention feeding back up to the ICC that registers the political affect or unstructured potential of the ICC's intervention, that is, how the ICC's procedures of justice can affect and be affected by Mato Oput, and form what we might call the cross-cultural complementarity of justice standards and procedures.

One such emerging standard involves victims' participation. At the ICC, the participation of victims in the legal process is intended to raise awareness of their rights under the Rome Statute, which provides the following: "to assist victims in obtaining legal advice and organizing their legal representation, providing their legal representation with adequate support assistance and information, and to ensure the effective participation of victims in proceedings before the Court."[49] With Mato Oput, one encounters the actual participation in the ritualistic process, which integrates the memories and feelings of the community through these procedures.

In this way, mutual complementarity can be conceived as a relational effect of a hybrid legal-moral propriety in which local tribal customs and international elements of crimes are combined through the dialogue between the international culture of punishment and local values of forgiveness. The interaction between these cultures is affective, and not simply a matter of imposing impartial standards as a condition of adaptation. The ICC, it should be noted, also contains a progressive list of specific elements of sexual crimes, which lie outside the local customs of Acholi justice. This legal-social gap between local and international justice raises the question of how the exclusion of harm perpetrated against Acholi women forces us to confront the effect of global moral propriety; that is, the application of a uniform set of procedural rules, which although predicated on recognizing and presenting different values, triggers the need to defend the difference and the integrity of the local propriety adversely affected or ignored by this application. How, in other words, can communal forgiveness of pain be fully effectual if its source is not recognized or made part of the confession itself? And does this become Mato Oput's own affective limitation and causal source of the political cycle of violence?

The answer seems to lie in the Acholi people's willingness to revise their traditional customs. This does not mean that they need to conform to the specificity of elements of crimes, but rather that they must generate their own outside normative pressures for being inclusive at the communal level. What I mean here is the construction of a generalizable sensibility about inclusion that is not directed from above or simply imposed top-down (which after all triggered the problematic propriety effect in the first place). Indeed, as some have pointed out, the "naming of harms" can lead to omissions that allow some harms to go unrecognized and to continue structuring the political cycle of violence.[50] Rape in this case needs to be felt by the local peoples as a symptom of the violence that divides their community; it must, in other words, resonate the brutal, divisive effects of war. This, in short, is what it means to create an affective mechanism of justice to control the effects of foreign normative pressures and local reactionary pressures.

Affecting Outreach

Another key, practical component of this affective mechanism of mutual complementary is the ICC's outreach program. Established at the fifth session of Assembly of States Parties (2005), it reflects the agreement among ICC officials to adopt a strategic plan for reaching out to the local population in hopes of furthering peace and reconciliation. For many, outreach is both a dynamic and evolving mechanism with an ambitious design.[51] As Patrick Vinck and Phuong Pham put it, "outreach was designed to demonstrate that judicial arbitrariness is no longer an acceptable mechanism,"[52] and that, in constituting a network of ICC officials, lawyers (legal practitioners), activists, media personnel, civil society groups, and local communal groups, it offers accurate and comprehensive information to communities regarding its role and the participation of the local communities in the activities of the court. Thus far, outreach has managed to show extensive coverage of trials and hearings to locals, hold workshops, set up radio talk shows and informational meetings, and conduct surveys about the ICC's activities.

Critics, however, argue that outreach "comes at the expense of domestic efforts to achieve justice,"[53] and to further "educate the stigma of rape."[54] Yet in responding to this criticism, the ICC's outreach unit has begun a more concerted and transparent campaign of enabling the Ugandan population to question gender norms. This has included the launching of an Internet-based Short Message Services (SMS) system to address the topic of gender crimes and the Court's activities. ICC authorities have also established a strong network of gender-based NGOs and community-based organizations and conducted several consultative meetings with over eighty-nine NGOs that have reached out to schools and universities.[55] In the 2009 Outreach Report, ICC officials recommended, among other things, strengthening the capacity of NGOs and the media and ensuring that the local journalists attending The Hague proceedings offer accurate information of the trial. Studies also suggest that there is a growing base of support for outreach and its role in producing the needed communicative links between global and local officials.[56]

In terms of local justice, it is worthwhile to recall that Mato Oput supporters stressed the need to incorporate gender into their truth telling and elder mediation processes. Tribal elders were expected to consult with ICC officials, NGOs, and communal groups in order to determine how best to express or specify the war crime elements of the perpetrators' (voluntary) guilt. Yet it was considered a voluntary moral measure on the part of both the ICC and Mato Oput officials to erect a new threshold promoting the justiciability of these elements and a new set of constraints on gender violence (via its interactivity with the ICC).

Outreach, in short, is not simply about raising awareness of the ICC's standards with local people but providing the Acholi people with the resources and opportunities to become aware of the relation between its justice system and the court's legal operations. As such, the ICC's outreach opens up channels of communication with the local peoples and creates the conditions for capacity building, intercultural dialogue, and participation. Still, this will require us to bring together the informal and formal modes of justice or to actualize value intensity by addressing how the overlooked points of intersection between the ICC's and Mato Oput's restorative dimension can transition us to a higher awareness of their mutual ties.

Conclusion

In this chapter, I discussed the intersection and gaps between Mato Oput's ritualistic customs and norms and the ICC's formal rules of procedure. Bridging these gaps involved a deeper understanding of the limits of local and international justice as well as the political stakes of accommodating the legal rules of a different system of cultural propriety. Indeed, they required us to confront the potential points of intersection of these two sets of procedure and what this meant for applying a bottom-up complementarity and working beyond the constraints of the ICC's uniform set of legal standards. In short, the ICC's top-down complementarity approach exposed the tensions between liberal decency, or the impartiality and rights standards for protecting individuals from harm, and the preservation of local customs and norms concerning dignity protection. The propriety effect of these tensions reflected the affective limitation of the Mato Oput's relation to the ICC's retributive mission or function.

To address the deeper implications of this effect, I discussed the unstructured potential of mutual complementarity, in particular the affective alignment between the ICC's formal retributive mechanisms and Mato Oput's informal restorative procedures. Here I sought to show the possibility of working beyond this affective limitation of the ICC's retributive dimension by locating the points of intersection between these formal and informal features of restorative justice. In showing the hybrid dimension of local and international justice procedures, I concluded that, while still a matter of much conjecture, the connection between local and international justice reflects a realistic possibility of advancing global moral propriety. Not only does it reflect the affirmation of the different rules of cultural propriety but it also entails working toward a more diverse set of international interests regarding justice.

CHAPTER SEVEN

The Roma's Moral Predicament and the European Union

I have seen people in whom virtue was so natural that it was not even noticeable; they followed duty without forcing themselves, performing it as if by instinct. Far from drawing attention to their unusual qualities by talking about them, it seemed as if knowledge of these qualities had not penetrated to them.

—Montesquieu, *Persian Letters*, 1721

One of the central issues discussed in chapter 3 was whether the effects of identity politics had destabilized the liberal global order. There, I analyzed the role of basic rights in extending liberal decency to identity politics, arguing that the extension revealed the political perils and stakes for decency in the post–Cold War era. Global moral propriety was supposed to represent a progressive movement in global politics. But the openness of liberal decency ended up creating effects that worked against the consistent application of decency standards. In other words, in advancing a uniform set of rules to extend and reinforce decency standards, the rapid spread of liberal decency led to many conflicting applications of decency, including right-wing populists' use of decency to justify their racist agendas. Decency in this sense continues to be shaped by the tensions between basic, conservative, and liberal decency, which have exposed the growing hostility of emotions in global politics.

Nowhere has this growing hostility been more evident than in the European Union, which, in the 1990s, set out to constitutionalize the liberal norms of nondiscrimination, minority rights, and the rule of law. As the largest ethnic minority group in Europe, the Roma have arguably received the most recognition and attention. Much of this can be attributed to their long history of oppression. In fact, no other minority group in Europe, with the exception of the Jewish people, has suffered more from the effects of discrimination than the Roma. And yet, the Roma's struggle for fair treatment and equal protection continues to this day, despite the recent political gains achieved through EU legislation and its recent initiative of intercultural dialogue.

Indeed, while the EU has adopted various initiatives of intercultural dialogue aimed at integrating the Roma in Europe, it has failed to work beyond the hostile anti-Roma sentiment fomented by nativist movements in Europe. Although the EU has certainly empowered the Roma over the years, it has not, I argue, managed to overcome the effects of the deep-seated prejudice against the Roma, which continues to reinforce the perception of the Roma's moral impropriety. The Roma's predicament is an example of the retrogressive intensity of decency in Europe, where nativists and populists have applied it to justify the preservation of tradition and law and order at the expense of the Roma. The retrogression of decency's identity politics, I will show, helps us to understand the limits of the EU's liberal multicultural order and the political perils of advancing its transnational moral propriety.

In this chapter, I shall examine the sticking points and disparities between the Roma's political mobilization and their traditional customs, showing how the Roma's political gains at the EU level have come to highlight the increasing political stakes and challenges of bridging the political and moral chasm between the Roma community and national customs, as well as the rising conflict between state-run populist politics and EU legislation. Here, I analyze the historical and political sources of such discrimination against the Roma (or Gypsies in a strictly historical context) in Eastern and Western Europe, before moving on to examine how the EU's transnational laws have failed to overcome the discriminatory stereotypes that persist in various countries, notably, Poland and Hungary, despite the Roma's efforts at building a political coalition consisting of different NGOs (political participation in the EU) and the EU's laws on minority rights.[1]

Persecution and the Noncivilized Peoples

A central theme we addressed in chapter 2 was the exclusionary nature of the civilizational standards of international law in the nineteenth century.

Many of these standards were used to support the self-serving interests and democratic values of European states, which allowed these states to treat non-Europeans as inferior and to marginalize them in international relations. In time, these standards would be replaced by the decency standards of the post–World War II architecture that stressed the dignity of all persons, the international rule of law, consensus, and equality. The idea of basic decency was that in redressing the essential social needs of all people, states also had to commit themselves to the principles of nondiscrimination and fair representation and to learn how to trust and cooperate with one another.

The EU sought to extend this idea through a series of special initiatives of cultural accommodation that provided the basis of rules for reconciling democratic freedom with the cultural rights of traditionally excluded minority groups. In the case of the Roma, the 1990 Convention of the EC, which stipulated an EU directive that would later form the basis of the Schengen Agreement in 1999, offered new opportunities for the Roma and others to adapt their values to the progressive standards of EU minority rights law.[2] As important as this new agenda was, it also involved the difficult task of resolving the deep-seated effects of the Roma's oppression that had shaped their identity.

Tradition and Identity

The Roma's persecution dates back several centuries. In the mid-twentieth century their plight reached a devastating climax. Like the Jews in Europe, the Gypsies (as they were called at the time) experienced severe discrimination from the Nazis, who later targeted them (albeit not officially) for extermination under the Final Solution (1941), the Nazi policy to exterminate all Jews.[3] All told, it is estimated that from 220,000 to 1.5 million Roma lost their lives during World War II. And yet, unlike the Jews, the Roma never gained statehood.[4] Their statelessness, along with their long history of discrimination, constituted a key component of their oppressed status as a minority group, making them not only the special focus of EU law and, later, of civil society building, but also the outsiders who were unable and unwilling to assimilate into Western society (or into European states' liberal democratic systems).[5] Together, such factors reinforced an underlying sympathy for their plight, but also confirmed their long-standing desire to remain outside the full legal scope of civilizational norms. What is important to note is how the word "Gypsies" was synonymous with uncivilized, and as such, the deep-seated tendency to treat the Roma as deviant, dirty, unkempt, uneducated, and lawless.[6] The Gypsies, in other words, were by nature unassimilable people who had to be forcibly integrated in order to become civilized. As Timofey Agarin writes:

> Integration and segregation are phenomena of the same kind: they entrench a dichotomy of "civilized European/uncivilized Roma" to affirm Europeans' myths of their civilizing mission, and as such, relegated Roma to an object-position—the targets of policies designed and implemented by the "subjects" of civilization.[7]

With the emergence of the post–World War II human rights regime, many hoped that the commitment to nondiscrimination would resolve the brutal effects of discrimination. However, its application raised an important question: To what extent should inclusion and participation reflect the new civilized standards of civil society building that could accommodate the cultural values and beliefs of illiberal and seemingly unassimilable groups? The very idea of forced assimilation suggested the fear that some groups would use the special protection to actively preserve their cultural identity. Still, for the Roma, there was little escaping the issue of the authenticity of their values and beliefs and the need to uphold their distinctive way of life in relation to European culture.[8] Their non-Europeanness, or Indian roots, had and continues to remain a source of pride. It is still Roma custom, for instance, to refer to Europeans as "others," or by the Romani word *gaje* (others). *Gaje* entitles all Roma to treat non-Roma as they see fit, meaning that it is European outsiders who lack the moral propriety to live according to Gypsy values. As Iskra Uzunova puts it, "Gypsies generally view the *gaje* as having no sense of justice or decency."[9] *Gaje*, in other words, is how Gypsies assert the duality between injustice and justice to affirm their own identity. For them, it demonstrates an innate sense of decency and fairness that does not need to be validated by the application of civilized standards or etiquette.[10] Earlier we saw how such standards helped support Victorian decency overseas, by allowing British moral propriety to be imposed on the colonial natives. The application of Victorian decency did the very opposite of what *gaje* has long sought to do: to preserve the integrity and difference of the Roma's cultural values. *Gaje* in this context means that the Gypsies' sense of decency is negatively tied to a timeless tradition, that it is rooted in the desire to remain free of European culture or to maintain their identity as non-Europeans. In short, *gaje* is not simply about otherness, but about preserving the Roma' community from outside efforts to corrupt or oppress it.

However, for many, this is precisely what makes the Roma unwilling to fully assimilate into civil society (or incapable of being integrated). By remaining unassimilable, the Roma have shown little willingness to reconcile their culture with national customs and laws of European states, since they believe that their own sense of justice and moral propriety predate the liberal constraints and civil manners of Europe. This outsider status thus raises two important issues: (1) whether their sense of propriety expresses an authenticity or inexpressible moral difference that cannot be judged or valued in accordance with European standards of civil conduct; and (2) if the political need of ending Roma suffering presupposes the political pressures and tensions within the Roma community itself, that is, between their traditional sentiment of preserving their culture and the basic and liberal decency associated with their political mobilization at the EU level.[11] I shall examine the latter in greater detail in the final section of this chapter. The former, though, reflects the difficult struggle to overcome the effects of deep-seated stereotyping such as the Roma's being thieves, vagabonds, and lazy, as well as the challenge this struggle poses to their willingness to fully participate in the EU's liberal multicultural programs/laws, an issue that we shall turn to next.

Liberalism and the Roma's Shame

Martha Nussbaum, as we saw earlier, treated shame as a hostile emotion, or a negative appraisal of one's behavior. Shame, she argued, was about how an individual feels by either not doing enough (or doing nothing at all) to promote a desirable good. But shame, it could be argued, can also be felt collectively and be shaped by the political tendency to repress past memories and to refrain, for that matter, from celebrating the past, for example, Germany. In the context of the Roma, individual and collective shame is not something that suppresses individual development (and the relationship with others), nor any traditional sentiment of preserving the past. Rather, it assumes a mostly positive function of maintaining the norms and roles of the community, that is, of stabilizing social expectations.

Collective shame can also be tied to *gaje* or the Roma's rejection of outside justice and, conversely, the Roma's affirmation of its communal structure, including female domesticity. While it is not a custom supported by today's progressive standards of liberal decency, such domesticity reveals the ongoing tension between liberal decency and Roma tradition. As we saw with the Western interpretation of the veil in the Cairo Women's Mosque Movement, decency was associated with compassion and the freedom of choice. Empowerment through these means meant diminishing the role of shyness, even though shyness was considered a pious private virtue and central to their identity as Islamic women. Much like shyness, shame seems to reinforce a restrictive set of rules of behavior that represses the needs of women while privileging male interests. The Roma, for this reason, have been understandably pressured to conform to these liberal standards of equal protection. But to argue that these are inherently desirable pressures overlooks the complexity of their cultural experience, particularly their past resistance to pressures that involved perhaps the most brutal forms of past mistreatment.

In the 1960s and 1970s, for instance, national governments initiated and maintained eugenic programs of Gypsy sterilization. Human rights organizations claimed that the program was part of a larger plan of genocide, or systematic extermination of the Roma from various Balkan countries. Bad governance and widespread social and patriarchal norms ensured that Romani women would lack access to these mechanisms to find redress. Another abusive policy/practice concerns the trafficking of young brides, which remains a custom among Roma communities (and for some, regarded as a form of human trafficking.). Here, Roma women's bodies have become a political battleground, in which the subjection of their bodies violates the very normative constraints on harming the dignity of others. It becomes important, then, to distinguish between the violations of basic individual rights and the cultural customs and practices that reinforce the vitality of Roma tradition and identity, since the distinction represents the Roma's moral ambivalence toward liberal rights and moral progress, or rather, the conflict between their interest in ending discrimination and their fear of destabilizing the norms and customs of the Roma community. The point of course is that preserving the Roma's traditional moral propriety has long remained their most stable defense against outside pressures or attacks.

Consider, for example, the function of Roma women's wear. Attire and labor is what distinguishes the women from men's daily tasks. However, it is the Roma women, not the men, who determine what to wear and what is and is not shameful. As one Romani woman put it, "Because we have shame, our women are decently dressed."[12] Romani women's traditional attire, which consists of the headscarf, a long skirt, and an apron, constitute the habituated items of pride in the division of the household. And while men may be publicly shamed for performing the same household chores of washing, it is the duty of men to respect the women's role and their onerous possession of shame. Ada Engebrigtsen, for example, argues that shame reflects the division between the people who "have a sense of shame and know how to avoid ridicule, and the people that don't know."[13] The division, she points out, remains crucial to the Roma's traditional social structure. For women, and not men, determine the structure of the community and the restrictions placed on their public role. This self-inhibiting constraint, as Engibrigtsen suggests, is structured in a way that enables the Romani community to maintain its traditional customs vis-à-vis modern liberal rights or moral equality. It seems to have less to do with men's honor and respect and domination over women than with a woman's capacity to possess her own moral independence and space within the communal structure.

From this perspective, the issue of Romani subjection is whether it delimits the men's competition for honor and respect in the public realm. The idea is that the woman's role does not necessarily give men the right to exclude her from taking part in the public sphere (where she may be able to exercise direct, as opposed to indirect, influence over male competition), but rather that her domestic role can be treated as a social determination of the man's acquisition of honor and respect in the public realm.[14] In blurring the line between traditional and basic decency at the local/communal level, this social determination makes it difficult to opt for basic decency to eliminate or transcend this social constraint on equality. The challenge becomes one of balancing Romani shame against the liberal norms of equal protection.

Again, for liberal cosmopolitans, shame remains an emotion that deprives one of positive self-judgment. Nussbaum treated it as one of the enemy emotions of compassion and love, which involved guilt and the low self-worth of the person.[15] Yet, for Romani women, shame remains a way of expressing their contribution to preserving the pride of the Romani community and its unique identity. In this way, the Western tendency to stigmatize shame reveals the disparity between Europe's liberal values and the non-liberal values of the Romani community—hence the difficult task of working beyond this complex bias against Romani women.[16] The role of shame inside the community suggests the different ways of feeling good or bad about something. As Robert Solomon puts it, "We learn what we feel not just by feeling it but sometimes by way of interpersonal feedback, including criticism and bad relations with others."[17] Solomon goes on to claim that emotions, even at the most "personal level," are often a mode of social action and therefore specific to the cultural practices of different groups.[18] This cultural-specific function of emotion might explain why Romani men feel structurally inhibited from demeaning women, for fear of disrupting Romani customs and their public role. In this way, shame allows us to understand the difference between Western liberal norms and the Roma's more informal way of life. This is not to excuse or look past the subjugating role of Romani women, but rather to understand their competing narratives of moral progress and cultural tradition.

To sum up: there exists a dichotomous bias between *gaje* and the deep-seated European prejudice against Roma moral propriety. Both seem to offset one another. However, the Western bias, because of its political power structure, exerts a pronounced effect. Indeed, many have suggested that the Roma not only lack shame but are incapable of reciprocating the benefits of compassion. For Alaina Lemon, such bias requires us to draw "a causal relation between pollution beliefs and social divisions both among Roma and between Roma and [*gaje*]."[19] By offering the binary between pollution and purity, Western scholars end up reinforcing the stereotype about the Roma as being untouchables (that is interchangeable with the Dalit who continue to be discriminated against and severely mistreated in pubic).[20] This modern-day bias, Lemon goes on to argue, is rooted in the misperception that the Roma, with their Indian origin, share a close affinity with the Dalits—that they continue to be born into India's lowest caste system and therefore fated to remain on the margins of society in Europe. Still, to treat the Roma in this manner suggests, as Lemon puts it, that the "tropes of Gypsies as genetically isolated untouchables circulate widely and in high places."[21] In short, the deep-seated, anti-Roma sentiment reinforces public perceptions that the Roma are untrustworthy and incapable of adjusting to the EU's liberal laws and value. This, in turn, has had the effect of increasing the Roma's own moral determination to politically mobilize at the EU level.

The Populist and Nativist Factor

The Roma's political mobilization at the EU level has been one of the more promising developments in EU politics. But it represents, I argue, an ongoing disparity between Roma activism and Romani tradition. Rather than alleviating the effects of prejudice, it calls attention to the political stakes and contradictory outcomes of working beyond the effects of such prejudice. In other words, recognizing the unique difference of the Roma can also become a source of reactionary national pressure against integration. In a sobering letter submitted to the *Central Europe Review*, one detractor wrote:

> I do not think that the Romanies will be ever capable of integrating themselves into European society. A specialist in the cultures of India has written in one book that the Romanies simply have different customs, a different culture, a different morality and so they are encountering problems.[22]

The perception here is that their lack of morality is intricately tied to moral indifference, or their inability to integrate. And it arises predominantly at the national level, where, as we saw in chapter 3, the Roma have been severely discriminated against and negatively impacted by the rise of nativist and xenophobic movements in EU countries, including in Poland, where President Jarosław Kaczyński, the leader of the Law and Justice Party, has stressed Christian devotion and the need for discriminatory laws against the Roma. The deepening discrimination by right-wing populist parties, as we shall see, shows how the Roma have become caught up in the widening gap between conservative and liberal decency in Europe. One might even argue that in inspiring violence against the Roma, nativist politicians have allowed some Roma, or the most persecuted in small villages in Eastern Europe, to fall into a virtual, political abyss between these two dueling decencies—much like the female victims of honor killings.

Still, Roma mobilization at the EU has meant greater participation, representation and legal protection in EU institutional bodies, such as the EU Parliament and the European Court of Justice. But such participation has neither stopped the populist attacks nor resolved the question of Roma cultural identity. As discussed in chapter 3, liberal multiculturalism has been at the forefront of tackling questions concerning the integration of cultural identities at the EU. Its aim has been to implement group-differentiated rights to preserve and transform the cultural identity of Europe's minority groups. Applying these rights was not simply intended to overcome the procedural constraints of liberalism (related to nondiscrimination or color blindness) and the cultural hierarchies and elitism that thwarted political transformation. It was also intended to target the degrees and sources of discrimination.[23] But, in the case of the Roma, this pragmatic project also seems to reinforce the need for cultural preservation in a way that destabilizes the liberal multicultural norms that are supposed to target the deep-seated bias against the Roma.

The Roma in this sense can be classified as the hard case of EU accommodation, in spite of their political mobilization.[24] For as early as the early 1990s, EU officials had been unwilling to label them as either a minority or immigrant group.[25] "Only in the second half of the 1990s," as one report states, "did specialized social and educational programs emerge for the Roma."[26] This might explain why the Roma themselves continue to embrace *gaje* to resist being identified as either a non-territorial European people or an entrenched cultural group in European states, which prefers to remain somewhere in between inclusion and exclusion.

On the other hand, the Roma's political mobilization has created its own political elite class at the EU level, where the goals of social mobility and political integration have remained at odds with the Roma's communal norms and values. If anything, this has revealed the unique challenge of depoliticizing the Western bias against the Roma. If Kymlicka is right—namely, that it is largely the subnational/cultural elites who use and determine the label of authenticity—then we should expect Roma elites to refrain from attacking and violating the cultural norms of Roma communities, especially in Czechoslovakia, Hungary, and Slovakia. But the reality is that it has been the national elites, not the subnational elites, who have exploited the deep-seated anti-Roma sentiment to greatest effect, and who have managed to offset many of the political gains of the Roma (e.g., special protection/recognition of their human rights).

In fact, the populist wave in Eastern Europe, as discussed earlier, has brought to power many nativists who have silently targeted the Roma. In Hungary, President Viktor Orbán is suspected to have supported the collusion between the criminal justice system and paramilitary groups that have attacked the Roma in the countryside. In public, he has done little to stop the attacks on the Roma in countryside villages. In 2013, when one of the founders of the Fidesz Party called the Roma "animals . . . unfit to live among people," Orbán remained silent.[27] Even after the European Court of Justice ruled that the government had done nothing to address the consequences of the attacks by vigilante groups in the countryside, the national government continued to do little to stop the violence. Nativist politics has not only spurred racist attacks that have killed Roma, but it has also legitimized these attacks (via their silence) and reinforced old negative stereotypes of Roma as the vagabond performers who pose a threat to children. In August 2016, for instance, the murder of a nine-year-old girl by a Roma man led to a backlash in a small Ukrainian village, where the residents began to threaten the Roma living inside the village. Authorities were eventually forced to rehouse five Roma families living in the village.[28]

The populist phenomenon is yet another example of anti-Roma sentiment, in which right-wing, nativist political parties have asserted a "race difference" to deny the Roma equal rights, such as equal access to education. For example, in Czechoslovakia, such treatment has taken the form of racial segregation that has led to the creation of "separate schools" for Romani children. As Dimitrina Petrova puts it, "The policy is built on the underlying stereotype that Roma are inferior and that Romani children are not ready for normal school. The result has been a denial of equal educational opportunity for most Romani children."[29] Even so, it is not clear if leveling the playing field at the EU level will enhance these opportunities and their effect on stopping racial profiling or discrimination, as illustrated in France where authorities have been quick to deport Roma suspected of illicit activities.[30] It seems more plausible to believe that political empowerment at the EU level has driven a wedge between their traditional customs and national populist politics, and normalized in the process, the irregularities between their EU activism and the biased national policies toward the Roma.[31]

The political pressures to root out this bias and to treat all Roma equal have had some influence in immobilizing the liberal constraints of the EU's transnational order and its multicultural policies. But is shoring up mutual support of the basic rights of Roma a compelling way to diminish the tension between their traditional values and the basic decency standards of the EU? Concerning this question, Asmet Elezovki states that

> this is a crucial time for dialogue with Roma communities. Throughout history the Roma have been a peaceful people, but problems

> may arise as radical groups grow or move into some communities to capitalise on Roma discontent. A latent risk exists, since enduring in extremely difficult conditions produces fruitful ground for conflict.[32]

As she suggests here, the risk of not actively addressing the history of discrimination against the Roma is that it might allow others to exploit their non-European tradition for political purposes, as the wave of populist attacks against them highlights. Unsurprisingly, this has helped make the Roma the key test case for Europe's evolving moral agenda of diversity promotion (and its progressive laws and standards of minority rights protection) and continuing efforts to open up further dialogue among its cultural minorities. On the other hand, it has also introduced new political pressures that have tested its initiatives for diversity.

A Fragile Liberal Transnational Order

The growing tension between the Roma and national law is as much the outcome of the EU's progressive advances in human rights as it is the result of many financial and political setbacks, including its failure to pass an EU constitution. But the EU remains arguably the most progressive example of what I will call a transnational moral propriety by stressing the interdependence of moral commitments, capacity building, intercultural dialogue, and participation. Intercultural dialogue in Europe stems from the EU's (and its member states') long-standing and innovative commitment to diversity and minority rights protection and participation. In 2008, the EU adopted intercultural dialogue as an agenda, which sought to promote an open exchange among groups including the Roma.[33] As the Lisbon Treaty stipulates, it lies

> at the heart of the European project . . . to provide the means for intercultural dialogue and dialogue between citizens to strengthen respect for cultural diversity and deal with the complex reality in our societies and the coexistence of different cultural identities and beliefs in intercultural dialogue.[34]

For its part, the European Commission adopted its own initiative of intercultural dialogue (2008), in which it focused on promoting dialogue among Roma and non-Roma.[35] At the same time, it has stressed the freedom of movement to diminish statist obstacles, in spite of the growing friction between nationalists and minorities in several European states. But while open borders have provided an important vehicle for integrating the domains of the EU's transnational cultural propriety, it has also exposed the challenge of linking the EU's diversity initiatives to the remediation of the special bias against the Roma.

Some of the early initiatives of the EU's agenda of moral diversity included special legal protection of minorities. In the 1990s, for example, the EU adopted various special minority rights laws that extended the principles of equal treatment and nondiscrimination. These included the Charter on Local Self-Government (signed into law on September 1, 1988), which established two legislative chambers, the Congress of Local and Regional Authorities of Europe,[36] and the Draft European Charter on Regional Autonomy, drawn up by the Third Session of the Congress of Local Authorities on July 5, 1996. Both laws represented the trend toward deeper accommodation or autonomization to remedy the years of discrimination suffered by ethnic minorities in Europe. As Markku Suksi notes, "The entrenchment of autonomy in the EU suggests a necessary and binding measure of the people's right to self-determination, since it places an obligation on the state not to worsen or abolish autonomous arrangements without consent of the inhabitants."[37] Here, the EU's aim was to offer basic protection to minority groups against potential state abuse. Nowhere was this more evident than in the Liechtenstein Draft Convention on Self-Determination through Self-Administration,[38] an initiative designed to promote the flexibility of autonomy. For the legal scholar Gudmundur Alfredsson, the EU's priority of cultural autonomy was considered a desirable instrument, since, as he writes, "it was very flexible and could be used constructively so as to cover different aspects of self-determination and thereby to tailor the degree of self-expression enjoyed by communities to whatever was appropriate in their particular circumstances."[39]

Cultural autonomy, then, became a way of advancing minority rights and targeting the needs of ethnic minorities with strong subnational identities. But this proved to be a fairly limited benefit for the Roma who remained dispersed and less willing to have their customs accommodated. For the most part, the Roma have developed political interests that encompass Roma local values, but do not necessarily seek to preserve their cultural heritage. This has placed the Roma struggle in an even more difficult predicament. For the more they mobilize politically the more it seems that they widen and obscure the gap between their political mobilization at the EU level and the preservation of Roma values. Moreover, it was never clear if there was a distinct set of Roma political interests that were tied to or derived from these customs and values. If the Roma politicians press ahead with cultural autonomy, there is concern that this will divide their communities against one another and impose, rather than cultivate, the mutually shared normative constraints on Roma discrimination.[40] The division, it could be argued, will not only reinforce the prejudice against the Roma and public perception of their moral impropriety but also raise uncertainty about linking human rights protection with the preservation of the Roma's customs and values.

Helen O'Nions, for example, insists that in the case of the Roma, it is necessary to devise a "complementary approach to human rights which emphasizes the importance of cultural identity and autonomy in addition to the prevention of discrimination and promotion of equality."[41] The idea that we discussed earlier was that neither liberal autonomy nor liberal multiculturalism was adequate to actively combat the effects of anti-Roma bias or stigmatization. This was because the Roma still placed considerable emphasis on their communal identity. Preserving this identity through group rights left some Roma isolated or more vulnerable to attacks.

Combatting the effects of this special bias thus required additional measures to counter the tendency to discriminate on the basis of perceived moral impropriety, and to integrate, for that matter, the EU's open-ended transnational moral propriety.[42] In this way, it can be said that the cultural shift to human rights widens this propriety gap by spurring people to see individual human rights and minority rights as the cure-all for the Roma's plight. As Eva Sobotka contends, the shift "offers a redefinition of the problem and the object of policy. This transformation has opened up possibilities for new voices by altering contexts and making new types of action possible, such as Roma rights campaigns, which seemed to emerge virtually out of nowhere."[43] But the Roma's political mobilization did not emerge out of nowhere; rather, it stemmed from the public perception in many societies that nondiscrimination was too permissive, and that to actively promote Europe's largest and most dispersed minority group, the European Union also had to recognize their special identity.

In the late 1990s, for instance, the EU Commission and the Council of Europe undertook sweeping efforts to recognize the special identity of the Roma. Under one of its directives, the Council of Europe declared, "The European identity of Roma is in need of special protection."[44] But in recognizing the special European identity of Roma, such legislation ended up creating the binary relationship between European and national minority. For Peter Vermeesch, the EU's efforts created a political space for state governments to transcend their nationalist politics.[45] These efforts suggest, as he writes,

> that, while other citizens belong to the nation-states, the Roma belong to Europe, thus latching onto the alleged "Europeanness" of the Roma (and their alleged lack of national belonging) in order to exclude them symbolically from their own national space and frame them not only as "Europeans" without any attachment to any particular nation-state, but also as ethnic outsiders and cultural deviants.[46]

The Roma question in Europe is also about how the Roma's political activity at the EU level can complicate efforts to eliminate their marginalization. Neither neoliberal or marketization policies (e.g., single currency) nor the EU's liberal multicultural policies can fully resolve this question and the uncertainty it has raised for resolving the deep divide between the Roma as non-Europeans and Europeans.

It is therefore possible that rather than empowering the Roma, the EU's recognition of the Roma's rights has encouraged some national governments to implement policies stigmatizing the Roma, for being "Gypsy."[47] And yet, the purpose of the European Commission's European Agenda for Culture is to work beyond this divide by influencing "policy-making in the European Union through which national, regional and local policies on diversity and intercultural engagement can improve."[48] Despite this recognition, the difficult question posed by the wave of populist movements in Eastern Europe is how the EU's transnational initiative is inviting the very reactionary pressures that limit and fracture its liberal model of diversity promotion. If it still relies on member state cooperation to enforce its intercultural dialogue initiative, then it could be the case that the national populists have finally exposed the political perils of upholding nondiscrimination norms in a wider community (e.g., the need for deportation and restrictions on access to public goods)? As I have argued, the mutual tension between the nationalists and Roma tradition has allowed the former to use Roma impropriety as a political tool to actively discriminate against the Roma and even kill them. The increasing divide between liberal and traditional decency therefore leaves us with the more important question of how the EU can overcome this growing tension while also attempting to work beyond its own liberal, normative constraints. There of course is no easy answer, but the deepening uncertainty of maintaining the liberal framework of decency standards brings us to freedom of movement and how this principle might shed further light on the moral predicament facing the Roma in Europe.

Freedom of Movement and the Roma as Migrant/Refugee

As already mentioned in chapter 3, freedom of movement remains one of the EU's founding principles. There, we discussed some of the challenges to its codification in the Schengen Agreement adopted in 2004, which formally dissolved all internal borders/customs among twenty-three of the twenty-seven EU member states. Under the Free Movement Directive (2004), each signatory of the agreement is obliged to implement the Directive "without discrimination between the beneficiaries of the Directive on grounds such as sex, race, color, ethnic, or social origin, language, religion, or beliefs."[49] In many respects, the Free Movement Directive has helped the Roma's political cause by legitimizing mobility as a right of all EU citizens. Free movement in this sense seems to cut to the source of the special bias against the Roma: namely their outsider, vagabond stigma. But instead of undoing the stigma of the Roma as lawless, roaming people, free movement seems to have subjected the Roma to more abuse by turning them into the exception to the sovereign state. In effect, free movement works against the Roma's political cause since Schengen only allows EU citizens to exercise free movement. That is to say, if the Roma are not perceived as full-fledged citizens, then it becomes easier to dichotomize between free movement protection and the protection of their vagabond lifestyle. The dichotomy intensifies with political pressure and the perception of threat. And because fear and victimization require images and symbols to personify such threat, there is perhaps no better symbol than the Gypsy folklore of moving caravans and thieves to (falsely) intensify these pressures.[50]

Another way of putting this is to say that the Roma now occupy the margins of these transitional boundaries where the perception of threat to security is produced. Driving this perception is the deep-seated Gypsy stigma. When it is combined with the persistence of Roma culture in many EU states, it constitutes a source of threat to a freedom principle that was supposed to advance their cause.[51] This contradictory effect testifies as much to the embedded bias of peoples as it does to the sovereign foundations of this principle. In other words, the EU's freedom of movement principle relies on state sovereignty to legitimize and validate its measures in EU law. This sovereign factor produces its own imaginary and practical constraints on the EU as an open border supra-state, including the advanced techniques of regulating and monitoring movement and the perceived benefits of living a nonsedentary lifestyle. What cannot be effectively monitored in this case must also be feared—or, better yet, treated with suspicion.

The Roma's long-standing custom of a nonsedentary lifestyle thus symbolizes an existential threat to the freedom of movement principle. Instead of transcending the moral impropriety of the Roma through its open modes of cooperation and customary compliance, it merely neutralizes the perception of this impropriety within its sovereign parameters, where it confronts Roma difference as a nonsovereign source of movement. The nonsovereign dimension of this informal movement (that never needed a right per se to exist) does not disappear, but rather reemerges as an exception to this transnational right/principle. This may be why the Roma continue to present a unique test to the EU's freedom of movement, as highlighted by the French government's exclusion of the Roma. By becoming the scapegoat or exception to the principle, they are the *homo sacer* (sacred or accursed man) of freedom of movement's legalization.[52] The accursed Gypsies, who are citizens of the EU, now define the fragile nature of the EU's liberal transnational order, and, by extension, the susceptibility of immigrants to this exceptionalizing logic used by states and their ruling populists to attack this liberal principle. Thus, for example, in the spring of 2015, British prime minister David Cameron argued that Britain was being forced to share a disproportionate burden of paying for immigrants. He reasoned that it was not obliged to allow an unrestricted number of migrants to access Britain, where social benefits were more generous than some EU countries, and that it was paying more than some countries, offering social benefits for which it was not being compensated.

The EU has also been criticized for not doing enough to assist migrants. The crisis, as we have seen, illustrates the limits of liberal morality, in which treating migrants and the Roma as lazy recipients of charity can fuel the anti-immigrant sentiment that freedom of movement was supposed to in part address. Here, it is important to emphasize the primacy of the Free Movement Directive of EU law and how it assumes primacy in virtually all matters, even though states can interpret the constitutionality of their laws or situations vis-á-vis European law.

In a case involving the threat of migrants to domestic order, the French Conseil d'État interpreted whether EU law, or the EU principle of non-discrimination, took precedence over French constitutional law.[53] It ruled that French courts could retain legal authority under the directive—which allows states, after a three-month trial period—to evaluate the status of migrants who may pose a threat to public safety.[54] Given this tension between the EU's nondiscrimination laws and national laws, there is reason, I have contended, to be skeptical of the concurrent relationship between freedom of movement and cultural pluralism/identity. First, the Directive allows member states considerable leeway in interpreting how to apply the principle—so long as it achieves the outcome desired under the principle. States, for instance, still reserve the right to deal with internal matters that present a conflict between national and EU law, or a threat to public safety in member states. In the case of France, French authorities continue to link the threat of riots to perceived cultural traits of Roma (stealing and other petty crimes) to justify their deportation from France.

The Roma thus remain victims of the fear that pervades so much of promoting freedom of movement: namely, that affirming such freedom leads to more security threats by terrorists and migrants. Under this condition, the deportation or relocation of the Roma becomes the exceptional measure to lifting any EU constraint on the state's capacity to enforce security. This illustrates just how the state, in enforcing its own codes of propriety, can, for domestic reasons, ignore the EU's liberal laws and consequently drive a nationalist wedge into the EU's transnational moral propriety. This wedging process is as much a product of a state's politicizing the issue of immigration as it is the EU's failure to apply intercultural dialogue as a counterweight to these nationalist pressures undermining the commitments to human rights and democracy and dividing national and individual capacity building. The failure, one could also argue, symptomizes the larger tendency to depoliticize—via technocratic, neutralizing measures of integration—the EU's application of its rules and standards concerning human rights protections. Paul

Linden-Retek, for example, claims that the technical rules and measures of the EU have ended up minimizing the political effects of human suffering and dislocation.[55] When, in other words, liberal solutions take on the depoliticized mantle of charity alone, they can legitimize detachment from the suffering of migrants and the need to adjust policies to meet this need, such as the Dublin Accord, which, in stipulating that the countries whose borders the migrants reach first had a duty to process asylum claims, placed disproportionate responsibility on Greece and Italy to handle the millions of new claims for asylum.

Like the refugees of the 2015 refugee crisis (as we saw in chapter 3), then, the Roma continue to feel the effects of their quasi statelessness—stateless in the sense that few have defined their loyalties to the state and more have proved willing and capable of channeling their political grievances to the EU. Many Roma exist somewhere in between EU and national law, insofar as their true loyalties lie in their identity claims against European values. But again, the question this raises is how the laws and perspectives of the EU can be changed to address this political reality of their sense of statelessness. The EU thus faces its own predicament in overcoming what the political scientist Seyla Benhabib argues is the blunted imagination of the West, which needs to be "challenged by the multiplicity of perspectives that constitute public life."[56] In this case, I have sought to frame this issue in terms of the promotion of a multiplicity of moral proprieties, that is, whether or not its policies are diminishing the friction among the four domains of moral cooperation, capacity building, intercultural dialogue, and participation. The EU's progressive laws involve the retrogressive tendencies of decency politics, which is another way of saying that transnational moral propriety can create the pressures that destabilize its development and goals.

Accordingly, it is this restrictive way of openly practicing decency, not liberalism itself (and its accommodation), that may be contributing to the perception of liberalism's limited morality and the mistreatment of Roma in both Eastern and Western EU member countries. The issue thus becomes one of understanding the long-standing tension between decency and difference—how, in this case, the perception of the Roma's moral impropriety reinforces the *gaje* in ways that might better explain how the bias against the Roma can situate itself in between the Roma and the EU. The political stakes could not be higher in light of the killings and deaths of so many non-Europeans at the borders and other areas.

Conclusion: Beyond the Bias

Stereotypes have long fueled fear, resentment, and distrust of the Roma. This long-standing negative sentiment constitutes the special bias against the Roma, which continues to act as a source of the political tensions between the Roma and state officials, and which reinforces perceptions of the Roma's moral impropriety. More importantly, it reflects how the increased friction among these actors has diminished the positive influence of the four domains of the EU's transnational moral propriety, including intercultural dialogue, capacity building, participation, and moral cooperation.

In examining this bias (partiality) and discrimination against the Roma, I also addressed how the exceptionalism of the Roma exposed the affective limitations of EU principles, including the gap between nondiscrimination and freedom of movement and the emotional values of the Roma. These limits, I claimed, showed how the Roma's political mobilization remained in tension with the traditional sentiment underlying their cultural identity. The political effects of this tension—between their treatment and the perception of their moral impropriety—suggest that the intensity of negative emotions is increasing. Rather than validating the flexibility of the normative constraints of EU law, the discrepancy between EU treatment and national populist laws is helping to produce pressures that are both hardening and dulling the normative pull or effect of these constraints. There nonetheless looms the need for a pluralistic transnational moral propriety that can meet the challenge of bridging this gap between the EU and Roma moral propriety.

CHAPTER EIGHT

Decency in the Age of Trump

To insist on a unified cultural framework as a precondition of politics, whether secular or religious, would be to preclude such a framework from political contestation.

—Judith Butler, *Frames of War*, 2010

Those who achieve a special position in history claim a right to it either by virtue of power or by virtue of their goodness.

—Reinhold Niebuhr, *Love and Justice*, 1957

Throughout this book I have contended that decency remains one of the least understood political concepts in the global arena. Despite its wide-scale use in the public discourse, there is little desire to contest its meaning or creedal value. Much of this, as we saw, stems from its cherished ties to tradition and morals, or the idea that we need to preserve decency in much the same way that we preserve tradition. Indeed, decency represents a basic belief in human morality that simply cannot be questioned—which is to say that it expresses a faith in human goodness that has come to assume a permanent role in promoting dignity protection. This is one way that it functions in an orthodox manner to promote the common good and why it encompasses a range of religious and secular beliefs in protecting individuals from humiliation. It is also why we need to develop a more nuanced notion of decency in the political discourse to better gauge its role in the global arena. After all, it is in this arena where conflicts and challenges can compel leaders and officials to project the unquestioned belief in the common good. In terms of the evolution of liberal decency, this meant elevating reason and liberal principles to combat injustice and cruelty. But as vital as this secular projection was, it also exposed the tensions among the three strands of decency. More importantly, it suggested that this unquestioned belief had become a source of tension, one that would eventually play out on the global stage.

The rise of British Empire in the nineteenth century marked the global projection of the liberal and conservative strands of decency. The question this event raised was how British decency could be applied as a universal concept of morality when its global projection remained dependent on national imperial power. In other words, the problem with wedding decency to British power overseas was that the faith in decency became intertwined with the effects of applying imperial power. British decency's application in this sense created the inhumane effects and violence that it was supposed to prevent. Great Britain's civic imperialism thus highlighted the first perilous application of decency to global politics, by disguising the very racial biases of civilizational progress that would eventually weaken the legitimacy of Victorian morality overseas and help create the unstable conditions for the rise of nationalist aggression.

Of course, these destructive effects were never lost on international leaders and policymakers in the twentieth century. As we saw, the post–World War II architecture would see the adoption of sweeping human rights documents and the emergence of many basic standards of decency. The end of the Cold War would thus set the stage for a more open-ended idea of decency to shape global affairs, one that not only involved new mechanisms and laws to overcome the effects of racial and ethnic violence but that also sought to strengthen moral commitments, capacity building, and cultural and political participation. By the late twentieth century, a new global moral propriety took shape, creating the possibilities of practicing decency via the openness and transformative application of liberal principles. Not surprisingly, many liberal thinkers at the time embraced this practical idea of universal decency as a remedy to the harmful effects of strict traditional customs and authoritarian rule.

Yet the effects and tensions did not disappear, nor did the conflict between universal values and cultural pluralism. Rather, they merely assumed a different, albeit less perceptible form of consensus achieved through the moral efficacy of a uniform set of rules. The strength of this consensus, as we saw, was also its liability or peril, for it simultaneously opened up a new space for identity politics to emerge and to redress, for that matter, the particular effects of exclusion and unfair treatment.

Indeed, it revealed not simply the failure to neutralize the effects of projecting liberal decency as a national value but also how decency could be used by right-wing populists to advance and defend their nationalist and racist agendas. The intermingling of decency's orthodox dimension with identity politics thus revealed the perils of its orthodox function and ties to national identity.

In this way, decency can create more problems than it solves. The question is how the projection of its orthodox character creates the conditions for more conflicting applications of decency in the global realm. Does confronting this reality require a heterodox idea of decency that is based on the conflicting and diverse ways of practicing decency in this realm? My answer up to this point has been that in trying to uncover its political reality, it becomes important to understand the different reasons for championing decency as a moral ideal and for preserving morality, tradition, and law and order. I have also suggested that decency's political tensions are not inherently destabilizing, but rather underscore the need to reconfigure the mutually accommodating commitments to global peace and the reconciliation of different, culturally based moral proprieties.

My aim in this concluding chapter is to apply my heterodox idea of decency to understand the grave challenge posed by Trumpism, or President Donald J. Trump's systematic attempts to undo the liberal order by insulting and breaking ties with key U.S. allies. I argue that Trumpism is not simply a perilous challenge to my heterodox idea but constitutes an existential threat to it. As already discussed in chapters 3 and 4, where I addressed deep pluralism and decency's affective mechanisms, the politics of decency can arise from the intensity of hostile emotions. Trumpism has managed to single-handedly expose the instability of this politics—but it has done so by falsely characterizing itself as an agent of anti-corruption and anti-elitism. In other words, by dismissing scientific and political truth, it has undermined not only the liberal and basic strands of decency but also the conservative one that it champions through the slogan of "Make America Great Again" (e.g., its focus on the deregulation of essential environmental pollution standards). In short, Trumpism is neither practicing nor bringing back any past moral propriety, but instead is operating as an alternative reality to the political reality of decency. In doing so, it represents, as I suggested in chapter 4, the heightened political intensity of emotion that is fracturing the politics of decency. This is why we need to critically engage decency's political reality, so that we can become better in recognizing and advancing its diverse qualities and redressing the very harmful effects against the most vulnerable parts of the population.

Decency in a Deepening Crisis

In recent years, writers have come to lament what they see as the decline of decency in politics.[1] Many argue that decency no longer holds a central place in the political imagination; that reclaiming it requires respect for human values and trust in democratic institutions. But decency, I have argued, is not in decline, but rather continues to play a deep, albeit increasingly complex role in today's politics. The trouble is that in treating it as either an overarching humane ideal, a national creedal value, or universal standard of basic, proper treatment, we have failed to engage the forces of identity politics that are testing and shaping it. We have in effect lost sight of how decency has become entangled in today's polarizing politics, that is, how it is being used to gain political advantage and to cast blame on others. To think that we can appeal to decency to move beyond the polarizing forces of identity politics is to confuse the cause and effect of its role in identity politics. Today's conflicting applications of decency, I have contended, reflect the rapid intensification of political tensions that have long driven and shaped the national and global politics of decency. Trumpism, then, is yet another, albeit extreme example of how the perceived decline of decency symptomizes the political reactiveness or uncertainty stemming from the intensity of these tensions. The political challenge of decency is thus a matter of knowing more about how these tensions can create ideological gaps, or how the pragmatic, middle ground tying together the mutual aims of conservative and liberal decency can suddenly turn into a zero-sum game of gaining political advantage that creates a crisis of common decency.

As early as the 2000s, conservative British commentators addressed this issue by arguing that the threat to British decency was tied to the support of the welfare state. Their reasoning was that its expensive social programs had suppressed moral individualism. For example, conservative writer James Bartholomew remarked: "It is as if people feel that the need for them to be decent is satisfied by the payment of taxes. This liberates them to be wholly selfish. The concept of decency and real—rather than politicized—social solidarity has gone out of the window."[2] By insisting that the welfare state had led to the decline of bravery, charity, civility, and kindness, Bartholomew claimed that the United States and the charity and public service programs started by President George W. Bush showed a renewed affinity with these qualities of traditional decency. In short, British conservatives saw British decency as a tool to not only condemn the Labour Party's politics of maintaining the welfare state but also to promote a neoliberal agenda stressing individual economic freedom, lower taxes, and smaller government.

Right-wing populists, however, have used decency in a very different way: namely, to defend against the effects of this neoliberal agenda. In appealing to decent workers or working-class interests, their agenda has involved placing pressure on the British government to exit from the European Union. This pressure, in turn, has allowed populists to drive a wedge between neoliberalism and traditional decency, and in the case of Trumpism, to test both liberal and conservative decency in Britain. For instance, British prime minister Theresa May, in response to a tweet by Donald Trump, which cited the propaganda of Britain First, a right-wing hate group, stated publicly that Trump's support of Britain First was wrong. "The group," she said, "seeks to spread mistrust and division in our communities. It stands against common British decency."[3]

But the populist attacks on common British decency are not simply about sowing distrust. They also demonstrate the increasingly volatile effect of nationalist identity politics on traditional British decency. The latter reflects the broad-based effort to politicize the use of decency, rather than cultivating any genuine sense of decency. As we saw in chapter 2, the rise of basic decency in international relations marked a common-sense framework for both reconciling and developing liberal and conservative strands of decency. From this perspective, decency could be understood as advancing simultaneously at the national and international levels, where the liberal and conservative strands of decency had become so increasingly interdependent that they eventually laid the ground for the influence of the Labour Party in the 1960s and its commitments to promoting progressive international standards and workers' rights. When "New Labour," under the leadership of Tony Blair, emerged in the 1990s, there was an even greater emphasis on nurturing this interdependence. Terms like the "radical middle" conveyed policy measures designed to reconcile communal values in the UK with EU ideals of transnational citizenship. Although Blair's efforts helped to work beyond the effects of deregulation and privatization, they represented the failure to deal with the growing global pressures of neoliberalism, which would culminate in the 2008 global financial crisis. The result was not simply the Great Recession but a crisis of (orthodox) decency, which opened up a political space for radical right-wing populists to operate by exploiting class bias and social prejudice and reverse the gains of this interdependence, such as a strong liberal order, and championing the workers' exclusion from the global economy.

Trump's brand of populism has filled this space to become the critical driver of the decency crisis. Not only has it allowed insults and insincerity to undermine civility and respect for all persons but it also has fractured liberal identity politics through the disingenuous use of equality to attack the special rights of immigrants and other vulnerable minorities. More than anything, Trumpism threatens to create a great divide within decency and to produce even further uncertainty surrounding any universal application of it, as highlighted again by Australian prime Minister Tony Abbott's speech to the UN General Assembly concerning the treatment of dead victims of the Malaysian Airlines Flight MH17, where he called for a "global test of decency." If anything, the current political crisis of decency forces us to understand its weakened role in stabilizing order or addressing the effects of tribalism. This may be why Francis Fukuyama has elected to revert to identity to invoke decency as a national creedal value (as part of America's civic nationalism) that can steer us beyond the tensions of identity politics. But in this way decency would do something that liberal cosmopolitans have rejected: to return more explicitly to the national context of U.S. values to overcome the seemingly emasculated political state of liberal decency. However, it is precisely this national context of universalizing decency that raises the question of how deep the crisis of decency really is, especially given Trumpism's alternative reality of facts and lies that continue to characterize its disingenuous approach to politics.

Beyond Basic Constraint and Orthodoxy?

The challenge posed by the current crisis of decency is that identity politics now tests both the national and global contexts of (orthodox) decency. The trouble with British decency, as we saw, was that it was never truly global in scope, at least not in terms of promoting others' customs and cultural habits. It was rather a national attempt to export British manners overseas through civic imperialism and the mission of civilizing others. Again, Britain's small morals largely determined the liberal trajectory of its global vision of moral progress overseas and the need for imposing a fixed conception of a natural order of humanity on a global scale.[4] Perhaps more importantly, it suggested that the hegemonic basis for enforcing these constraints would always make it a partial project.

If this is true, then the post–World War II architecture may well have marked an important shift from British partiality toward an impartiality that was finally capable of effectively structuring the normative constraints of international order through consensus. But basic decency, as I argued earlier, remained limited in the global realm because of the power politics that restricted the application of liberal decency and its normative constraints. The whole idea of global moral propriety was to work past this restriction, primarily by stressing the voluntary notion of moral commitment and a rule of consensus that was meant to be inherently inclusive. But it was this action that required the fragile role of impartiality to uphold the international rules and to extend the normative constraints of tolerance to identity politics (or cultural accommodation). This, as we saw, represented a new tension that extended all the way to the very need for refraining from imposing values on others. As Karl Popper, the twentieth-century philosopher, wrote:

> The use of political means for imposing our scale of values upon others is a very different matter. Pain, suffering, injustice and their prevention, these are the eternal problems of public morals, the "agenda" of public policy. The higher values should very largely be considered as "non-agenda," and should be left to the realm of laissez-faire.[5]

Popper's mistake, though, was to believe that impartiality could neutralize these political effects and pressures. It was as if to say that there was a natural, given link between decency and liberalism that could anchor and support the permanent constraints of tolerance in a liberal democratic society.

But nationalist identity politics continues to challenge the extension of these normative constraints. By politicizing the strict propriety of national customs in countries with severe discriminatory laws against the LGBTQ community, it has exposed the widening rift between not only liberal and conservative decency but also conservative and basic decency. Indeed, there is still the tendency to forget just how powerful the national prejudice against LGBTQ members can become when it is politicized or linked to the defense of a national identity under threat by Western liberal values. If anything, this should remind us of the powerful sentimental forces that inform the reactionary politics of conservative decency. The fact that we are all creatures of habits and customs and learn to abide by accepted rules of conduct means that our human instinct for self-preservation can be just as powerful as the humane instinct of saving others. Indeed, the memory of the past can become an important conduit for conveying this human instinct. In the last volume of *Á la Recherche du Temps Perdu* (Remembrance of Things Past), Marcel Proust wrote about the symbols that allowed him to recover moments in the past, like the madeleine cake, which resonated with the smell and taste of his love for things already lived.[6] But for Proust it was not just what we could recover but also what we learned to unconsciously repress in the course of upholding customs. Indeed, in the opening scene of *Sodom and Gomorrah*, he describes in allusive detail a homosexual act in Monsieur Charlus's garden. Yet instead of condemning the act, he begins to delve into its mysteriousness and its peculiar place in the social reality of higher society circles, asking whether it can ever be reconciled with the conventional manners, tastes, and habits of French upper-class society in the nineteenth century. The threat of such offensive behavior, he suggests, must be kept in check by the accepted rules of propriety, meaning that society needs to remain silent on its existence. Silence in this respect reinforces the bias and prejudice in politics, by serving as an unconscious and accepted means of repressing and harming the identity of others. When the effect of this silence enters into political consciousness, it leads to angry demands to be heard, to have one's existence and dignity recognized. If this means returning to a past social order to regain such recognition, then the issue is whether the special rights granted under the current order should be respected and recognized (e.g., those of the LGBTQ community and other minorities). This is the issue that looms over the Trump administration.

But Trumpism is not simply about defending a past social order. It is also a movement that aims to use the existing tensions between conservative and liberal decency in identity politics against decency itself. By associating liberal identity politics with the authoritarian quality of political correctness, it has managed to use this quality to attack the basic rights of these minorities. The elusive and particularly destructive nature of Trumpism, though, is that it relies on dishonesty and cruelty to extend its reactionary brand of conservative decency. This at least is how it inverts its own conservative decency and the heterodox idea of decency: by creating an alternative reality that is always offensive, but never defensive; that shows how offensiveness can support its alternative reality (to dramatic effect), even though it is this offensiveness that undermines the very notion of alternativeness/heterodoxy. In other words, there can be no logical alternative to this alternative reality; and yet, it is in this way that its reality becomes self-refuting to the extent that the truth is no longer the truth but a tool to compete against and defeat one's enemies. There is, in this alternative reality, no room for apologies—only the endless space for impulsive, unrestrained action. Moreover, to admit to any weakness would mean submitting to the actual truth of human fallibility and the constraints of the system. Trumpism in this sense represents a false confrontation with decency's political reality, since it displaces the tensions driving this reality and absorbs all contradictions into its alternative, self-consuming reality. Accordingly, the effects of this false confrontation highlight the extreme perils of the instrumentalizing power of decency, where the confrontation with the limits of liberal and conservative morality means eliminating not only these limits through impulsive action but either isolating one from another or destroying the tensions between these various elements of decency. This is why cruelty and violence become necessary in Trumpism, since there is no element of decency left to resist its impulsivity, no belief in moral truth to provide a final check or say on policy.

Nowhere is this idea more evident than with the separation of migrant children from their parents at the U.S. border. The Trump administration's policy of forcible separation cuts directly to the extreme perils facing decency by eliminating the very need to confront the tension between conservative and liberal responses to effective immigration reform. Getting tough means in this case inflicting cruelty on the life and dignity of the most disadvantaged. The question is how does such cruelty signify the wrong kind of confrontation with moral exclusion by seeking to eliminate identity/difference and the human dignity of migrants? How, in other words, should we understand the moral vacuum of such resentment that fuels such cruelty and false confrontation?

Reclaiming Decency

To answer this question, we need to return to the issue of the intensity of emotion and affect, in particular, how Trump's heated emotional responses tend to remain untethered to the idea of decency. As I have contended, Trumpism undermines both the orthodox and heterodox idea of decency by reclaiming a past social order that effectively divorces us from the progressive qualities of decency, while championing decency's retrogressive tendency that I discussed in chapter 3. If, in other words, Trumpism means disengaging from the diverse emotions involved in applying (and integrating) the idea of decency, then its disruptiveness prevents the investment in the values and morality of fair and respectful treatment. Throughout this book I have referred to this in terms of affective disinvestment, a condition in which the intensity of emotion lacks any affective mechanisms to reconnect us to or move beyond the normative constraints of the system of governance (via intercultural dialogue). In the case of the caravan of migrants from Central America seemingly charging toward the U.S. border, Trump used the terms "aliens" and "invaders" to exaggerate the threat they posed to national security. And in an effort to block their entry, he sent his own cavalry—more specifically, 15,000 active duty troops—to the border to stop them. Meanwhile, local militias voluntarily moved to the border to assist these efforts at increasing border security.

These moves may have earned political points for taking border security more seriously, but together they show how fear, hate, and distrust can drive hardline policies that refuse to confront the reality of the caravan: namely, that most, if not almost all, the people, are innocent people fleeing the gang-related violence in countries such as El Salvador and Honduras where there is little or no rule of law. In addition, it should be noted that the United States deported these very same gang members back to their own countries, where their growing influence over society has limited the government's ability to stop the (gang-related) violence. The idea, then, is that hostile emotions can become divorced from the reality that determined their existence and intensity. Rather than investing in the values supporting the legal mechanisms of accommodation, populist resentment detaches itself from the very affective mechanisms that can resolve the effects of forced migration. In short, affective disinvestment allows us to understand populism's false engagement with the political reality of these effects.

This brings us back to the idea that emotions can express the diverse practices of decency across culture. Delving into the differing cultural contexts allowed us to test the moral limits of liberalism (or the common good) and to expose the nuanced link between culture and decency. As we saw with the Roma predicament, political mobilization has failed to resolve the effects of their marginalization; instead, it has revealed the deep division between their Europeanness and non-Europeanness, and the tension between the Roma's political gains and their traditional community. Such tension is the reason, one could argue, that the EU Council has focused its attention on the Roma through their agenda of intercultural dialogue. But whether this has made any substantial difference still needs to be determined, especially if we are to effectively address the question of the Roma who continue to adhere to the traditional norms and customs of their communities. On the other hand, it is precisely this tension that the nativists have seized upon to attack the Roma via the rogue, vigilante groups that enjoy the silent support of their national governments, and that the EU seems unable to stop, much less overcome.

Still, this is where the affective mechanism of complementarity may help inform our understanding of heterodox decency or what I am calling the affective reinvestment in the new conditions of communication and interaction. Complementarity, as I suggested earlier, cannot escape its political affects or ramifications. Its application stands at the political intersection of local and global efforts to implement and enforce the mechanisms of legal rules and judgments. Yet the tendency of many Western scholars is simply to treat decency as a basic value (judgment) of accountability. To achieve the hybridization of justice sentiments, it is not enough to merely adjust the liberal norms of justice; one must focus on the possibilities of affective mutual accommodation of contending political and legal proprieties. This was one way in which I sought to situate the politics of affect in the evolving intersection of international criminal justice and local justice. For the Acholi people, vengeance not only intensifies the divisions within local communities—it also tests the integrity of their tribal ethos.

In short, decency can be deployed in a number of ways to affect political outcomes. The pressures that determine these applications in the political arena can also intensify the emotions dividing people on various issues, including immigration and combating terrorism. Today, this intensification has reached levels that seem to contradict the very core idea of decency: namely, treating all people humanely and with respect, especially the most innocent. Yet the need to promote ethnic and racial inclusion, rather than helping us to confront and redress prejudice, has given way to hostile claims of white working-class exclusion, media bias, and even willful ignorance about scientific facts.

The Future of Decency in Global Politics

The final question we need to ask, then, is whether controlling for such prejudice through today's high-tech mechanisms of communication will help us to modulate these effects and therefore make us more decent. One can certainly argue that social media, while serving as a forum for abuse of women and minorities (e.g., Facebook's role in promoting attacks on the Rohingya in Myanmar, and the sexual attacks on women who speak out), has helped to connect people and to directly expose the actions of those defying societal norms and practices against abuse. In recent years, for instance, it has provided an open forum for people to voice their past abuse and mistreatment. As the most high-profile particular forum, the hashtag #MeToo movement finally enabled silenced women (and men) to call attention to their unreported incidents of sexual misconduct perpetrated by public officials, entrepreneurs, and political representatives. The result has been a new reckoning with past abuses, which has encouraged people to confront the harmful effects of past and existing social norms.

But the #MeToo movement also underscores how the Internet facilitates both tolerance and intolerance, connection and disconnection, and even hatred. In particular, it has exposed the political tensions between those speaking out and those leveling hostile accusations that the movement has gone much too far. The Brett Kavanaugh hearings, as mentioned earlier, revealed intense anger on both sides regarding the source of improper sexual misconduct. Supporters of the judge were quick to defend his reputation and to voice their own anger about the harm inflicted on him. However, many of these supporters also accepted the credibility of Christine Blasey Ford's testimony. Confronting these political effects of male bias thus produced contradictory applications of decency and its moral dissonance. If anything, it meant that we still need to get at the source of the abuse itself: that there can only be one true victim and that recognizing this fact involves treating victimhood as an end in itself, not simply as a means of excluding others' experiences.

It is therefore worth stressing the need for more critical scrutiny of social media's role in creating such political tension. Facebook, for instance, still must find ways of disabling the fake news that has created political uncertainty and promoted further confirmation bias. In an interview, the former president Barack Obama commented on how the social media had become a source of division: "One of the biggest challenges we have to our democracy is the degree to which we don't share a common baseline of facts. . . . That's what's happening with these Facebook pages where more and more people are getting their news from. At a certain point you just live in a bubble."[7] In short, Facebook and Twitter officials have not been able to design algorithms capable of fully deciphering what is and is not fake news (this has led to increasing congressional scrutiny of its own practices). In some cases, the indecipherability has had severe effects on the media in general. In November 2017, for instance, President Trump took to Twitter to attack the international division of CNN, which had reported evidence pointing to the practice of slavery inside Libya.[8] The Libyan government, however, then referred to his tweet to express uncertainty about the report, which had the effect of not simply undermining the original report but also of raising the political and human stakes of covering the news, since it placed these reporters in greater danger.

The social media in this respect has closed off as much as it has opened up encounters among individuals, groups, and organizations. This is not to say that it represents an inherently flawed process of resolving the effects of bias through its many sophisticated, seemingly unbiased algorithms. Rather, it is that the presumption of unbiased algorithms can be misleading, insofar as these algorithms can also determine the preferences of its users by automatically selecting news and events based on their activity or likes and preferences. This has led some to conclude that the social media has become the elephant in the kitchen on confirmation bias: that it is failing to promote not just civility but also the heterodox idea of decency in which we learn to reconcile biases rather than simply combating the bias of the enemy.

Still, it would be misleading to say that these combative attacks show that decency in general is coming to an end. Clearly, the greatest test facing decency is not simply the instability of the liberal international order but also the idea that we still need to reclaim the progressive qualities of decency from Trumpism's seeming colonization of its retrogressive dimension. Biases, in other words, do not die, but take different forms that continue to define the way we identify with the world, whether for liberal or conservative sentimental reasons. But to confront this political reality is not to surrender to or excuse the political attempts to manipulate these biases. It is to recognize that the struggle for decency is about the diverse ways of practicing an inviolable humane sentiment: namely, protecting the needs and rights of the innocent and most vulnerable from harm and violence. It is also to demonstrate that the violence committed against the innocent is the most reprehensible pain that connects the multiplicity of cultural proprieties in the open-ended struggle to be decent.

In *The Doomsday Machine*, Daniel Ellsberg argues that the political stakes of decency could never be higher in terms of starting a nuclear war.[9] Much of this is due to the fact that there is no person to prevent the leader of the United States from initiating a nuclear war. As Ellsberg notes, there have been numerous instances where, if it were not for the restraint of radar operators, such as when a flock of geese was mistaken for incoming missiles on the radar, nuclear war would have ensued. This, of course, makes the nuclear standoff with North Korea all the more instructive of the need for diplomatic decency in which decency standards are consistently upheld through a propriety of negotiation or proper respect for the rules of conduct for preventing war.[10] For as pressures mount between the United States and North Korea, many are left to wonder if the end of the world will boil down to two leaders insulting or dreading one another, as in this case of Kim Jong-un calling President Trump a "dotard," and Trump, in a speech delivered in Alabama on September 23, 2017, labeling the North Korean leader "little rocket man."[11] Even though Kim recently pledged to enter into a treaty with South Korea to denuclearize the entire Korean Peninsula, the specter of nuclear war still looms over the talks.

These and other man-made threats are not likely to disappear, nor diminish in their intensity. This may be why today's proxy wars have had such destructive impact on global moral propriety and its domains of moral commitments, capacity building, and participation in global politics. But, again, much of this can be attributed to how our solutions to moral conflicts tend to require a distance from the political reality shaping the contradictory applications of decency. As I claimed in chapter 3, populism was not caused by liberal identity politics: it had already infiltrated the production of global moral propriety. And yet, in framing the hostility of populist movements as symptomatic of the liberal system, many tend to downplay the legitimate needs or experience of these populist followers. For many liberal thinkers, it becomes all too easy to see inclusion as *the ideal way* to work permanently beyond tribalism and its propriety effects.

It is therefore not surprising that decency continues to reflect a moral orthodoxy of the common good. But the problem with depoliticizing decency is that it ignores the contradictory forces shaping its trajectory. The result is that we end up obscuring the relational possibilities of a diverse sensibility of fair treatment. The future of decency may have less to do with when good men do nothing than with the rise of strongmen around the world who can use this precept to undermine the very need for such a diverse sensibility in justice. Still, a more theoretically robust notion of decency may well begin to allow us to scrutinize these hollow beliefs and to move from an orthodox to a heterodox idea of decency.

Notes

Chapter 1

1. U.S. Senate 1954.

2. That is to say, it has come to play an important part in politicking or political campaigning. See, e.g., Samuels 2017.

3. Allen 2017.

4. Ibid., 135.

5. Fukuyama 2018.

6. Ibid., 106.

7. Krugman 2018.

8. Ash 2016, 26.

9. Senator John Cornyn of Texas invoked Joseph Welch's famous statement of "have you no decency" but omitted the words "sense of."

10. See. e.g., Ikenberry 2017; Nye 2017; Mazarr 2017; Mounk 2018; Kirchick 2018.

11. Mishra 2016, 49.

12. See, e.g., Mishra 2017; Hall 2013; Margalit 1990.

13. Allen 2017, 135–38.

14. Rawls 1999.

15. Miller 2007.

16. See, e.g., Nussbaum 2013, 6–8; Talbott 2005; Beitz 2009.

17. There has been considerable attention paid to what has become known as a "third wave" of global justice, which situates itself between the statism of Rawls's theory of justice (first wave) and the globalism of liberal cosmopolitan thinkers (second wave). A third wave of thinkers, which includes David Miller, examines the plurality of grounds for promoting justice. I shall steer clear of situating my analysis within this debate, since the debate largely avoids the implications of international cultural pluralism found in Rawls's *The Law of Peoples*.

18. See Davetian 2009. For an historical context of British decency, see Wilson 2007. A contemporary assessment of the loss of civility can be found in. Carter 1998.

19. Oxford English Dictionary 2018.

20. Packer 2018.
21. Paige 2002.
22. See Acemoglu and Robinson 2012, 308.
23. "Obama's Speech on Libya" 2011.
24. See Mitchell 2014.
25. Nussbaum 2013, 11.
26. Brubaker 2017.
27. Rancière 2010, 10.
28. Ahmed 2014.
29. Massumi 2015, 81.
30. See, e.g., Mhurchú and Shindo 2016; Inayatullah and Blaney 2004; Connolly 1991.
31. I shall herein refer to Connolly's pluralism as "deep pluralism."
32. Connelly 2005, 1995.
33. Berlin and Jahanbeloo 1991, 114.
34. Hobbes, *Leviathan* 1996, 69.
35. See Davetian 2009.
36. See Hall 2013.
37. Peter Gay used the term the politics of decency in this manner. See Gay 1969.
38. Hitchens 2012, 235.
39. Quoted in Sivananda 1957, 406.
40. Subramuniyaswami 2006, 197.
41. See Paige 2009.
42. Gomes de Matos 2009, 22.
43. Charter for a World without Violence 2010.
44. See Fabre 2012; Walzer 2006.
45. Cf. McMahan 2009, 6.
46. See Atwell 2004.
47. See Schwartz 1992, 12–15.
48. See Bell 2007.
49. Burke 1991, 8:248–49; see also Burke 2008.
50. See Burke 2000.
51. Orwell 1952, 81.
52. Popper 1962, 236–38.
53. UN General Assembly 1948.
54. Ibid.
55. UN High Commissioner for Refugees 2011.
56. Organization for Security and Co-operation in Europe (OSCE) 1975.
57. African Charter on Human and Peoples' Rights 1981.
58. European Community 1986.
59. Shue 1996.
60. See, e.g., Held 1995; Etzioni 2004; Kaldor 2003.
61. It was common to hear such terms as collective belonging, global citizenship, and global society to convey the idea of universal decency.
62. The European Institute of Comparative Cultural Research, "What Is Intercultural Dialogue?" http://www.interculturaldialogue.eu/web/intercultural-dialogue.php

63. United Nations Framework Convention on Climate Change, Paris Agreement, 2015.
64. UN General Assembly 2005.
65. Mitchell 2014.
66. Ibid.
67. Kymlicka 2007, 183.
68. See Duncombe and Dunne 2018, 25–26.
69. Colgan and Keohane 2017, 39.
70. See Bartholomew 2014.
71. See Mishra 2017.
72. Gettlemen and Raj 2018, 8.
73. Ibid.
74. Rubin 2016.
75. Scott 2007.
76. Wagner 2016.
77. Nichols 2017, 66.
78. Pehe 2011.

Chapter 2

1. Davetian 2009, 321–24.
2. Ibid.
3. Hobbes 1996, 69.
4. See Cassirer 1951.
5. See Gay 1969.
6. See Israel 2001.
7. Ibid., 171–72.
8. See Spinoza 1955.
9. See Israel 2010.
10. Gay 1969, 295.
11. Israel 2010, 165.
12. Ibid., 166.
13. Gay regarded them as the perfectionist conscience of their time and even the precursors of positivism. See Gay 1969, 397.
14. See Rousseau 1992; Toulmin 1990.
15. Locke deliberately excluded the Catholics and limited tolerance to the Protestant sects.
16. Locke 2006, 289.
17. Voltaire 1995.
18. Ibid., 3, 49.
19. Gay 1969, 399.
20. Montesquieu 1989, 114, 256.
21. Hobbes 1996, 69–70.
22. Rousseau 1987, 79.
23. In *A Vindication of the Rights of Woman*, Mary Wollstonecraft took Rousseau to

task for denying women their rightful and natural place in the struggle for freedom. She argued that Rousseau had arbitrarily justified the very oppression and intolerance against women that he condemned. See Wollstonecraft 2004, 179–82.

24. Kant 2007, 49.
25. Ibid.
26. Shaftesbury 1884, 42.
27. See Smith 2009.
28. Ibid., 28.
29. Raphael 2007, 41-42.
30. Smith 2009, 59.
31. Ibid., 61.
32. Ibid., 38.
33. See Griswold 1999, 39. The idea of limiting friendly relations may have struck many supporters of civilization as destabilizing, but in fact, as Griswold puts it, "its instability makes intelligible the decline of sympathy—which one would have thought the glue holding community together—into a group or narcissism."
34. Smith 1937, 423.
35. Ibid.
36. Ibid., 740.
37. Constant 1988, 80.
38. Burke 1987, 70.
39. Pitts 2012, 77.
40. Mehta 1999, 76.
41. Appiah 2010, 115.
42. Ibid., 115.
43. Burke 1987, 45.
44. See Burke 2008.
45. Ibid.
46. O'Neill 2016, 4–5.
47. See Burke 2000.
48. Davetian 2009, 184. See also Otter 2002.
49. Wilson 2007, 29–30.
50. Ibid., 30.
51. Bell 2011, 185.
52. Ibid., 138.
53. Ibid., 139.
54. Ibid., 186–88.
55. Briggs 2009, 392.
56. Ibid., 393.
57. Davetian 2009, 180.
58. Quoted in Wilson 2007, 21. In Byron's concessional poem, the tragic hero Manfred is depicted as a hero posing as an imperfect, flawed character, who holds little or no respect for the artificial ways of the world and who wonders in search of the self in nature, his ultimate refuge.
59. Magill 2012, 108.
60. Ibid., 107.

61. Davetian 2009, 178.
62. Ibid., 207.
63. Wilson 2007, 158.
64. Ibid., 20–21.
65. Elias 1981, 270.
66. Ibid.
67. Davetian 2009, 185.
68. Ibid., 186.
69. Darwin 1859.
70. Quoted in Wright 1930, 11–12.
71. Mill 1962, 142.
72. Sylvest 2007, 53, 60.
73. Gong 1984, 14–15.
74. See Pitts 2012.
75. Ibid., 50.
76. See Comte 1957.
77. See Fitzmaurice 2012.
78. See Koskenniemi 2001.
79. Such displacement breaks with the long tradition of natural law in nation building. As Emer de Vattel maintained, "Nations do not acknowledge any other law than that which nature has established." Vattel 2008, 11.
80. Fitzmaurice 2012, 139.
81. Koskenniemi 2001, 105–6.
82. Spencer 1982, 27.
83. Pitts 2007, 69.
84. This is one reason why the practice of capitulations in the Ottoman Empire proved a particular sticking point in extending the standards of civilization to the Ottomans. Capitulation was an arrangement made by the sultan, in which foreigners were granted privileges. Christians confused it as treaties.
85. Koskenniemi 2001, 135.
86. Halévy 1947, 304–5.
87. Gong 1984, 51.
88. Elias 1981, 366.
89. Anghie 2004, 168.
90. Freud 1961, 49–50.
91. See Boahen 1987.
92. Anghie 2004, 94.
93. Davidson 1992, 67–68.
94. Koskenniemi 2001, 131.
95. Ibid., 135.
96. den Otter 2007, 92.
97. James 1963, 111.
98. Gandhi 1990, 89.
99. Ibid., 238.
100. Van Reybrouck 2010, 214–16.
101. Fanon 1963, 41.

102. As a trained psychologist, Fanon studied the connections between skin color and inferior self-images, concluding that darker skin colors tended to correspond to negative self-images.

103. Gibson 1999, 493.

104. Anghie 2004, 184.

105. Ibid., 189.

106. Ibid.

107. See Roach 2005b, 22–23.

108. Italy's invasion of Abyssinia, for example, amounted to a clear-cut violation of Articles 12, 14, and 15 of the League Covenant, in which all members were required to consult the Council and Permanent Court of International Justice before declaring or committing war against another nation. See Covenant of the League of Nations 1919.

109. Benjamin 1968, 259.

110. Lauterpacht 1938

111. Schmitt 1996.

112. See Orwell 1936.

113. Stewart 2003, 29.

114. Orwell 1933, 204.

115. Stewart 2003, 26.

116. Davetian 2009, 213.

117. Tocqueville 1945, 252.

118. Pragmatism took root in America with the ideas of William James, Charles Peirce, Oliver Wendell Holmes, and John Dewey. See Menand 2001.

119. See Turner 1892.

120. Davetian 2009, 252.

121. Meacham 2006, 24.

122. Ibid., 158.

123. Ibid., 120.

124. Ibid., 207.

125. See Mouw 1992.

126. See Black 1978.

127. In their attempt to preserve traditional customs and family values in America, the Moral Majority has found common cause with the secular aims of liberal decency by aligning with liberal feminists to fight the exploitation of women in the pornography industry and sex trafficking.

128. Morsink 2009, 25–26.

129. Quataert 2009, 56–58.

130. Ibid.

131. See Moyn 2010, 46–47. For a critique of human rights as a liberal ideology of the West, see Mutua 2002.

132. Ehrenfreud 2013, 8–9.

133. Roach 2012, 65.

134. Jackson 1945.

135. Ibid.

136. The United States, for all its moral interest in the rapid evolution of international criminal justice norms, has become one of the most vocal skeptics of the ICC.

137. The UN General Assembly ultimately decided that South Africa's discriminatory treatment ran counter to the spirit of Chapter 37 of the UN Charter. See UN General Assembly 1966.

138. Quoted in Andemicael 1976, 123.

Chapter 3

1. See Jones 2016.
2. Niblett 2016.
3. Malik 2016.
4. Nussbaum 2015, 68; see also Rawls 1999.
5. See Connelly 2005, 1991.
6. See Shue 1996.
7. Ibid., 81.
8. See Kateb 2011, 16, 66.
9. For a critique of the ticking time bomb theory, see Waldron 2010. On the issue of the death penalty posing a challenge to the notion of an evolving standard of decent punishment, see Atwell 2004.
10. Fierke 2015, 50.
11. Rosen 2012, 114.
12. Roorda 2014, 34.
13. United Nations 2000.
14. International Labour Organization 1999.
15. European Commission 2013.
16. See Mackie 1977.
17. Lieberman 2007, 4.
18. See UN Security Council 2009.
19. European Institute of Comparative Cultural Research, "What Is Intercultural Dialogue?" http://www.interculturaldialogue.eu/web/intercultural-dialogue.php
20. European Commission, Intercultural Dialogue. https://ec.europa.eu/culture/policy/strategic-framework/intercultural-dialogue_en
21. UNESCO, "Intercultural Dialogue." https://en.unesco.org/themes/intercultural-dialogue
22. See Marteens 2011.
23. Miller 2007.
24. See, e.g., Kuper 2005; Caney 2005; Tan 2004.
25. See, e.g., Bull 1977; Vincent 1986; Linklater 2009.
26. See Clark 2007.
27. See Margalit 1990.
28. Ibid., 29.
29. Ibid., 121.
30. Ibid.
31. Ibid., 129.
32. For an excellent analysis of this point and relationship between humiliation and global conflict, see Lindner 2009 and Lindner 2018; see also Saurette 2006, 495–522.

33. UN General Assembly 1998.
34. See Roach 2005a.
35. See, e.g., Pogge 2008; Buchanan 2000.
36. Rawls 1999, 3.
37. Ibid., 37.
38. Ibid.
39. Ibid., 38.
40. See Walzer 1983, 273.
41. See Walzer 1994, 16–17.
42. Rawls 1999, 67.
43. Ibid., 38.
44. See Reidy 2004, 310; see also Martin and Reidy 2006.
45. See Talbott 2005, 79–80.
46. Ibid., 164–65.
47. See Nussbaum 2013.
48. Ibid., 10.
49. Ibid., 17.
50. Miller 2007, 125.
51. Ibid., 181.
52. See, e.g., Beitz 2009; Kuper 2004, 22–23.
53. Beitz 2009, 145–46.
54. Kuper 2004, 20–21.
55. Ibid.
56. Seth 2014, 20; Landau, Verjee, and Mortensen 2014.
57. See, e.g., Williams 1996; Gutmann and Thompson 1996; Horton and Mendus 1999.
58. Edyvane 2012.
59. Kymlicka 2007, 85.
60. Ibid., 121.
61. Ibid., 12.
62. Ibid., 81.
63. Ibid., 164.
64. Kymlicka also argued how spreading liberal multiculturalism could backfire in postcolonial states that have come to see it as a form of Western imperialism. Ibid., 166.
65. Ibid.
66. Santora and Erlanger 2018, 6.
67. Kingsley 2018, 18.
68. Massumi 2015, 11.
69. See Santos 2002.
70. See Campbell and Schoolman 2008; cf. Wenman 2015.
71. Campbell and Schoolman 2008, 11.
72. Connolly 2005, 43.
73. Ibid., 47.
74. Ibid., 60.
75. Connolly 1991, 91.
76. Connolly 2005, 64

77. It also differs from a relativistic notion of decency, which affirms the power of faiths to subvert the hegemonic culture within territorial sovereign spaces.
78. Connolly 2005, 50.
79. Feldman 2015, 4.
80. Ibid., 10.
81. Agamben 1998.
82. See Foucault 1977.
83. Grant and Mirof 2018.
84. Juss 2004, 290.
85. See, e.g., Kotef 2015; Cresswell 2007.
86. It should be noted that freedom of movement encompasses three freedoms—entry, residence, and exit—and expresses a basic right that "is an integral part of the enjoyment of anything as right" (Article 13 of the Universal Declaration of Human Rights). See also Article 12 of the International Covenant on Civil and Political Rights (1966) and Article 12 of the African Charter on Human and People's Rights.
87. Bigo 2011, 32.
88. See, e.g., Jones 2017; Brown 2010.
89. King 2016.

Chapter 4

1. Nigel Thrift. Quoted in Leys 2011, 442.
2. Ibid.
3. See Massumi 2015; Protevi 2009.
4. Oprisko 2012, 29.
5. Berlin 1959, 54.
6. Weber 1978, 25.
7. Weber 1992, 119–22.
8. Nietzsche 1956, 160.
9. Ibid., 170.
10. Ibid., 171.
11. Deigh 2008, 87.
12. Solomon 2007, 16.
13. Ibid., 19.
14. Fierke 2015, 50–52.
15. Ben Ze'ev 2000, 249.
16. Nussbaum 2013, 10.
17. Ibid., 144.
18. Ibid., 11.
19. Kant 2007, 45.
20. Nussbaum 2015, 68.
21. Kant 1951, 73–74.
22. Panagia 2009, 23.
23. Ibid., 22.
24. Goldie 2002, 247–48.
25. Fierke 2015, 48.

26. Elster 1999, 262.
27. See Edkins 2003.
28. Connolly 2002, 75–76.
29. Ibid., 76.
30. Ruth Leys argues it is the problematic tendency to reduce affect to the unconsciousness. See Leys 2011, 442.
31. Connolly 2002, 77.
32. Ekman 1992, 552.
33. Wiersbicka 1994, 133–96.
34. Ibid., 254–55.
35. Solomon 2007, 254.
36. See Pinker 2008. For an in-depth discussion of the different scenarios (in the courtroom) of the trolley and footbridge scenario, see Cathcart 2014.
37. When groups of people were asked to choose between saving the workers on the platform and the fat man, a majority consistently chose to save the fat man.
38. See Williams 2012, 258.
39. Ibid., 259.
40. See Massumi 2015.
41. Ibid., 104.
42. Ibid.
43. See Thrift 2008.
44. Protevi 2009, 35.
45. See Damasio 2003.
46. Massumi 2015, 6, 8.
47. Ibid., 5.
48. Ibid.
49. See Ahmed 2014.
50. See Ahmed 2004.
51. Protevi 2009, 46.
52. Deleuze and Guattari 1991, 164.
53. Deleuze and Guattari 1987, 256.
54. Massumi 2015, 73.
55. Ibid., 95.
56. Ibid., 98.
57. See Marx 1976.
58. Massumi 2015, 71.
59. See Solomon 2018.
60. See, e.g., Mercer 2005; Crawford 2003; Payne 2015.
61. Scheff 1997, 4.
62. See, e.g., Demertzis 2013; Ross 2006; Koschut et al. 2017.
63. See Hutchison and Bleiker 2014, 491–95.
64. Massumi 2015, 82.
65. Ibid., 97.
66. United Nations 2012.
67. See Zebrowski 2016.
68. See O'Malley 2010.
69. See, e.g., Joseph 2013; Reid 2012.

70. Grove and Adey 2015, 82.
71. Massumi 2015, 67.
72. Ibid., 69.
73. Rancière 2010, 42–43.
74. See, e.g., Bellamy 2010; Evans 2008.
75. Rancière 2010, 38.

Chapter 5

1. See Bellaigue 2017.
2. Badawi 1978, 14–15.
3. Ibid., 51.
4. See Al-Afghani and al-Dahriyyin 1956; Badawi 1978, 31.
5. Sagiv 1995, 84–85.
6. Hatina 2007, 126–29.
7. See Fuda 1985.
8. Quoted in Sagiv 1995, 114.
9. Gamal Abdel Nasser's Arab nationalism expressed the Arab people's demands for unity and control over their political fate. Hence, the collective identity of the Arab people provided a common framework for solidarity that dictators had sought to suppress.
10. Hatina 2007, 9–10.
11. In Western countries, the rule of law refers to the impartial application of legal principles and the rules and procedures to administer law, or the adjudication of such rules that operate above partisan politics.
12. Hatina 2007, 153.
13. Compared to the 1980s and 1990s, the rise of Islamic fundamentalism would lead many thinkers to push for a more democratic application of *ijtihad*, one in which political leaders, officials, and others could be recognized and authorized to interpret the Islamic texts to advance their political agenda.
14. Sagiv 1995, 29–30.
15. Ibid., 31.
16. Lynch 2016.
17. See Rubin 2002.
18. Ibid., 58.
19. Note that compared to the Clash of Civilizations thesis, which treats religion as the central source of structural conflict in the modern world, this rigid distinction leaves little, if any, room for long-term cooperation.
20. Sullivan and Abed-Kotob 1999, 90.
21. See Kassem 2004.
22. Ibid., 28.
23. One of the important and unique features of Islam in Egypt is its pervasiveness, with nearly 90 percent of the population being Muslim; 7 to 10 percent are Coptic Christian.
24. Pahwig 2015, 190.
25. Ibid., 201.
26. See Badran 2014.

27. Gause 2011, 89.
28. Cook 2016.
29. The takeover was not officially labeled a coup or recognized as such by many states, including the United States.
30. Cook 2016, 113.
31. This action was counterbalanced by deals with many of the Islamic groups, including Hamas, to win support of these groups and to perhaps build a more moderate Islamic force that could contain the Salafists who had attacked Egyptian military forces in the Sinai Peninsula.
32. "Egyptian President Increasingly Turns to Religion" 2016, 11.
33. Mansour 2016.
34. Quoted in Bellaigue 2017.
35. Cole 1994, 23–25.
36. Ibid., 27.
37. See Gocek and Balaghi 1994.
38. Ibid., 6.
39. Mahmood 2005, 51.
40. Ibid., 25.
41. Hessini 1994, 30–39.
42. Ibid., 31.
43. Quoted in Mahmood 2005, 160.
44. Ibid., 161.
45. See Butler 1993.
46. See Butler 1998.
47. Mahmood 2005, 167.
48. Ibid., 162.
49. Ibid., 15.
50. Ibid., 157.
51. See Abu-Lughod 2013.
52. The most prominent case involved a young woman who was stoned to death outside of a court building in Lahore, Pakistan, where she had sought to have her right to marry validated or upheld. See Tharoor 2014.
53. Quoted in Tharoor 2014.
54. See Fattah and Fierke 2009, 72. The authors argue that shamed-based, as opposed to guilt-based, cultures can produce harsh(er) bodily reactions.
55. Weir 2013, 326.
56. See UN General Assembly 1979.
57. Kato 2017.
58. Ibid.
59. Ibid.

Chapter 6

1. See Greenawalt 2009, 131–34. In the 2009 Office of the Prosecutor report, for example, Luis Moreno-Ocampo stated that the ICC's complementarity principle "does not exclude alternative forms of justice." Quoted in Greenawalt 2009, 132.

2. See Bosco 2014.
3. See Vilmer 2016.
4. See Glasius 2009.
5. See, e.g., Moffett 2014; Gegout 2013; Branch 2007.
6. See Kersten 2016.
7. See Justice and Reconciliation Project 2007.
8. See Branch 2007. The ICC, it should be noted, does not accept any blanket amnesties and has refused to comply with the demands for dropping the indictments, even though the national government implemented a national amnesty law in 2000 to allow perpetrators to confess their guilt in exchange for amnesty.
9. See, e.g., Allen 2006; Unger and Wierda 2009.
10. See, e.g., Roach 2009; Jeffrey 2011, 78–95; Nouwen and Werner 2010.
11. Branch 2007, 193.
12. As of April 2019, there were 123 states that had ratified the Rome Statute (to become a state party), and eleven situations or areas where the ICC has been conducting its prosecutorial and judicial operations. Note that at the 2010 Review Conference held in Kampala, Uganda, states parties finally agreed to incorporate a comprehensive definition along with the specified elements of the crime of aggression.
13. See Roach 2012.
14. Vilmer 2016, 1325.
15. South Africa's threat, if carried out (it has yet to be as of April 2019), risks turning angry sentiment against the court's interventionism in African affairs. This reflects the potentially heavy political cost to the ICC's standing and ability to uphold and expand the global rule of law through its framework principle of complementarity.
16. See, e.g., El Zeidy 2008; Kleffner 2008.
17. Eventually, officials decided that there would be three ways to trigger the investigatory powers of the ICC. First, the OTP would be allowed to either take over a case or exercise its *proprio motu* power with the authorization of the pretrial chamber, when it determined that the crimes committed within the territory of a state party rose to the level of severe gravity. Second, the UN Security Council could issue a resolution authorizing the ICC to investigate a situation of violence involving gross human rights atrocities within a nonstate party. Note that the UN Security Council has already referred the situations of the Darfur genocide (2005) and the violence in Libya (2011) to the ICC, while the ICC prosecutor has initiated its own investigations in Kenya, Mali, and the Côte d'Ivoire. Third, state parties reserve the power to refer a situation. Uganda, the Democratic Republic of Congo, and the Central African Republic, for example, have elected to refer situations within their own state borders (also called self-referrals).
18. Stahn 2008, 89.
19. See Branch 2007.
20. See Owor and Murithi 2011.
21. Locals use the metaphor the "cooling of hearts" to express the psychological redress for the perpetrators and victims.
22. Allen and Vlassenroot 2010.
23. Justice and Reconciliation Project 2007.
24. Ibid., 4.
25. See Keller 2008.

26. *Gacaca*, it should be noted, has also raised concern regarding state power, in particular the tacit practice of victors' justice in which the Rwandan government has held only the Hutu perpetrators of genocide accountable, immunizing, in effect, Tutsi military personnel from prosecution. See Longman 2011, 304.

27. Note that many Christian groups remain open to and accepting of Mato Oput. See Quinn 2010, 107.

28. Finnström 2010, 137. On the issue of religious tension, see Quinn 2009, 2010.

29. See Minow 1998, 22. On this point of the false dichotomy between universalism and particularism, see also Teitel 1999.

30. Minow 1998, 23.

31. See Justice and Reconciliation Project 2007.

32. Ambos, Large, and Wierda 2009, 268.

33. See Justice and Reconciliation Project 2010.

34. Ibid., 10–12. Despite these concerns, some fighters have signaled their willingness to follow the path of Mato Oput. Two LRA fighters, for example, Sunday Otto and Richard Odong, surrendered to the government in exchange for (conditional) amnesty. And although the Ugandan government has yet to act on their requests for conditional amnesty, the two have confessed their guilt and requested to be tried under Mato Oput in order to begin rebuilding their lives. It should be stressed that Mato Oput offers the substantive hope that these fighters will confess and seek to reunite with their community, thereby redressing the deep-seated grievances that can perpetuate and erupt into new violence.

35. Note that the Ugandan government has signaled some willingness to compensate, though it has not yet specified how it would do so under the peace accords.

36. Justice and Reconciliation Project 2007, 6.

37. UN General Assembly 1998, article 5(d).

38. Quinn 2009, 185–87.

39. Ibid., 185.

40. See Hazan 2017.

41. It should be added that the ICC is unlikely to drop its indictments not only because it needs to uphold its mission of promoting the global rule of law, but also because the national war crimes court alternative would deprive many victims of their formal judicial rights. The Ugandan national court, in other words, would lack the resources and capacity to provide comparable (if any at all) assistance to victims. Local peoples would have to lean more on Mato Oput for redress, even though supporters of Mato Oput have already signaled their acceptance of the ICC's special role of trying the very worst perpetrators.

42. For a detailed discussion of this topic, see Ambos 2009.

43. See Funk 2009. It is important, as already stated, that we not overstate any definitive results of the link between these legal mechanisms. After all, the victims' program and outreach are nascent features of the ICC. As such, the practical link between the ICC restorative mechanism and traditional justice mechanism needs to be addressed on a case-by-case basis.

44. See International Criminal Court 2011.

45. Ibid.

46. See UN General Assembly 1998. Article 79 of the Rome Statute provides several conditions for deciding amounts. These include: "The Court may order money and other property collected through fines or forfeitures to be transferred, by order of the Court, to the Trust Fund; 3) the Trust Fund shall be managed according to criteria to be determined by the Assembly of States Parties."

47. See Schabas 2007, 338.

48. Rose 2008, 546–47.

49. See UN General Assembly 1998, article 16(1)(b)(c).

50. See Stanley 2009.

51. It should be noted that outreach efforts were implemented at these tribunals, but were never well developed. Some studies suggest that this contributed to more harm and injustice in the affected regions. For an excellent discussion of these events, see Peskin 2008.

52. Vinck and Pham 2010, 442.

53. Baylis 2009, 52.

54. Bartels et al. 2010, 4.

55. International Criminal Court 2009, 3.

56. Research on the Central African Republic indicates that ICC outreach has had some positive and transformative impact. Vinck and Pham, for instance, conducted various surveys, which showed that much of the awareness of the ICC in the Central African Republic came primarily from radio and television, and less from its workshops and discussion sessions. Yet the effect has varied along class or socioeconomic group lines, with high levels of awareness coming from well-educated citizens. On the issue of neutrality, only 10 percent found the ICC not to be neutral. But of the minority holding this opinion of the lack of neutrality, 34 percent attributed the lack of neutrality to the ICC's assisting the national government.

Chapter 7

1. See Russinov 2002.

2. See Roma Integration 2020 2015.

3. I use the term "Gypsy" in a historical and cultural context.

4. See Landanya and Szelenyi 2006.

5. See McGarry 2010.

6. Paradoxically, it was these very discriminatory laws that enabled the Nazis to carry out their sinister campaign against civilization.

7. See Agarin 2014; Bogdal 2011.

8. In much the same way, the Basques (or *Vascos*) in northern Spain legitimize their unique cultural identity in terms of preserving the Euskadi language.

9. Uzunova 2010, 295.

10. Much like the word *gringo* (or a person of light or white complexion from northern countries), which is used by Latin Americans to disparage the ignorance and presumptuousness of foreigners from the North, *gaje* expresses non-Roma's lack of awareness of appreciation for their own way of life. And, like *gringo*, it is intended to

assert a unique way life shared by the Roma: to express a tacit cultural pride that binds many together.

11. See Donnelly 2012.
12. Engebrigtsen 2007, 63.
13. Ibid., 64–65.
14. Ibid., 99.
15. Nussbaum 2013, 287.
16. See Kushi 2016, who contends that "the Roma women's oppression now lies at the intersection of three factors: reproductive healthcare, human trafficking and sex work, and 'educational deficiencies'."
17. Solomon 2007, 23.
18. Ibid.
19. Lemon 2000, 83.
20. The Dalit continue to be discriminated and severely mistreated in public, for example, the recent action by one shop owner in Allahabad to shoot and kill a Dalit couple who could not pay the remaining 23 cents for food.
21. Lemon 2000, 83; see also the UN High Commissioner for Refugees 1993.
22. Quoted in Vermeersch 2002, 374.
23. Kymlicka 1995, 26.
24. What is interesting to note here is that in Kymlicka's theory of multicultural membership, African Americans represented a hard case of accommodation, since they could not be categorized as either immigrants or as a national minority.
25. Tamás 2007.
26. Ibid., 168.
27. See Cernusakova 2017.
28. BBC News 2016.
29. Petrova 2007, 146.
30. See Mahoney 2012.
31. See Gheorghe 2002.
32. Elezovski 2007, 139.
33. See Council of Europe, Committee of Ministers 2008.
34. European Union 2007, article 167.
35. See European Commission 2007.
36. See European Commission 1985.
37. Suksi 1998, 165.
38. See United Nations 1993.
39. Quoted in Alfredsson 1996, 72. Emil Cardenas and Maria Fernando Canas, for instance, maintain that local self-administration provides a "means of upholding the necessary balance between various communities or minorities in pluralist societies against the tribalism associated with the abuse of the idea of self-determination." See Cardenas and Canas 1997, 162.
40. See O'Nions 2007.
41. Ibid., 6.
42. See European Union 2012.
43. See Sobotka 2003.

44. See European Commission 2004.
45. See Vermeersch 2012, 1096.
46. Ibid., 1099.
47. See Vermeersch 2005.
48. See European Commission 2007.
49. Quoted in Mahoney 2012, 664.
50. See Kotef 2015, 4–7.
51. See Roughneen 2010.
52. See Agamben 1998.
53. See Bell 2011.
54. On the related issue of Muslim migrants, the French government had been accused, in the wake of the Charlie Hebdo attack in January 2015, of remaining lax on the threat posed by Islamic terrorists to public safety. But, in fact, the driving force was the economic discrimination against Muslims in France, which motivated them to join and pledge their loyalty to the Islamic State.
55. Linden-Retek 2016.
56. Benhabib 2012, 50.

Chapter 8

1. See Remnick 2016.
2. Bartholomew 2014.
3. Master 2017.
4. This might explain why, during the late interwar period and even in the aftermath of colonialism and decolonization, many became sentimental about the loss of Victorian morality and decency.
5. Popper 1962, 237.
6. Proust 1928.
7. Obama 2018. One of these facts President Obama was alluding to was the denial of human CO_2 impact on the climate global warming. Confirmation bias has, as we have seen, driven the need for fake news feeds.
8. See "Fake News!" 2017.
9. See Ellsberg 2017.
10. See Gomes de Matos 2000.
11. The war of words was set off by Trump's announcement in a speech delivered to the UN General Assembly to wipe out North Korea.

References

Abu-Lughod, Lila. *Do Islamic Women Need Saving?* Cambridge: Harvard University Press, 2013.

Acemoglu, Daron, and James A. Robinson. *Why Nations Fail: The Origins of Power, Prosperity, and Poverty*. New York: Crown Business, 2012.

African Charter on Human and Peoples' Rights. Adopted June 27, 1981. OAU Doc. CAB/LEG/67/3 rev. 5, 21 I.L.M. 58 (1982). Entered into force 21 October 1986.

Agamben, Giorgio. *Homo Sacer: Sovereign Power and Bare Life*. Palo Alto: Stanford University Press, 1998.

Agarin, Timofey. "Angels with Dirty Faces? European Identity, Politics of Representation and Recognition of Romani Interests." *Ethnicities* 14, no. 6 (2014): 549–60.

Ahall, Linda, and Thomas Gregory, eds. *Emotions, Politics, and War*. Abingdon, UK: Routledge, 2015.

Ahmed, Sara. "Affective Economies." *Social Text* 22, no. 2 (2004): 117–39.

Ahmed, Sara. *The Cultural Politics of Emotions*. Abingdon, UK: Routledge, 2014.

Al-Afghani, Jamal al-Din, and Al Raad al Dahriyyin. *Modern Islam in Egypt*. Cairo: University of Cairo Press, 1956.

Alfredsson, Gudmundur. "Different Forms of and Claims to the Right of Self-Determination." In *Self-Determination: International Perspectives*, edited by Donald Clark and Robert Williamson. New York: St. Martin's Press, 1996.

Allen, Michael. *Civil Disobedience in Global Perspective: Decency and Dissent over Borders and Inequalities*. The Hague: Springer, 2017.

Allen, Tim. *Trial Justice: The International Criminal Court and the Lord's Resistance Army*. London: Zed Books, 2006.

Allen, Tim, and Koen Vlassenroot, eds. *The Lord's Resistance Army: Myth and Reality*. London: Zed Books, 2010.

Ambos, Kai. "The Legal Framework of Transitional Justice: A Systematic Study with Special Focus on the Role of the ICC." In *Building a Future on Peace and Justice: Studies on Transitional Justice, Peace and Development*, edited by Kai Ambos, Judith Large, and Marieke Wierda. The Hague: Springer, 2009.

Ambos, Kai, Judith Large, and Marieke Wierda, eds. *Building a Future on Peace and*

Justice: Studies on Transitional Justice, Peace and Development. The Hague: Springer, 2009.

Andemicael, B. *The OAU and the UN: Relations between the Organization of African Unity and the United Nations*. New York: African Publishing Company, 1976.

Anghie, Antony. *Imperialism, Sovereignty and the Making of International Law*. Cambridge: Cambridge University Press, 2004.

Appiah, Kwame Anthony. *The Honor Code: How Moral Revolutions Happen*. New York: W. W. Norton, 2010.

Ash, Timothy Garton. "Is Europe Disintegrating?" *New York Review of Books* 64, no. 1 (January 19, 2016): 25–31.

Atwell, Mary Welek. *Evolving Standards of Decency: Popular Culture and Capital Punishment*. New York: Peter Lang, 2004.

Badawi, M. A. Zaki. *The Reformers of Egypt*. London: Croom Helm, 1978.

Badran, Sammy Zeyad. "The Contentious Roots of the Egyptian Revolution." *Globalizations* 11, no. 2 (2014): 277–87.

Bartels, S., D. Scott, R. L. Leaning, R. R. Mukwege, R. Lipton, and M. Van Rooyen. "Surviving Sexual Violence in Eastern Democratic Congo." *International Journal of Women's Studies* 11, no. 4 (2010): 37–49.

Bartholomew, James. "The Death of Decency." *Spectator*, November 13, 2014. https://www.spectator.co.uk/2004/11/the-death-of-decency//

Baylis, Elaine. "Reassessing the Role of International Criminal Law: Rebuilding National Courts through Transitional Networks." *Boston College Review* 50, no. 1 (2009).

BBC News. "Ukraine Moves Roma Families amid Village's Rage at Murder." *BBC News*, August 29, 2016. https://www.bbc.com/news/world-europe-37212817

Beck, Ulrich. *World at Risk*. London: Polity Press, 2008.

Beitz, Charles. *The Idea of Human Rights*. Oxford: Oxford University Press, 2009.

Bell, Duncan. *The Idea of Greater Britain: Empire and the Future of World Order, 1860–1900*. Princeton: Princeton University Press, 2007.

Bell, Duncan, ed. *Victorian Visions of Global Order: Empire and International Relations in Nineteenth-Century Political Thought*. Cambridge: Cambridge University Press, 2007.

Bell, John. "French Administrative Law and the Supremacy of European Courts." *European Public Law* 11, no. 4 (2011): 487–510.

Bellaigue, Christopher de. "The Islamic World Did Liberalise—but Then Came the First World War." *Spectator*, February 25, 2017. http://www.spectator.co.uk/2017/02/the-islamic-world-did-liberalise-but-then-came-the-first-world-war/

Bellamy, Alex J. "Mainstreaming RtoP in the UN System: Dilemmas, Challenges and Opportunities." *Global Responsibility to Protect* 5, no. 2 (2013).

Benhabib, Seyla. *The Rights of Others: Aliens, Residents and Citizens*. Cambridge: Cambridge University Press, 2012.

Benjamin, Walter. *Illuminations: Essays and Reflections*. Edited and with an introduction by Hannah Arendt. New York: Shocken Books, 1968.

Ben-Ze'ev, Aaron. *The Subtlety of Emotions*. Cambridge, MA: MIT Press, 2000.

Berlin, Isaiah. *The Crooked Timber of Humanity*. Princeton: Princeton University Press, 1959.

Berlin, Isaiah, and Ramin Jahanbegloo. *Conversations with Isaiah Berlin: Reflections of a Historian of Ideas*. New York: Charles Scribner & Sons, 1991.

Bigo, Didier. "Freedom and Speed in Enlarged Borderzones." In *The Contested Politics of Mobility: Borderzones and Irregularity*, edited by Vicki Squire, 32. London: Routledge, 2011.

Black, Gregory. *The Catholic Crusade against Morals, 1940–1975*. Cambridge: Cambridge University Press, 1978.

Bleiker, R., and E. Hutchison. "Fear No More: Emotions and World Politics." *Review of International Studies* 34, no. 3 (2008): 115–35.

Boahen, A. Abdu. *African Perspectives on Colonialism*. Baltimore: Johns Hopkins University Press, 1987.

Bogdal, K. M. "Europa Erfindet die Zigeuner." *Eine Geschichte von Faszination und Verachtung*. Berlin: Suhrkamp, 2011.

Bosco, David. *Rough Justice: The International Criminal Court in a World of Power Politics*. Oxford: Oxford University Press, 2014.

Branch, Adam. "Uganda's Civil War and the Politics of ICC Intervention." *Ethics and International Affairs* 21, no. 2 (2007): 179–98.

Brassett, J., S. Croft, and N. Vaughn-Williams, eds. "Introduction: Agenda for Resilience in Politics and International Relations." *Politics* 33, no. 4 (2013): 221–28.

Briggs, Asa. *The Age of Improvement 1783–1867*. New York:Longman, 2009.

Brown, Wendy. *Walled States, Waning Sovereignty*. Cambridge, MA: MIT Press, 2010.

Brubaker, Rogers. "Populism's Perfect Storm." *Boston Review*, July 11, 2017. http://bostonreview.net/politics/rogers-brubaker-populisms-perfect-storm#.WWeORsIt8sU.linkedin

Buchanan, Allen. *Justice, Legitimacy and Self-Determination: Moral Foundations for International Law*. Oxford: Oxford University Press, 2007.

Buchanan, Allen. "Rawls's Law of Peoples: Rules for a Vanished Westphalian World." *Ethics* 110 (2000): 697–721.

Bull, Hedley. *The Anarchical Society: A Study of Order in World Politics*. New York: Columbia University Press, 1977.

Burke, Edmund. *The Evils of Revolution*. London: Penguin Books, 2008.

Burke, Edmund. *On Empire, Liberty, and Reform: Speeches and Letters*. Edited by David Bromwich. New Haven: Yale University Press, 2000.

Burke, Edmund. *Reflections on the Revolution in France*. Edited by J. G. A. Pockock. Indianapolis: Hackett, 1987.

Burke, Edmund. "Two Letters Addressed to Members of the Present Parliament on the Proposals for Peace with the Regicide Directory of France." In *The Writings and Speeches of Edmund Burke*, edited by Paul Langford, 8:248–49. Oxford: Oxford University Press 1991.

Butler, Judith. *Bodies That Matter: On the Discursive Limits of Sex*. London: Routledge, 1993.

Butler, Judith. *Frames of War: When Is Life Grievable?* London: Verso, 2010.

Butler, Judith. "Performative Acts and Gender Constitution: An Essay on Phenomenology and Feminist Theory." *Theater Journal* 40, no. 4 (1998): 519–31.

Campbell, David, and Martin Schoolman, eds. *The New Pluralism: William Connolly and the Contemporary Global Condition*. Durham, NC: Duke University Press, 2008.

Caney, Simon. 2005. *Justice across Borders*. Oxford: Oxford University Press.

Cardenas, Emil, and Maria Fernando Canas. "The Limit of Self-Determination." In *Self-Determination and Self-Administration: A Sourcebook*, edited by W. Danspeckgruber and A. Watts. Boulder, CO: Lynne Rienner, 1997.

Carter, Stephen L. *Civility: Manners, Morals, and the Etiquette of Democracy*. New York: Basic Books, 1998.

Cassirer, Ernst. *The Philosophy of the Enlightenment*. Princeton: Princeton University Press, 1951.

Cathcart, Thomas. *The Trolley Problem or Would You Throw the Fat Guy off the Bridge? A Philosophical Conundrum*. New York: Workman Publishing, 2014.

Cernusakova, Barbora. "The Roma People's Hungarian Hell." *Politico*, January 28, 2017. https://www.politico.eu/article/the-roma-peoples-hungarian-hell/

Chandler, David. "International State-Building and the Ideology of Resilience." *Politics* 33, no. 4 (2013): 274–86.

Chandler, David. "The Responsibility to Protect? Imposing the 'Liberal Peace.'" *International Peacekeeping* 11, no. 1 (2004): 59–81.

Charter for a World without Violence. "8th World Summit of Nobel Peace Laureates, Article 13." 2010. http://nonkilling.org/center/2010/11/04/cgnk-at-the-11th-world-summit-of-nobel-peace-laureates/

Clark, Ian. *International Legitimacy and World Society*. Oxford: Oxford University Press, 2007.

Cole, Juan R. L. "Gender, Tradition, and History." In *Reconstructing Gender in the Middle East: Tradition, Identity, and Power*, edited by Fatma Muge Gocek and Shiva Balaghi. New York: Columbia University Press, 1994.

Colgan, Jeff D., and Robert O. Keohane. "The Liberal Order Is Rigged: Fix It Now or See It Wither." *Foreign Affairs* 96, no. 3 (May–June 2017): 36–44.

Comte, Auguste. *A General View of Positivism*. London: Robert Speller and Sons, 1957.

Connolly, William E. *Ethos of Pluralization*. Minneapolis: University of Minnesota Press, 1995.

Connolly, William E. *Identity/Difference: Democratic Negotiations of Political Paradox*. Ithaca, NY: Cornell University Press, 1991.

Connolly, William E. *Neuropolitics: Thinking Culture, and Speed*. Minneapolis: University of Minnesota Press, 2002.

Connolly, William E. *Pluralism*. Durham, NC: Duke University Press, 2005.

Constant, Benjamin. *Constant: Political Writings*. Edited by Biancamaria Fontana. Cambridge: Cambridge University Press, 1988.

Cook, Steven A. "Egypt's Nightmare: Sisi's Dangerous War on Terror." *Foreign Affairs* 95, no. 6 (November–December 2016): 75–89.

Council of Europe, Committee of Ministers. "White Paper on Intercultural Dialogue." 118th Session of the Committee of Ministers, CM (2008) 30 final, May 2, 2008. https://pjp-eu.coe.int/documents/1017981/1668213/whitepaper_coe.pdf/fdfa4648–8e93–45cd-a01c-82e6599ee00a

Covenant of the League of Nations, 28 April 1919. "Article 22(a)." Accessed May 8, 2018. http://www.refworld.org/docid/3dd8b9854.html

Crawford, Neta. "Institutionalizing Passion in World Politics: Fear and Empathy." *International Theory* 6, no. 3 (2004): 535–57.

Crawford, Neta. "The Passion of World Politics." *International Security* 24, no. 4 (2003): 116–56.

Cresswell, Tim. *On the Move: Mobility in the Modern Western World.* London: Routledge, 2007.

Damasio, Antonio. *Looking for Spinoza: Joy, Sorrow, and the Feeling Brain.* New York: Harcourt, 2003.

Danspeckgruber, W., and A. Watts, eds. *Self-Determination and Self-Administration: A Sourcebook.* Boulder, CO: Lynne Rienner, 1997.

Darwin, Charles. *On the Origin of Species by Means of Natural Selection, or, the Preservation of Favoured Races in the Struggle for Life.* London: J. Murray, 1859.

Davetian, Benet. *Civility: A Cultural History.* Toronto: University of Toronto Press, 2009.

Davidson, Basil. *The Black Man's Burden: Africa and the Curse of the Nation-State.* New York: Random House, 1992.

Deigh, John. *Emotions, Values and Law.* Oxford: Oxford University Press, 2008.

Deleuze, Gilles, and Felix Guattari. *A Thousand Plateaus: Capitalism and Schizophrenia.* Minneapolis: University of Minnesota Press, 1987.

Deleuze, Gilles, and Felix Guattari. *What Is Philosophy?* New York: Columbia University Press, 1991.

Demertzis, Nicolas. *Emotion in Politics: The Affect Dimension in Political Tension.* New York: Palgrave Macmillan, 2013.

den Otter, Sandra. "'A Legislating Empire': Victorian Political Theorists, Codes of Law, and Empire." In *Victorian Visions of Global Order: Empire and International Relations in Nineteenth-Century Political Thought*, edited by Duncan Bell. Cambridge: Cambridge University Press, 2007.

Donnelly, Jack. *Universal Human Rights.* 3rd ed. Ithaca: Cornell University Press, 2012.

Duffield, Mark. "Challenge Environments of Danger: Resilience and 'Aid Industry.'" *Security Dialogue* 43, no. 3 (2012): 475–92.

Duncombe, Constance, and Tim Dunne. "After Liberal World Order?" *International Affairs* 94, no. 1 (January 2018): 25–42.

Dworkin, Ronald. *Justice for Hedgehogs.* Cambridge: Harvard University Press, 2011.

Edkins, Jenny. *Trauma and Memory of Politics.* Cambridge: Cambridge University Press, 2003.

Edyvane, Derek. "Tolerance and Pain." *Critical Review of International Social and Political Philosophy* 14, no. 3 (2012).

"Egyptian President Increasingly Turns to Religion to Bolster His Authority." *New York Times*, January 10, 2016.

Ehrenfreud, Robert. *The Nuremberg Legacy: How the Nazi War Crimes Trials Changed the Course of History.* London: Palgrave Macmillan, 2013.

Ekman, Peter. "Are There Basic Emotions?" *Psychological Review* 99, no. 3 (1992): 550–53.

Elezovski, Asmet. "Roma Integration into the European Union." In *Roma Diplomacy*, edited by Valeria Nicloae and Hanna Slavik. London: IDEBATE Press, 2007.

Elias, Norbert. *The Civilizing Process.* London: Blackwell, 1981.

Ellsberg, Daniel. *The Doomsday Machine: The Confessions of a Nuclear War Planner.* New York: Bloomsbury, 2017.

Elster, Jon. *Strong Feelings: Emotion Addiction and Human Behaviour.* Cambridge, MA: MIT Press, 1999.

El Zeidy, Mohamed. *The Principle of Complementarity in International Criminal Law: Origins, Development, and Practice*. The Hague: Brill, 2008.

Engebrigtsen, Ada L. *Exploring Gypsiness: Power, Exchange, and Interdependence in a Transylvanian Village*. New York: Berghahn Books, 2007.

Etzioni, Amitai. *From Empire to Community: A New Approach to International Relations*. New York: Palgrave Macmillan, 2004.

European Commission. "A Decent Life for All." 2013. http://ec.europa.eu/europeaid/documents /2013-02

European Commission. "European Agenda for Culture." Resolution of the Council of 16 November 2007 on a European Agenda for Culture. Document 32007G1129(01). https://eur-lex.europa.eu/legal-content/EN/TXT/?uri=CELEX:32007G1129%2801%29

European Commission. "European Commission Directorate-General for Employment and Social Affairs." Luxembourg: Office of Official Publications of the European Communities, 2004. http://ec.europa.eu/employment_social/social_inclusion/docs/final_joint_inclusion_report_2003_en.pdf

European Commission. "The European Draft Charter on Local Self-Government." ETS No. 122. October 15, 1985.

European Commission. "Intercultural Dialogue." 2008. https://ec.europa.eu/culture/policy/strategic-framework/intercultural-dialogue_en

European Community. "The Single European Act, Signed on 17 February 1986 by the Nine Member States and on 28 February 1986 by Denmark, Italy and Greece."

European Union. "Council of Europe, Intercultural Dialogue." 2012. https://ec.europa.eu/culture/policy/strategic-framework/intercultural-dialogue_en

European Union. *Treaty of Lisbon Amending the Treaty on European Union and the Treaty Establishing the European Community*. December 13, 2007. 2007/C 306/01. Accessed December 26, 2018. https://www.refworld.org/docid/476258d32.html

Evans, Gareth. *The Responsibility to Protect: Ending Mass Atrocities Once and for All*. Washington, DC: Brookings Press, 2008.

Fabre, Cecile. *Cosmopolitan War*. Oxford: Oxford University Press, 2012.

"Fake News! Libya Seizes on Trump Tweet to Discredit CNN Slavery Report." *Guardian*, November 28, 2017. https://www.theguardian.com/world/2017/nov/28/libya-slave-trade-cnn-report-trump-fake-news

Fanon, Frantz. *The Wretched of the Earth*. New York: Grove Books, 1963.

Fattah, Khaled, and Karin M. Fierke. "A Clash of Emotions: The Politics of Humiliation and Political Violence in the Middle East." *European Journal of International Relations* 15, no. 1 (2009): 67–93.

Feldman, Gregory. *We Are All Migrants*. Palo Alto: Stanford University Press, 2015.

Fierke, Karin. "Human Dignity: Basal Emotion and Global Emotionology." In *Emotions, Politics, and War*, edited by Linda Ahall and Thomas Gregory. Abingdon, UK: Routledge, 2015.

Fierke, Karin. *Political Self-Sacrifice: Agency, Body, and Emotion in International Relations*. Cambridge: Cambridge University Press, 2013.

Finnström, Sverker. "Reconciliation Grown Bitter? War, Retribution, and Ritual Action in Northern Uganda." In *Localizing Transitional Justice: Interventions and*

Priorities after Mass Violence, edited by Rosalind Shaw, Lara Waldorf, and Pierre Hazan. Palo Alto: Stanford University Press, 2010.

Fitzmaurice, Andrew. "Liberalism and Empire in Nineteenth-Century International Law." *American Historical Review* 117, no. 1 (February 2012): 122–40.

Foucault, Michel. *Discipline and Punish*. New York: Harcourt, 1977.

Freud, Sigmund. *Civilization and Its Discontents*. New York: W. W. Norton, 1961.

Fuda, Faraj. *Qabl al-Suqut* [Before the fall]. Cairo: University of Cairo, 1985.

Fukuyama, Francis. "Against Identity Politics: The New Tribalism and the Crisis of Democracy." *Foreign Affairs* 97, no. 5 (September–October 2018): 90–114.

Fukuyama, Francis. *Identity: The Demand for Dignity and the Politics of Resentment*. New York: Farrar, Straus and Giroux, 2018.

Funk, Markus. *Victims' Rights and Advocacy at the International Criminal Court*. Cambridge: Cambridge University Press, 2009.

Gandhi, Mahatma. *The Essential Writings of Mahatma Gandhi*, edited by Raghavan Iyer. Oxford: Oxford University Press, 1990.

Gause, F. Gregory. "Why Middle East Studies Missed the Arab Spring." *Foreign Affairs* 90, no. 4 (July–August 2011).

Gay, Peter. *The Enlightenment, an Interpretation: The Science of Freedom*. New York: W. W. Norton, 1969.

Gegout, Catherine. "The International Criminal Court: Limits, Potential and Conditions for the Promotion of Peace and Justice." *Third World Quarterly* 34, no. 5 (2013): 800–818.

Gehring, Jacqueline. "Roma and the Limits of the Free Movement in the European Union," In *Democratic Citizenship and the Free Movement of People*, edited by Wilhelm Maas. The Hague: Brill, 2013.

Gettlemen, Jeffrey, and Suhasini Raj. "Caste Is Still Enforced in a Changing India, with Fists and Blades." *New Yok Times*, November 18, 2018.

Gheorghe, Nicolae. "In Search of New Deal for the Roma: ERRC Interview with Nicolae Gheorghe." In *Race, Justice and Strategies for Equality*, edited by Claude Cahn. London: International Debate Education Association, 2002.

Gibson, Nigel. "Radical Mutations: Fanon's Untidy Dialectic of History." In *Rethinking Fanon*, edited by N. Gibson. New York: Humanity Books, 1999.

Glasius, Marlies. "What Is Global Justice and Who Decides? Civil Society and Victims' Responses to the International Criminal Court's First Investigations." *Human Rights Quarterly* 31, no. 2 (May 2009): 496–520.

Gocek, Fatma Muge, and Shiva Balaghi, eds. *Reconstructing Gender in the Middle East: Tradition, Identity, and Power*. New York: Columbia University Press, 1994.

Goldie, Peter. "Emotions, Feelings, Intentionality." *Phenomenology and Cognitive Sciences* 1 (2002): 235–54.

Gomes de Matos, Francisco Cardoso. *Nurturing Nonkilling: A Poetic Plantation*. Honolulu: Center for Global Nonkilling, 2009.

Gong, Gerrit W. *The Standard of 'Civilization' in International Society*. Oxford: Clarendon Press, 1984.

Grant, Mary Lee, and Nick Mirof. "U.S. Militias Head to the Border, Stirred by Trump's Call to Arms." *Washington Post*, November 4, 2018. http://www.msn.com/en-us/

news/us/us-militia-groups-head-to-border-stirred-by-trump%e2%80%99s-call-to-arms/ar-BBPiGxA?ocid=ientp

Greenawalt, Alexander. "Complementarity in Crisis." *Virginia Journal of International Law* 50, no. 1 (2009): 108–62.

Griffiths, Paul. *What Emotions Really Are: The Problems of Psychological Categories.* Chicago: University of Chicago Press, 1997.

Griswold, Charles L. *Adam Smith and the Virtues of Enlightenment.* Oxford: Oxford University Press, 1999.

Grove, Kevin, and Peter Adey. "Security and the Politics of Resilience: An Aesthetic Response." *Politics* 35, no. 1 (2015): 78–84.

Gutmann, Amy, and Dennis Thompson. *Democracy and Disagreement.* Cambridge: Harvard University Press, 1996.

Halévy, Elie. *The Age of Peel and Cobden: A History of the English People 1841–1852.* London: Ernest Benn, 1947.

Hall, John A. *The Importance of Being Civil: The Struggle for Political Decency.* Princeton: Princeton University Press, 2013.

Harris, Sam. *The Moral Landscape: How Science Can Determine Human Values.* New York: Free Press, 2010.

Hatina. Meir. *Identity Politics in the Middle East: Liberal Thought and Islamic Challenge in Egypt.* London: Tauris Academic Publishers, 2007.

Hayner, Priscilla B. *Unspeakable Truths: Transitional Justice and the Challenge of Truth Commissions.* Abingdon, UK: Routledge, 2011.

Haynes, Jeffrey. "The Arab Uprising: Islamists and Democratization." *Mediterranean Politics* 18, no. 2 (2013): 170–88.

Hazan, Pierre. "Uganda's Amnesty Law and the Peace / Justice Dilemma." *Info.Net,* October 7, 2017. http://www.justiceinfo.net/en/component/k2/33820-uganda-s-amnesty-law-and-the-peace-justice-dilemma.html

Held, David. *Democracy and the Global Order.* Palo Alto: Stanford University Press, 1995.

Hessini, Leila. "Wearing the Hijab: Choice and Identity." In *Reconstructing Gender in the Middle East: Tradition, Identity, and Power,* edited by Fatma Muge Gocek and Shiva Balaghi, 30–39. New York: Columbia University Press, 1994.

Hitchens, Christopher. *Long Live Hitch: Three Classic Books in One Volume.* New York: Atlantic Books, 2012.

Hobbes, Thomas. *Leviathan.* Edited by Richard Luck. Cambridge: Cambridge University Press, 1996.

Horton, John, and Susan Mendus. *Toleration, Identity, and Difference.* New York: St. Martin's, 1999.

Hunt, Lynn. *Inventing Human Rights: A History.* New York: W. W. Norton, 2007.

Hutchison, Emma, and Roland Bleiker. "Theorizing Emotions in World Politics." *International Theory* 6, no. 3 (2014): 491–51.

Ikenberry, John G. "The End of the Liberal International Order?" *International Affairs* 94, no. 1 (January 2017): 7–23.

Inayatullah, Naeem, and David L. Blaney. *International Relations and the Problem of Difference.* London: Routledge, 2004.

International Commission on Intervention and State Sovereignty. "The Responsibility to Protect." Ottawa: International Development Research Centre, 2001.

International Criminal Court. "Kisumu: Registry and the Common Legal Representative for Victims Consults with Victims." ICC-CPI-20110921-PR724 (2011).
International Criminal Court. "The Netherlands Contributes 250,000 to the Trust Fund for Victims." ICC-TFV-20110824-PR713.
International Criminal Court. *Outreach Report, 2009.* www.icc.org
International Labour Organization. "Report of the General Director: Decent Work." Geneva, 87th Session, June 1999. http://www.ilo.org/public/english/standards/relm/ilc/ilc87/rep-i.htm
Israel, Jonathan. *Radical Enlightenment: Philosophy and the Making of Modernity, 1650–1750.* Oxford: Oxford University Press, 2001.
Israel, Jonathan. *A Revolution of the Mind: Radical Enlightenment and the Intellectual Origins of Modern Democracy.* Princeton: Princeton University Press, 2010.
Jackson, Patrick Thaddeus. *Civilizing the Enemy: German Reconstruction and the Invention of the West.* Ann Arbor: University of Michigan Press, 2006.
Jackson, Robert H. "Opening Statement before the International Military Tribunal." Robert H. Jackson Center, November 1945. https://www.roberthjackson.org/speech-and-writing/opening-statement-before-the-international-military-tribu nal/
James, C. L. R. *Beyond a Boundary.* Durham, NC: Duke University Press, 1963.
Jeffrey, Renee. "Forgiveness, Amnesty, and Justice: The Case of the Lord's Resistance Army in Northern Uganda." *Cooperation and Conflict* 46, no. 1 (2011): 78–95.
Jones, Reece. *Violent Borders: Refugees and the Right to Move.* London: Verso, 2016.
Joseph, Jonathan. "Resilience in the UK and French Security Strategy: An Anglo-Saxon Bias?" *Politics* 33, no. 4 (2013): 253–64.
Juss, Satvinder S. "Free Movement and the World Order." *International Journal of Refugee Law* 16, no. 3 (2004): 289–335.
Justice and Reconciliation Project. "Special Report: The Cooling of the Hearts." Gulu District NGO Forum. Vancouver, BC: Liu Institute for Global Issues, July 2007.
Kaldor, Mary. *Global Civil Society: An Answer to War.* Cambridge, UK: Polity Press, 2003.
Kant, Immanuel. *Critique of Judgment.* New York: Hafner Press, 1951.
Kant, Immanuel. *Kant: Political Writings.* Edited by H. S. Reiss. Cambridge: Cambridge University Press, 2007.
Kassem, Mary. *Egyptian Politics: The Dynamics of Authoritarian Rule.* Boulder, CO: Lynne Rienner, 2004.
Kateb, George. *Human Dignity.* Cambridge: Harvard University Press, 2011.
Kato, Miwa. "Women of Egypt," *Cairo Review of Global Affairs* 24 (Winter 2017). https://www.thecairoreview.com/essays/women-of-egypt/
Kaye, David. "Who's Afraid of the International Criminal Court?" *Foreign Affairs* 90, no. 3 (2011): 118–30.
Keller, Linda. "Achieving Justice: The ICC and Ugandan Alternative Mechanisms." *Connecticut Journal of International Law* 23 (2008): 209–79.
Kersten, Mark. *Justice in Conflict: The Effects of the International Criminal Court's Interventions on Ending Wars and Building Peace.* Oxford: Oxford University Press, 2016.
King, Natasha. *The Politics of Immigration Control and Resistance.* London: Zed Books, 2016.

Kingsley, Patrick. "Taking an Ax to Democracy as Europe Fidgets." *New York Times*, February 11, 2018.
Kirchick, James. *The End of Europe: Dictators, Demagogues, and the Coming Dark Age.* New Haven: Yale University Press, 2018.
Kleffner, Jan. *Complementarity in the Rome Statute and National Criminal Jurisdiction.* Oxford: Oxford University Press, 2008.
Koschut, Simon, Todd H. Hall, Reinhard Wolf, Ty Solomon, Emma Hutchison, and Roland Bleiker. "Discourse and Emotions in International Relations." *International Studies Review* 19, no. 3 (2017): 481–508.
Koskenniemi, Martti. *The Gentle Civilizer of Nations: The Rise and Fall of International Law, 1870–1960.* Cambridge: Cambridge University Press, 2001.
Kotef, Hagar. *Movement and the Ordering of Freedom.* Durham, NC: Duke University Press, 2015.
Krugman, Paul. "Fall of the American Empire." *New York Times*, June 18, 2018. https://www.nytimes.com/2018/06/18/opinion/immigration-trump-children-american-empire.html
Kuper, Andrew. *Democracy beyond Borders: Justice and Representation in Global Institutions.* Oxford: Oxford University Press, 2004.
Kuper, Andrew, ed. *Global Responsibilities: Who Must Deliver on Human Rights?* Abingdon, UK: Routledge, 2005.
Kushi, Sadita. "Romani Women of the Balkans: Battling Intersectional Oppression." *Open-Democracy*, January 18, 2016. https://www.opendemocracy.net/sidita-kushi/romani-women-of-balkans-still-battling-intersectional-oppression
Kymlicka, Will. *Multicultural Citizenship.* Oxford: Clarendon Press, 1995.
Kymlicka, Will. *Multicultural Odysseys: Navigating the International Politics of Diversity.* Oxford: Oxford University Press, 2007.
Landanya, Janos, and Ivan Szelenyi. *Patterns of Exclusion: Constructing Gypsy Ethnicity and the Making of an Underclass in Transitional Societies of Europe.* Boulder, CO: East European Monographs, 2006.
Landau, Elizabeth, Zain Verjee, and Antônia Mortensen. "Uganda President: Homosexuals Are Disgusting." *CNN*, February 21, 2014.
Lauterpacht, Hersch. *League of Nations, Collected Papers.* Cambridge: Cambridge University Press, 1938.
Lebow, Richard N. *The Tragic Vision of Politics: Ethics, Interests, and Orders.* Cambridge: Cambridge University Press, 2003.
Lemon, Alaina. *Between Two Fires: Gypsy Performances and Romani Memory from Pushkin to Post-Socialism.* Durham, NC: Duke University Press, 2000.
Leys, Ruth. "The Turn to Affect: A Critique." *Critical Inquiry* 37, no. 3 (Spring 2011): 434–72.
Lieberman, Marcel S. *Commitment, Value, and Moral Realism.* Cambridge: Cambridge University Press, 2007.
Linden-Retek, Paul. "How Refugees Can Save Europe." *Boston Review*, January 27, 2016. http://bostonreview.net/world/paul-linden-retek-refugees-european-project
Lindner, Evelin. *From Humiliation to Dignity: For a Future of Global Solidarity.* Lake Oswego, OR: Dignity Press, 2019.

Lindner, Evelin. *Emotion and Conflict: How Human Rights Can Dignify Emotion and Help Us Wage Good Conflict.* Westport, CT: Praeger, 2009.

Linklater, Andrew. *Critical Theory and International Politics.* London: Routledge, 2008.

Linklater, Andrew. "Prudence and Principle in International Society: Reflection on Vincent's Approach to Human Rights." *International Affairs* 85, no. 5 (2009): 1179–91.

Locke, John. *An Essay Concerning Toleration.* Oxford: Oxford University Press, 2006.

Longman, Timothy. "An Assessment of Rwanda's Gacaca Court." *Peace Review* 24 (2011): 546–51.

Lynch, Marc. "In Unchartered Waters: Islamic Parties beyond Egypt's Muslim Brotherhood." December 16. Washington, DC: Carnegie Endowment for International Peace, 2016.

Mackie, John L. *Ethics: Inventing Right and Wrong.* New York: Penguin, 1977.

Magill, R. Jay, Jr. *Sincerity.* New York: W.W. Norton, 2012.

Mahmood, Saba. *Politics of Piety: The Islamic Revival and the Feminist Subject.* Princeton: Princeton University Press, 2005.

Mahoney, Diane E. "Expulsion of the Roma: Is France Violating EU Freedom of Movement and Playing by French Rules or Can It Proceed with Collecting Roma Expulsions Free of Charge?" *Brooklyn Journal of International Law* 37, no. 2 (2012): 649–82.

Malik, Kenan. "Liberalism Is Suffering but Democracy Is Doing Just Fine." *Guardian*, December 31, 2016.

Mamdani, Mahmood. *When Victims Become Killer: Colonialism, Nativism, and the Genocide in Rwanda.* Princeton: Princeton University Press, 2001.

Mansour, Mohammad. "Why Sisi Fears Egypt's Liberals: Behind the Recent Crackdown of Civil Society." *Foreign Affairs*, May 18, 2016.

Marcel, Gabriel. *Homo Viator.* Paris: Aubier, 1975.

Margalit, Avishai. *The Decent Society.* Cambridge: Harvard University Press, 1990.

Marteens, Kerstin. "Civil Society and Accountability of the United Nations." In *Building Global Democracy: Civil Society and Accountable Global Governance*, edited by Jan Aart Scholte. Cambridge: Cambridge University Press, 2011.

Martin, Robert, and David A. Reidy. *Rawls's Law of Peoples: A Realist Utopia?* London: Blackwell, 2006.

Marx, Karl. *Capital: Volume 1.* London: Penguin Press, 1976.

Massumi, Brian. *Politics of Affect.* London: Polity, 2015.

Master, James. "May Says Trump Was 'Wrong" to Share Anti-Muslim Videos." *CNN*, November 30, 2017.

Mazarr, Michael J. "The Once and Future Order: What Comes after Hegemony." *Foreign Affairs* 96, no. 1 (January–February 2017): 271–85.

McGarry, Aidan. *Who Speaks for Roma? Political Representation of a Transnational Minority Community.* London: Continuum, 2010.

McMahan, Jeff. *Killing in War.* Oxford: Clarendon Press, 2009.

Meacham, Jon. *American Gospel: God, the Founding Fathers, and the Making of a Nation.* New York: Random House, 2006.

Mearsheimer, John J. *The Tragedy of Great Power Politics.* New York: W. W. Norton, 2001.

Mehta, Uday Singh. *Liberalism and Empire: A Study in Nineteenth-Century British Political Thought*. Chicago: University of Chicago Press, 1999.

Menand, Louis. *The Metaphysical Club: A Story of Ideas in America*. New York: Farrar, Straus and Giroux, 2001.

Mercer, Jonathan. "Rationality and Psychology in International Relations." *International Organization* 59, no. 1 (2005): 77–106.

Mhurchú, Aoileann Ní, and Reiko Shindo, eds. *Critical Imaginations in International Relations*. Abingdon, UK: Routledge, 2016.

Mill, John Stuart. *Utilitarianism, On Liberty, and Essay on Bentham*. New York: New American Library, 1962.

Miller, David. *National Responsibility and Global Justice*. Oxford: Oxford University Press, 2007.

Miller, William I. *Humiliation: And Other Essays on Honor, Social Discomfort, and Violence*. Ithaca: Cornell University Press, 1993.

Minow, Martha. *Between Vengeance and Forgiveness: Facing History after Genocide and Mass Violence*. Boston: Beacon Press, 1998.

Mishra, Pankaj. *The Age of Anger: A History of the Present*. New York: Farrar, Straus and Giroux, 2017.

Mishra, Pankaj. "The Globalization of Rage." *Foreign Affairs* 95, no. 6 (November–December 2016): 46–54.

Mitchell, Paul. "UN Supports Australian Resolution on MH17 Crash." *Sydney Morning Herald*, July 22, 2014.

Moffett, Luke. *Justice for Victims before the ICC*. Abingdon, UK: Routledge, 2014.

Montesquieu, Baron. *The Spirit of the Laws*. Cambridge: Cambridge University Press, 1989.

Morsink, Johannes. *Inherent Human Rights: Philosophical Roots of the Universal Declaration*. Philadelphia: University of Pennsylvania Press, 2009.

Mounk, Yascha. "How Populists Uprisings Could Bring Down Liberal Democracy." *Guardian*, March 18, 2018. https://www.theguardian.com/commentisfree /2018/mar/04/shock-system-liberal-democracy-populism

Mouw, Richard L. *Uncommon Decency: Christian Civility in an Uncivil World*. Downers Grove, IL: Intervarsity Press, 1992.

Moyn, Samuel. *The Last Utopia: Human Rights in History*. Cambridge: Belknap Press of Harvard University, 2010.

Mulligan, Kevin. "From Appropriate Emotions to Values." *Monist* 81, no. 1 (1998): 161–88.

Mutua, Makau. *Human Rights*. Philadelphia: University of Pennsylvania, 2002.

Niblett, Robin. "Liberalism in Retreat. *Foreign Affairs* 96, no. 1 (November 2016): 17–24.

Nichols, Tom. "How America Lost Faith in Expertise." *Foreign Affairs* 96, no. 2 (March–April 2017): 60–73.

Nietzsche, Friedrich. *The Birth of Tragedy and The Genealogy of Morals*. Translated by Francis Golffing. New York: Doubleday, 1956.

Nouwen, Sarah H. M., and Wouter G. Werner. "Doing Justice to the Political: The International Criminal Court in Uganda and Sudan." *European Journal of International Law* 21, no. 4 (2010): 941–65.

Nussbaum, Martha C. *Political Emotions: Why Love Matters for Justice*. Cambridge: Harvard University Press, 2013.

Nussbaum, Martha C. "Political Liberalism and Global Justice." *Journal of Global Ethics* 11, no. 1 (2015): 68–79.

Nussbaum, Martha C. *Upheavals of Thought: The Intelligence of Emotions*. Cambridge: Cambridge University Press, 2001.

Nye, Joseph S., Jr. "Will the Liberal Order Survive? The History of an Idea." *Foreign Affairs* 96, no. 1 (January–February 2017): 10–16.

Obama, Barack. "Obama: Social Media Dividing Our Country." *NBC News*, January 10, 2018.

"Obama's Speech on Libya." *New York Times*, February, 23, 2011. http://www.nytimes.com/2011/02/24/us/politics/24obama-statement-libya.html?mcubz=0

O'Malley, Peter. "Resilient Subjects: Uncertainty, Warfare and Neoliberalism." *Economy and Society* 39, no. 4 (2010): 488–509.

O'Neill, Daniel. *Edmund Burke and the Conservative Logic of Empire*. Berkeley: University of California Press, 2016.

O'Nions, Helen. *Minority Rights Protection in International Law: The Roma of Europe*. Aldershot, UK: Ashgate, 2007.

Oprisko, Robert L. *Honor: A Phenomenology*. Abingdon, UK: Routledge, 2012.

Organization for Security and Co-operation in Europe (OSCE). *Conference on Security and Co-operation in Europe (CSCE): Final Act of Helsinki*, 1 August 1975. Accessed April 15, 2019. https://www.refworld.org/docid/3dde4f9b4.html

Orwell, George. *Down and Out in Paris and London*. New York: Harcourt, 1933.

Orwell, George. *Homage to Catalonia*. London: Harcourt Press, 1952.

Orwell, George. "Shooting the Elephant." *New Writing* 2 (Autumn 1936): 1–7.

Otter, Chris. "Making Liberalism Durable: Vision and Civility in the Late Victorian City." *Social History* 27, no. 1 (January 2002): 1–15.

Owor, Lino, and Tim Murithi. "Transitional Justice and War Crimes in Northern Uganda, Justice and Reconciliation Project." JRP-IJR Policy Brief No. 1, 2011.

Oxford English Dictionary (OED). "Civility." *OED Online*. July 2018. Oxford University Press. http://www.oed.com/viewdictionaryentry/Entry/11125

Packer, Z. Z. "Polite Society." *New York Times Magazine*, December 2, 2018.

Pahwig, Sumita. "Secularizing Islamism and Islamicising Democracy: The Political Ideational Evolution of the Egyptian Muslim Brotherhood." *Mediterranean Politics* 19, no. 2 (2015): 189–216.

Paige, Glenn. *Nonkilling Global Political Science*. Honolulu: Center for Nonkilling, 2009.

Panagia, David. *The Political Life of Sensation*. Durham, NC: Duke University Press, 2009.

Payne, Kenneth. "Fighting On: Emotion and Conflict Termination." *Cambridge Review of International Affairs* 28, no. 3 (2015): 480–97.

Pehe, Jiri. "Havel and the Politics of Common Decency." *Star*, December 19, 2011.

Peskin, Victor. *International Justice in Rwanda and the Balkans: Virtual Trials and the Struggle for State Cooperation*. Cambridge: Cambridge University Press, 2008.

Petrova, Dimitrina. "The Denial of Racism." In *The Roma, a Minority in Europe: Historical, Political and Social Perspectives*, edited by Roni Stauber and Raphael Vago. Budapest: Central European University Press, 2007.

Pinker, Steven. "The Moral Instinct." *New York Times Magazine*, July 13, 2008.

Pitts, Jennifer. "Boundaries of Victorian International Law." In *Victorian Visions of*

Global Order: Empire and International Relations in Nineteenth Century Political Thought, edited by Duncan Bell, 67–88. Cambridge: Cambridge University Press, 2007.

Pitts, Jennifer. "Empire and Legal Universalisms in the Eighteenth Century." *American Historical Review* 117, no. 1 (2012): 92–121.

Pitts, Jennifer. *A Turn to Empire: The Rise of Imperial Liberalism in Britain and France.* Princeton: Princeton University Press, 2005.

Pogge, Thomas. "An Egalitarian Law of Peoples." *Philosophy and Public Affairs* 23, no. 3 (1994): 196–220.

Pogge, Thomas W. *World Poverty and Human Rights.* Cambridge: Polity Press, 2008.

Popper, Karl. *The Open Society and Its Enemies: The High Tide of Prophecy of Hegel, Marx, and the Aftermath.* Vol. 2. Princeton: Princeton University Press, 1962.

Price, Richard M., ed. *Moral Limit and Possibility in World Politics.* Cambridge: Cambridge University Press, 2008.

Protevi, John. *Political Affect: Connecting the Social and the Somatic.* Minneapolis: University of Minnesota Press, 2009.

Proust, Marcel. *Remembrance of Things Past* [*À la Recherche du Temps Perdu*]. Translated by Scott Moncrieff. New York: Modern Library, 1928.

Quataert, Jean H. *Advocating Dignity: Human Rights Mobilizations in Global Politics.* Philadelphia: University of Pennsylvania Press, 2009.

Quinn, Joanna. "The Thing behind the Thing: Christian Responses to Traditional Practices of Acknowledgement in Uganda." *Review of Faith and International Affairs* 8, no. 1 (2010): 3–12.

Quinn, Joanna. "What of Reconciliation? Traditional Mechanism of Acknowledgment in Uganda." In *Reconciliation(s): Transitional Justice in Postconflict Societies*, edited by Joanna R. Quinn, 185–87. Montreal: McGill-Queen's University Press, 2009.

Rancière, Jacques. *Dissensus: On Politics and Aesthetics.* London: Continuum, 2010.

Raphael, David D. *The Impartial Spectator: Adam Smith's Moral Philosophy.* Oxford: Oxford University Press, 2007.

Rawls, John. *The Law of Peoples.* Cambridge: Harvard University Press, 1999.

Reid, Julian. "The Disastrous and Politically Debased Subject of Resilience." *Development Dialogue* 58 (2012): 67–81.

Reidy, David A. "Rawls on International Justice: A Defense." *Political Theory* 32, no. 3 (2004).

Remnick, David. "An American Tragedy." *New Yorker*, November 9, 2016. https://www.newyorker.com/news/news-desk/an-american-tragedy-2

Roach, Steven C. "Arab States and the Role of Islam in the International Criminal Court." *Political Studies* 53, no. 1 (March 2005a): 143–61.

Roach, Steven C. *Cultural Autonomy, Minority Rights, and Globalization.* Aldershot, UK: Ashgate, 2005b.

Roach, Steven C., ed. *Governance, Order, and the International Criminal Court: Between Realpolitik and a Cosmopolitan Court.* Oxford: Oxford University Press, 2009.

Roach, Steven C. "How Political Is the ICC? Pressing Challenges and the Need for Diplomatic Efficacy." *Global Governance* 19, no. 3 (2013): 507–23.

Roach, Steven C. "Multilayered Justice in Northern Uganda: ICC Intervention and

Local Procedures of Accountability." *International Criminal Law Review* 1, no. 1 (2013): 249–68.

Roach, Steven C. *Politicizing the International Criminal Court: The Convergence of Politics, Ethics, and Law*. Lanham, MD: Rowman & Littlefield, 2006.

Roach, Steven C. "Should the International Criminal Court Impose Justice?" *Yale Journal of International Affairs* 7, no. 1 (2012): 64–70.

Roma Integration 2020. *The Report: The Decade of Roma Inclusion, 2005–2015*. http://www.romadecade.org/decade-documents-decade-progress-reports

Roorda, Niko. *Fundamentals of Sustainable Development*. Abingdon, UK: Routledge, 2014.

Rose, Cecily. "Looking beyond Amnesty and Traditional Justice and Reconciliation Mechanisms in Northern Uganda: A Proposal for Truth-Telling and Reparations." *Boston College Third World Law Journal* 28, no. 2 (2008): 546–47.

Rosen, Michael. *Dignity: Its History and Meaning*. Cambridge: Harvard University Press, 2012.

Ross, Andrew. "Coming in from the Cold: Constructivism and Emotions." *European Journal of International Relations* 12, no. 2 (2006): 197–222.

Roughneen, Dualta. *The Right to Roam: Travelers and Human Rights in the Modern Nation-State*. Newcastle: Cambridge Scholars Publishing, 2010.

Rousseau, Jean-Jacques. *The Basic Political Writings*. Translated by Donald A Cress. Indianapolis: Hackett Publishing, 1987.

Rousseau, Jean-Jacques. *Confessions*. New York: Alfred A. Knopf, 1992.

Rubin, Alissa J. "Penalizing Women for Covering Too Little, and Then Too Much." *New York Times*, August, 28, 2016.

Rubin, Barry. *Islamic Fundamentalism in Egyptian Politics*. New York: Palgrave Macmillan, 2002.

Russinov, Runyan. "The Bulgarian Framework Programme for Equal Integration of Roma." In *Race, Justice and Strategies for Equality*, edited by Claude Cahn. London: International Debate Education Association, 2002.

Sagiv, David. *Fundamentalism and Intellectuals in Egypt, 1973–1993*. London: Frank Cass, 1995.

Samuels, Brett. "Flake on Jones Victory: 'Decency Wins'." *The Hill*, December 12, 2017. https://thehill.com/homenews/senate/364603-flake-on-jones-victory-decency-wins

Santora, Mark, and Steven Erlanger. "In Poland, Connecting with the Past, and the Voters." *New York Times*, March 4, 2018.

Santos, Boaventura de Sousa. *Toward a New Legal Common Sense*. Cambridge: Cambridge University Press, 2002.

Saurette, Paul. "You Dissin Me? Humiliation and Post 9/11 Global Politics." *Review of International Studies* 32, no. 3 (2006): 495–522.

Saurette, Paul. *The Kantian Imperative: Humiliation, Common Sense and Politics*. Toronto: University of Toronto Press, 2005.

Schabas, William A. *An Introduction to the International Criminal Court*. 3rd ed. Cambridge: Cambridge University Press, 2007.

Scheff, T. J. *Bloody Revenge: Emotion, Nationalism and War*. London: Palgrave, 2000.

Scheff, T. J. *Emotions, the Social Bond, and Human Reality: Part/Whole Analysis.* Cambridge: Cambridge University Press, 1997.

Scheler, Max. *The Nature of Sympathy.* Translated by Peter Heath. Hamden, CT: Archon, 1954.

Schmitt, Carl. *The Concept of the Political.* Chicago: University of Chicago Press, 1996.

Schwartz, Shalom H. "Universals in the Content and Structure of Values: Theoretical Advances and Empirical Tests in 20 Countries." *Advances in Experimental Psychology* 25 (1992): 1–65.

Scott, Joan Wallach. *The Politics of the Veil.* Princeton: Princeton University Press, 2007.

Seth, Leyla. "You're Criminal if Gay." *New York Review of Books* 61, no. 5 (March 2014).

Shaftesbury, Earl of. *An Inquiry Concerning Virtue and Merit.* London: Rudolf, Lechner and Sohn, 1884.

Shue, Henry. *Basic Rights: Subsistence, Affluence, and U.S. Foreign Policy.* 2nd ed. Princeton: Princeton University Press, 1996.

Sivananda, Sri Swamin. *Bhagavad Gita.* Durban: Dive Life Society of South Africa, 1957.

Smith, Adam. *Theory of the Moral Sentiments.* London: Penguin Books, 2009.

Smith, Adam. *The Wealth of Nations.* New York: Random House, 1937.

Sobotka, Eva. "The Roma in Politics in the Czech Republic, Slovakia, and Poland." European Roma Rights Center, 2003. http://www.errc.org/roma-rights-journal/roma-in-politics-in-the-czech-republic-slovakia-and-poland

Solomon, Robert C. *The Passions: Emotions and the Meaning of Life.* Indianapolis: Hackett Publishing, 1993.

Solomon, Robert C. *True to Our Feelings: What Emotions Are Really Telling Us.* Oxford: Oxford University Press, 2007.

Solomon, Ty. "Ontological Insecurity: The Circulation of Affects and the Arab Spring." *Journal of International Relations and Development* 21, no. 4 (2018): 934–58.

Sontag, Susan. *Regarding the Pain of Others.* New York: Farrar, Straus and Giroux, 2003.

Spencer, Herbert. *The Man Versus the State.* Indianapolis: Liberty Classics, 1982.

Spinoza, Baruch. *On the Improvement of the Understanding: The Ethics.* London: Dover Publications, 1955.

Stahn, Carsten. "Complementarity: A Tale of Two Notions." *Criminal Law Forum* 19 (2008): 87–113.

Stanley, Elizabeth. "Transitional Justice: From the Local to the International." In *The Ashgate Research Companion to Ethics and International Relations*, edited by Patrick Hayden, 275–92. Aldershot, UK: Ashgate, 2009.

Stauber, Roni, and Raphael Vago, eds. *The Roma, A Minority in Europe: Historical, Political, and Social Perspectives.* Budapest: Central European University Press, 2007.

Stewart, Anthony. *George Orwell, Doubleness and the Value of Decency.* London: Routledge, 2003.

Subramuniyaswami, Satguru Sivaya. *Dancing with Siva: Hinduism's Contemporary Catechism.* Delhi: Motilal Banarsidass, 2006.

Suksi, Markku. "On the Entrenchment of Autonomy." In *Autonomy: Applications and Implications*, edited by Markku Suksi. The Hague: Kluwer Law International, 1998.

Sullivan, Denis J., and Sana Abed-Kotob. *Islam in Contemporary Egypt: Civil Society vs. the State*. Boulder, CO: Lynne Rienner, 1999.

Sylvest, Casper. "The Foundations of Victorian International Law." In *Victorian Visions of Global Order: Empire and International Relations in Nineteenth-Century Political Thought*, edited by Duncan Bell, 47–66. Cambridge: Cambridge University Press, 2007.

Talbott, William J. *Which Rights Should Be Universal?* Oxford: Oxford University Press, 2005.

Tamás, Pál. "Central European Roma Policy: National Minority Elites, National States and the EU." In *The Roma: A Minority in Europe: Historical, Political and Social Perspectives*, edited by Roni Stauber and Raphael Vago, 163–75. Budapest: Central European University Press, 2007.

Tan, Kok-Chor. *Justice without Borders: Cosmopolitanism, Nationalism, and Patriotism*. Cambridge: Cambridge University Press, 2004.

Taylor, Charles. *A Secular Age*. Cambridge: Belknap Press of Harvard University Press, 2007.

Teitel, Ruti. *Transitional Justice*. Oxford: Oxford University Press, 1999.

Tharoor, Ishaan. "Husband of Pakistani 'Honor Killing' Victim Killed His First Wife." *Washington Post*, May 29, 2014.

Thoits, Peggy. A. "The Sociology of Emotions." *Annual Review of Sociology* 15 (1989): 317–42.

Thrift, Nigel. "Non-Representational Theory: Space, Politics, and Affect." Abingdon, UK: Routledge, 2008.

Tocqueville, Alexis de. *Democracy in America*. Vol. 1. New York: Alfred A. Knopf, 1945.

Toulmin, Stephen. *Cosmopolis: The Hidden Agenda of Modernity*. Chicago: University of Chicago Press, 1990.

Turner, Frederick Jackson. *The Closing of the American Frontier*. Madison: University of Wisconsin Press, 1892.

Unger, Thomas, and Marieke Wierda. "Pursuing Justice in Ongoing Conflict: A Discussion of Current Practice." In *Building a Future on Peace and Justice: Studies on Transitional Justice, Peace and Development*, edited by Kai Ambos, Judith Large, and Marieke Wierda. The Hague: Springer, 2009.

UN General Assembly. "2005 World Summit Outcome." Resolution Adopted by General Assembly on September 16, 2005. A/Res/60/1.

UN General Assembly. *Convention on the Elimination of All Forms of Discrimination against Women*. December 18, 1979. A/RES/34/180. http://www.refworld.org/docid/3b00f2244.html

UN General Assembly. *Convention on the Prevention and Punishment of the Crime of Genocide*. Approved and Proposed for Signature and Ratification or Accession by General Assembly Resolution 260 A (III) of December 9, 1948.

UN General Assembly. "GA Res. 2145 (XXI)." October 27, 1966.

UN General Assembly. *Rome Statute of the International Criminal Court (last amended 2010)*. July 17, 1998, ISBN No. 92-9227-227-6. http://www.refworld.org/docid/3ae6b3a84.html

UN General Assembly. "Universal Declaration of Human Rights." 217 [III] A) (1948). Paris. http://www.un.org/en/universal-declaration-human-rights/

UN High Commissioner for Refugees (UNHCR). *The 1951 Convention Relating to the Status of Refugees and Its 1967 Protocol.* September 2011. http://www.refworld.org/docid/4ec4a7f02.html

UN High Commissioner for Refugees (UNHCR). *The Untouchables: A Survey of the Roma People of Central and Eastern Europe.* March 1993. https://www.refworld.org/docid/580605e74.html

United Nations. "Draft Convention on Self-Determination through Self-Administration." UN Doc. A/48/PV 36. October 1993.

"United Nations Framework Convention on Climate Change, Paris Agreement." Adopted November 4, 2015. UN/CP21. http://unfccc.int/paris_agreement/items/9485.php

United Nations. "UN Millennium Goals." General Assembly, adopted 2000. http://www.un.org/millenniumgoals/

United Nations. "UN Secretary-General Report to the General Assembly and Security Council: The Responsibility to Protect: State Responsibility and Prevention." August 2012. A/67/929–S/2013/399.

UN Security Council. *Report of the Secretary-General on the United Nations Operation in Cyprus.* May 15, 2009. S/2009/248. http://www.refworld.org/docid/4a1a62892.html

U.S. Senate, Committee on Government Operations. "Special Senate Investigation on Charges and Countercharges Involving Secretary of the Army Robert T. Stevens, John G. Adams, H. Struve Hensel and Senator Joe McCarthy, Roy M. Cohn, and Francis P. Carr." 83rd Cong., 2nd Sess., part 59, p. 2429. Washington, DC: U.S. Government Printing Office, 1954.

Uzunova, Iskra. "Roma Integration in Europe: Why Minority Rights Are Failing." *Arizona Journal of International law and Comparative Law* 27 (2010): 283–327.

Van Reybrouck, David. *Congo: The Epic History of a People.* Translated by Sam Garrett. New York: Harper Collins, 2010.

Vattel, Emer de. *The Law of Nations.* Edited by Bela Kapossy and Richard Whatmore. Indianapolis: Liberty Fund, 2008.

Vermeersch, Peter. "Marginality, Advocacy, and the Ambiguities of Multiculturalism: Notes on Romani Activism in Central Europe." *Identities: Global Studies in Culture and Power* 12, no. 4 (2005): 451–78.

Vermeersch, Peter. "Reframing the Roma: EU Institutions and the Politics of Reinterpretation." *Journal of Ethnic and Migration Studies* 38, no. 8 (September 2012): 1195–2012.

Vermeersch, Peter. "Romani Political Mobilization in Central and Eastern Europe." *European Yearbook of Minority Issues* 1, no. 1 (2002): 373–94.

Velleman, J. David. *Practical Reflection.* Princeton: Princeton University Press, 1989.

Vilmer, Jean Baptiste Jeangene. "The African Union and the International Criminal Court: Counteracting the Crisis." *International Affairs* 92, no. 6 (November 2016): 1319–42.

Vincent, John. *Human Rights and International Relations.* Cambridge: Cambridge University Press, 1986.

Vinck, Patrick, and Phuong N. Pham. "Outreach Evaluation: The International Criminal Court in the Central African Republic." *International Journal of Transitional Justice* 4, no. 3 (2010).

Voltaire. *Treatise on Tolerance*. Cambridge: Cambridge University Press, 1995.

Wagner, Alex. "Bill O'Relly's Ugly Carnival." *Atlantic*, October 6, 2016.

Waldron, Jeremy. *Torture, Terror, and Trade-offs: Philosophy for the White House*. Oxford: Oxford University Press, 2010.

Walzer, Michael. *Just and Unjust Wars: A Moral Argument with Historical Illustrations*. 4th ed. New York: Basic Books, 2006.

Walzer, Michael. "On Humanitarianism." *Foreign Affairs* 90, no. 4 (2011): 69–80.

Walzer, Michael. *Spheres of Justice: A Defense of Pluralism and Equality*. New York: Basic Books, 1983.

Walzer, Michael. *Thick and Thin: Moral Argument at Home and Abroad*. Notre Dame, IN: University of Notre Dame Press, 1994.

Weber, Max. *Economy and Society*. Vol. 1. Berkeley: University of California Press, 1978.

Weber, Max. *The Protestant Ethic and the Spirit of Capitalism*. London: Routledge, 1992.

Wehner, Peter. "Can We Find Our Way Back to Lincoln?" *New York Times*, July 17, 2016.

Weir, Allison. "Feminism and the Islamic Revival: Freedom as a Practice of Belonging." *Hypatia* 28, no. 2 (2013): 323–40.

Wiersbicka, Anna. "Emotion, Language, and Cultural Scripts." In *Emotion and Culture: Empirical Studies of Mutual Influence*, edited by Shinobu Kitayama and Hazel Rose Markus, 133–96. Washington, DC: American Psychological Association, 1994.

Wenman, Mark. "William E. Connolly: Resuming the Pluralist Tradition in American Political Science." *Political Theory* 43, no. 1 (2015): 54–79.

White, G. M. "Affecting Culture: Emotion and Morality in Everyday Life." In *Emotion and Culture: Empirical Studies of Mutual Influence*, edited by Shinobu Kitayama and Hazel Rose Markus, 219–40. Washington, DC: American Psychological Association, 1994.

Williams, Bernard. "Toleration: An Impossible Virtue." In *Toleration: An Elusive Virtue*, edited by David Heyd. Princeton: Princeton University Press, 1996.

Williams, Caroline. "Affective Processes without a Subject: Rethinking the Relation between Subjectivity and Affect with Spinoza." *Subjectivity* 3, no. 2 (2012).

Wilmot, Jennifer. "A Commitment to Politics: The Trajectory of the Muslim Brotherhood during Egypt's 2011–13 Political Opening." *Contemporary Arab Affairs* 8, no. 3 (2015): 379–97.

Wilson, Ben. *The Making of Victorian Values: Decency and Dissent in Britain, 1789–1837*. London: Penguin, 2007.

Wollstonecraft, Mary. *A Vindication of the Rights of Woman*. London: Penguin, 2004.

Wright, Quincy. *Under the League of Nations*. Chicago: University of Chicago Press, 1930.

Zebrowski, Chris. *The Value of Resilience: Securing Life in the Twenty-First Century*. Abingdon, UK: Routledge, 2016.

Index

Printed and bound by CPI Group (UK) Ltd, Croydon, CR0 4YY
16/09/2026
14963487-0006